W9-DCO-729

DAVID ALAN JOHNSON

THE LAST WEEKS OF ABRAHAM LINCOLN

★ ★ ★ ★ ★ ★ ★

A DAY-BY-DAY ACCOUNT *of* HIS PERSONAL, POLITICAL, *and* MILITARY CHALLENGES

Prometheus Books

59 John Glenn Drive
Amherst, New York 14228

Published 2018 by Prometheus Books

Cover design by Nicole Sommer-Lecht
Cover image © Alamy Stock Photo
Cover design © Prometheus Books

The internet addresses listed in the text were accurate at the time of publication. The inclusion of a website does not indicate an endorsement by the author or by Prometheus Books, and Prometheus Books does not guarantee the accuracy of the information presented at these sites.

Inquiries should be addressed to
Prometheus Books
59 John Glenn Drive
Amherst, New York 14228
VOICE: 716–691–0133 • FAX: 716–691–0137
WWW.PROMETHEUSBOOKS.COM

22 21 20 19 18   5 4 3 2 1

Library of Congress Cataloging-in-Publication Data Pending

Printed in the United States of America

To Laura, as always

CONTENTS

CONTENTS

ACKNOWLEDGMENTS

I received a great deal of assistance from librarians and historians in gathering all the material needed to put this book together, and I would like to single out a few individuals who went out of their way to help me out.

I would like to thank Jeffrey Bridgers at the Library of Congress for his assistance with photos.

Dr. James Cornelius of the Abraham Lincoln Presidential Library and Museum was also a great help. I would like to thank him for answering all of my many and persistent questions.

Also, many sincere thanks go out to the staff of the Union, New Jersey, Public Library. Thank you to Laura, Eileen, Denise, Susan, and all of their colleagues for their assistance.

And last, but certainly not least, many thanks to Laura Libby for all of her help and understanding, and for putting up with me once again, as she has done with every one of my other books.

INTRODUCTION

The last six weeks of Abraham Lincoln's life are among the most important and eventful in the history of the United States. Among the events that took place between March 4, 1865, and April 15, 1865, were Lincoln's Second Inauguration as president of the United States, climactic battles leading up to the end of the Civil War, Robert E. Lee's surrender to Ulysses S. Grant at Appomattox, and the assassination of President Lincoln at Ford's Theatre on April 14, 1865.

Not every day during the last days of Lincoln's life was eventful. Some were filled with nothing more than the business of politics and of running his office. The president also needed time to recuperate from the strain and tension of the war and spent some days confined to his bedroom. But on March 28, aboard the steamer *River Queen*, the president met with General Ulysses S. Grant, general-in-chief of all Union forces, General William Tecumseh Sherman, and Admiral David D. Porter, to discuss the prosecution of the war as well as postwar strategy for rebuilding the South. As Carl Sandburg put it, "They were hammering out a national fate."[1] After General Lee's surrender at Appomattox on April 9, Lincoln shifted his thoughts to postwar reunification of the country.

Lincoln's Second Inaugural Address, which he delivered on March 4, 1865, set the tone for how he wanted the war to be fought and what he envisioned for the immediate postwar period. The president wanted a terrible war, a war that would permanently end the rebellion and destroy the armies of the Confederacy, but he also looked forward to a generous peace. "With malice toward none; with charity for all," he said, "let us strive to finish the work we are in; to bind up the nation's wounds."[2]

But before there could be a magnanimous peace, the war would have to be brought to an end. Not much fighting took place during the early weeks of March 1865. The roads in Virginia were still muddy and unusable from the winter rains, and attacks were limited to skirmishes and contacts between Union and Confederate pickets. General Grant waited for the roads to dry before carrying out his spring offensive against General Robert E. Lee and his army. Grant hoped this would be the last campaign of the war. Lincoln was hoping for the same thing.

General Philip Sheridan's Army of the Shenandoah had chased Confederate general Jubal Early out of Virginia's Shenandoah Valley and had destroyed most of the farms in the area by late March. General Sherman kept pushing his men through North Carolina toward Virginia, where he hoped to link up with Grant. Grant had not yet begun his campaign against Lee, but the president sent him an order forbidding him from discussing any subject but military matters with General Lee when the war in Virginia came to an end. Specifically, Lincoln told Grant that he was not to discuss or negotiate any political questions. Politics was the domain of President Lincoln himself, not General Grant or any other general.

General Grant's main anxiety was that General Lee and his army would escape from Petersburg one night, before Grant was aware of it. If Lee moved to North Carolina and joined forces with General Joseph E. Johnston's Army of Tennessee, the war would be prolonged for at least another year, possibly longer. Grant did not have the luxury of concerning himself with "political questions." His first priority was to stop Lee and destroy his army, and think about negotiations after Lee had surrendered.

President Lincoln met with General Grant, as well as General Sherman and Admiral Porter, aboard the *River Queen* to discuss war strategy. Just as important, at least in Lincoln's point of view, they also talked about rebuilding the country after the war. General Sherman noted that the president's first priority was to end the war as quickly as practicable, but he also saw that Lincoln wanted to show clemency to the South after the fighting ended.

But the war was not over yet. The spring offensive in Virginia was actually begun by Robert E. Lee, not by General Grant. Lee's forces not only captured Fort Stedman on March 25, which was part of Grant's Petersburg defenses, but also threatened to break Grant's siege of Petersburg. Lee's success was only temporary, however. Grant's counterattack forced Lee to abandon both Petersburg and Richmond.

On the afternoon following the Fort Stedman attack, President Lincoln visited the battlefield. The dead and wounded had not yet been removed from the field, and the president saw the fighting from a soldier's viewpoint. The visit made Lincoln even more anxious to end the war than before.

The president's wife, Mary Lincoln, suffered from her own mental strain and nervousness, which added to her husband's anxieties. Mrs. Lincoln had frequently been called "a crazy woman." Friends and acquaintances knew that she was not well. Mrs. Lincoln was extremely nervous and anxious. Her condition was frequently the cause of awkward scenes. She often perceived slights and offenses where none were intended and flew into embarrassing rages that made her feel humiliated and ashamed afterward. The president was very sympathetic toward Mary and her condition. Friends remarked that his manner toward Mrs. Lincoln was always "gentle and affectionate." Even though she frequently embarrassed the president with public outbursts, which were directed at him as well as others, Lincoln always remained calm and did his best to keep her calm as well. Mrs. Lincoln's state of mind did nothing to help the president with his own worries and concerns.

The trip on the *River Queen* seemed to cheer the president and lift his spirits. But with the arrival of spring the war started again, along with all the stress and strain that went with it. President Lincoln was not at ease over the fighting that he knew was to come. A steady rain turned all the roads into quagmires for several days after Fort Stedman. On the last day of March, General Sheridan was turned back by a Confederate attack at a small town called Dinwiddie Court House. On the following day, April 1, Sheridan personally led a charge against the Confederate flank at the Battle of Five Forks.

Five Forks was a Confederate rout. General Grant ordered an attack all along the line, which turned out to be the final assault at Petersburg. Grant sent President Lincoln a telegram to report the success of the attack, telling Lincoln that everything looked highly favorable, which was a gigantic understatement.

By noon on April 2, almost the entire line of Confederate trenches had been overrun. Petersburg itself surrendered on the following day, and General Grant entered the town on horseback. President Lincoln visited Grant in Petersburg; the two of them talked about politics, about the possibility of General Sherman coming north to support Grant, and about showing leniency toward the Confederacy after the war ended. Clemency for the South was an important topic for the president. General Lee was now in full retreat, heading west along the Appomattox River and trying his best to break away from Grant and escape to North Carolina. After about half an hour, the president said goodbye to Grant and left Petersburg. Shortly after Lincoln's departure Grant received word that Richmond had surrendered. He regretted that he had not heard the news while he was still with the president.

General Grant kept the pressure on Lee—"Still plodding along following up Lee," a Union officer wrote.[3] The two armies finally made contact on April 6, at Sayler's Creek. General Lee lost seven thousand men, most of them captured, and suffered another loss at Farmville on the following day. General Grant sent Lee a note, asking him to surrender. Lee declined. The last battle of the war took place at Appomattox Court House on April 9. Federal troops moved in front of

Lee—General Sheridan's cavalry, followed by two infantry corps—blocking any further hopes of a Confederate escape. Lee surrendered to Grant on the afternoon of April 9, 1865.

General Grant telegraphed the news of Lee's surrender the same afternoon, and Washington began celebrating that day. The president was as relieved to hear Grant's message as everyone else in Washington and throughout the North. But now that the war was over, Lincoln began making plans for the postwar period and the rebuilding of the South.

Appointing Ulysses S. Grant as general-in-chief was one of Abraham Lincoln's most important decisions as a wartime president, if not *the* most important decision. It took three years, and a number of disastrous losses by several Union generals, before Lincoln was able to find the man who had the drive and gumption to outfight and out-general Robert E. Lee. President Lincoln knew what he wanted, as well as what he needed, in a commanding general, but could not find him until he brought U. S. Grant to Virginia from the west.

Shortly after General Grant received his promotion to lieutenant general, President Lincoln wrote a letter to the general to say that he was confident in his abilities as a commander. He began by saying that he wanted to express his "entire satisfaction" with what General Grant had accomplished up to that point in time, "so far as I understand it."[4] After this opening, he told Grant, "The particulars of your plans I neither know, nor seek to know," and followed by informing the general that he did not want to "obtrude any constraints or restraints upon you." Lincoln also complimented General Grant on the fact that he had managed to avoid any battlefield disasters, and invited Grant to contact him if he might think of anything "which is within my power to give." The president closed his letter of confidence with, "And now with a brave Army, and a just cause, may God sustain you."

General Grant's reply indicated as much confidence in President Lincoln as Lincoln had shown in him. He wrote that the president's satisfaction with his record so far, along with his confidence in future campaigns, was "acknowledged with pride," and that he would do his best not to disappoint either the president or the country. The general also said that he had no cause for complaint against either the Lincoln administration or Secretary of War Stanton, and was astonished at the readiness with which everything he had asked for had been given to him. The last sentence of Grant's letter said exactly what President Lincoln wanted to hear: "Should my success be less than I desire and expect, the least I can say is, the fault is not with you."

General Grant made it clear that his goal was precisely the same as President Lincoln's: to win the war. He was not going to complain or find fault or make excuses for himself, the way past commanding generals had done. Lincoln realized that Grant had the ability and the single-mindedness to take charge of the army himself, and he would not blame the president for any of his failures. The president had complete faith in his newly appointed commander in chief. If Grant could go to Virginia and accomplish the same things he had accomplished at Shiloh, Fort Donelson, and Vicksburg, Lincoln was not going to worry about how he planned to go about it.

The stresses and strains of being a wartime president and overall commander had finally ended for Lincoln, but he was about to find out that being a peacetime president came with its own set of problems and anxieties. Lincoln's policy of leniency toward the South did not make him very popular with many Northerners, including members of his own party. The Radical Republicans had no use for either Lincoln or his program for clemency. They wanted to hang Jefferson Davis, Robert E. Lee, and all other high-ranking Confederates, and punish the seceded Confederates for treason.

But the president was not all that concerned with the Radical Republicans or with their opinion regarding his outlook for the postwar United States. He was just as unscrupulous as any of the Radicals and was determined to do anything that needed to be done to push his postwar programs for reunification through Congress.

The president had every confidence in himself and in his ability to carry out his agenda for reunification. But on the night of April 14, 1865, he was shot by John Wilkes Booth, a Southern firebrand who wanted to do something "heroic" for the South. Abraham Lincoln died early on the following morning.

Lincoln's death ended his plan for a magnanimous peace. He wanted the reconstruction of the former Confederate states to be generous and lenient. Instead, "Reconstruction" would come to mean just the opposite—vengeance toward the South and corruption by Carpetbaggers and vindictive politicians. Lincoln's successor, Andrew Johnson, along with the Radical Republicans, carried out their own program, which was to treat the seceded states as traitors and to punish them accordingly. The United States evolved into a different country because Abraham Lincoln was not able to finish his second term or carry out his postwar program for rebuilding and reuniting the country.

A SACRED EFFORT

According to custom, the president always traveled from the White House to his inauguration in a shiny carriage, as part of the inauguration parade. The inauguration parade traditionally consisted of floats, marching bands, marching soldiers, and the president's carriage, accompanied by a phalanx of marshals. On the morning of March 4, 1865, Grand Marshal Ward Lamon, who knew Lincoln from the days when they both lived in Illinois, drove to the White House to escort his old friend to the ceremony at the Capitol Building. The pre-inaugural festivities were already in the process of being organized, and Marshal Lamon wanted to make certain that the president would not be late for his own parade.

But when he arrived at the White House, Lamon was informed that the president had already left for the Capitol. He had some work to do, some bills to sign, and decided to take care of these routine details before going off to his inauguration. As far as Lincoln was concerned, the morning of March 4, 1865, was just an ordinary working morning.

Actually, President Lincoln was not as casual about the day as he seemed to be. He knew that he was lucky to be going to his own inauguration that afternoon and was very much aware that he had come perilously close to losing last November's election. Abraham Lincoln nearly did not have a second term to look forward to. During the previous summer, it looked as though he was not going to win the election, and that his rival, George B. McClellan, would be sworn in as president. At the time, General Ulysses S. Grant was deadlocked with General

Robert E. Lee at Petersburg, about twenty miles south of Richmond, and General William Tecumseh Sherman had stalled north of Atlanta, Georgia. At least this was what voters in the North were reading in their newspapers. The Democrats were saying that the war was a total failure, and the public listened and believed. "You think I don't know I am going to be beaten," Lincoln said, "*but I do* and unless some great change takes place *badly beaten.*"[1]

The great change that Lincoln was hoping for took place in September, when General Sherman captured Atlanta. After the fall of Atlanta, which was one of the turning points of the war, public opinion immediately turned in Lincoln's favor. On Election Day, November 8, 1864, voters sent Lincoln back to the White House for four more years. But if it had not been for General Sherman, Lincoln realized that he would only have been in Washington long enough to watch President-Elect McClellan take the oath of office, and that he would have been on his way back home to Springfield, Illinois, immediately after the ceremony. Lincoln was happy and relieved that he would be commander in chief during the last days of the war instead of George B. McClellan.

"The city is quite full of people," Secretary of the Navy Gideon Welles wrote in his diary on the previous day, March 3, 1865, in a staggering understatement.[2] Abraham Lincoln's second inauguration had certainly filled Washington, DC, with people—it was overcrowded, jammed, and congested. All the hotels in town were cram-packed. Every nook, cranny, and cubbyhole had been turned into a sleeping space. The Willard, Washington's grandest and most fashionable hotel, even had cots set out in the halls as well as in the parlors, the ballrooms, and in all the public rooms. Everyone wanted to see President Lincoln take his oath of office, or at least wanted to be able to say that they had been in Washington when the great event took place.

But not everybody in Washington had come to wish the president well. "General Halleck has apprehensions that there may be mischief," Gideon Welles went on to remark, with some apprehensions of his own. "I do not participate in these fears," Secretary Welles wrote, "and yet I will not say that it is not prudent to guard against contingencies."[3] Major General Henry W. Halleck was chief of staff. Although his headquarters were in Washington, General Halleck was responsible for the administration of the entire United States Army. He was also very concerned with the safety and well-being of the president. It would not look good if anything happened to the president when the chief of staff was in town, especially on Inauguration Day.

Actually, General Halleck's concerns over the president's safety were more than justifiable, and they were not just self-serving. Along with the flood of tourists and sightseers that had come for the inauguration, there were also more than a few malcontents and Confederate sympathizers in town. Many of these individuals hated the president and wanted to see him dead—they blamed Lincoln for the fact that the South was now on the brink of losing all hope for independence. One such person was a twenty-six-year-old actor from Maryland named John Wilkes Booth.

President Lincoln was not at all concerned with security or with his own safety on the morning of his second inauguration; he was too busy signing bills in a room of the Senate wing. Outside the Capitol, the weather was cold, rainy, and generally miserable. The inauguration parade, minus the president, slowly made its way along Pennsylvania Avenue in spite of the weather, and also in spite of the fact that the steady rain had turned all the streets into rivers of mud. The mud was several inches thick in places and sometimes brought the parade to a complete stop—the marching soldiers and parading horses and patriotic floats sank into the goo and stayed there until they could be extracted from their predicament.

By about noon, Lincoln finished his bill-signing tasks and began walking toward the Senate Chamber. The inauguration was to have been held outside, in front of the Capitol Building, but, because the weather would not cooperate, the ceremony was moved inside. At 11:45, all the government officials began making their way into the Senate Chamber. Hannibal Hamlin, the departing vice-president, and Andrew Johnson, the incoming vice-president elect, filed in together.

Vice-President Hamlin opened the proceedings with a short farewell speech, in which he thanked everyone present for their kindness and consideration during the past four years. It was a routine address; not many of the attendees paid much attention to it. Secretary of State William Seward, along with other members of the president's cabinet, arrived to take their seats while Vice-President Hamlin was in the middle of it. This distracted everyone in the room, including Hamlin, who stopped speaking until all the men were seated.

After all the cabinet members had made their way into the Senate Chamber, the justices of the Supreme Court, led by Chief Justice Salmon P. Chase, filed in and sat down. While this was going on, a group of women in the visitor's gallery kept up a steady stream of chattering and laughing, paying no attention to either Hamlin or what he was saying. Vice-President Hamlin asked them to stop, but they paid no attention to him and kept on talking.

Hamlin had not been very happy during his four years in office, and he did not have a very high opinion of the office of the vice-president in general. As far as he was concerned, the vice-president had no power, no influence, and no respect. The way he was being treated while he was giving his farewell speech only reinforced his low opinion of the position. He did not even have the authority to make a bunch of talkative women shut their mouths.

In spite of all the distractions, the vice-president kept on speaking. No sooner had he restarted his speech than the president's wife, Mary Lincoln, entered the chamber and took her seat in the diplomat's gallery, causing another distraction. This little comedy of errors ended when Vice-President Hamlin finally reached the end of his address. As he read his final lines, guests were still entering the Senate Chamber.

After Hamlin finished, President Lincoln entered the chamber and sat down in the front row—he was a few minutes late, but at least he did not interrupt Hamlin's speech. But Hannibal Hamlin's farewell address was only a minor fiasco. It was about to be followed by a much larger one—Vice-President Andrew Johnson's inaugural address.

Earlier that day, Johnson had complained to Hannibal Hamlin that he did not feel well, and that he should not even be in Washington. He was still recovering from an attack of typhoid fever and had asked Lincoln for permission to take the oath of office at his home in Nashville, Tennessee. But the president wanted his running mate in town for the ceremony, so Johnson obligingly made the trip to Washington.

On the morning of the inauguration, Johnson was still feeling the effects of his illness. When he arrived at Vice-President Hamlin's office, someone brought him a large, tumbler-sized glass of whisky, which was supposed to steady his nerves as well as lessen any lingering effects of the fever. Before leaving for the Senate Chamber, Johnson had another large whisky. According to some accounts, he also had a third. By the time he made his way into the Senate Chamber and onto the rostrum to begin his speech, Andrew Johnson was absolutely and thoroughly drunk. He was not falling-down drunk, but he had enough whisky in him to slur his speech and interfere with his reflexes. Everyone in the chamber, including the president, could not help but notice Johnson's condition.

As he stood in front of a Senate Chamber that was filled to capacity, Johnson began his rambling address by reminding Secretary Seward, Secretary of War Edwin M. Stanton, and the Secretary of the Navy (he could not remember Gideon Welles's name) that they derived their power and authority from the people, and not from President

Lincoln—apparently, he thought this was a new and revolutionary idea. His voice was raspy and unsteady. He was obviously under the influence. Secretary Welles turned to Stanton, who was sitting just to his right, and said, "Johnson is either drunk or crazy." Stanton agreed. "There is evidently something wrong," he said.

"The Vice President made a rambling and strange harangue, which was listened to with pain and mortification by all his friends," Secretary Welles wrote in his diary. "My impression was that he was under the influence of stimulants, yet I know not that he drinks." Welles remembered that Johnson had been "sick and feeble, perhaps he may have taken medicine or stimulants. . . . Whatever the cause, it was all in very bad taste."[4]

Everybody present, including all the attendees in the chamber, were stunned by Johnson's performance. A reporter from the *New York Herald* commented that Andrew Johnson's address was "remarkable only for its incoherence, which brought a blush to the cheek of every senator and official of the government."[5] Vice-President Hamlin tried to catch Johnson's attention by tugging on his coattails, but the vice-president elect kept rattling on in spite of all attempts to stop him. Johnson's speech was supposed to last six or seven minutes; it went on for seventeen.

President Lincoln was as embarrassed as everyone else by the spectacle Johnson was making of himself. He sat with his head down, staring at his shoes, not able even to look at his new vice-president. Johnson eventually did stop speaking, either because Hannibal Hamlin's coat tugging finally caught his attention or because he ran out of breath.

When it became evident that Johnson had reached the end of what the New York *World* called his "incoherent address,"[6] the clerk arrived with a Bible, and the oath of office was administered. Johnson took the oath in a very loud, raspy voice, gave the book a very wet kiss, and sat down. President Lincoln and everyone else present seemed relieved that the incident had ended.

The rain had stopped by this time—it ended at around 11:40, according to most accounts. The sky was still dark and overcast, but at least it was no longer raining. Arrangements were quickly made to continue the inauguration ceremony outside the building, where many more people could see and hear the president give his inaugural address. Lincoln, Johnson, and all the other dignitaries were escorted out of the building to a wooden platform in front of the Capitol. As he made his way out of the building with the rest of the procession, President Lincoln told one of the marshals that Johnson must not be allowed to speak again. It was bad enough that he made a fool of himself within the confines of the Senate Chamber. Lincoln did not want his vice-president, who had now been sworn in, to repeat his performance in front of thousands of people.

As soon as he stepped outside, onto the platform, Lincoln was struck by the size of the crowd that had come to see and hear him. The *New York Times* called the gathering "a grand crush."[7] A good many soldiers were among those present. Some had come from nearby camps; others were convalescing patients in Washington hospitals. As soon as the president came into view, the "exceedingly large" mass of people began shouting and applauding, and continued their applause as a military band played "Hail to the Chief."[8]

At the precise moment when Lincoln began walking toward the rostrum, the sun broke through the clouds. Chief Justice Salmon P. Chase thought the sudden burst of sunshine must be a favorable omen. The sergeant at arms of the Senate had already signaled the crowd to quiet down.

At six feet, four inches tall, the president towered above most of those around him. The fact that he was also very thin, and has been diplomatically described as gaunt, made him appear even taller. He was fifty-six years old, but many of his friends and acquaintances thought he looked much older. One of the president's aides, John Hay, observed that Lincoln had changed a great deal during the past four years, and that he was very different from the vigorous and active president-elect of 1861. Mary Lincoln thought that her husband looked tired and careworn. The war had certainly taken its toll. Four years of constant stress and strain had turned Abraham Lincoln into a worn and weary old man.

When the president arrived at the rostrum, he put on his steel-rimmed glasses and looked down at his inaugural address. The speech was in type—not handwritten—and was arranged in two columns on a single sheet of paper. After a moment, he began reading.

"Fellow countrymen," he said. "At this second appearing to take the oath of the presidential office, there is less occasion for an extended address than there was at the first." His first inaugural address was certainly a very different speech than the one he was about to give. On March 4, 1861, Lincoln had asked the South to reconcile their differences with the North and to do everything possible to avoid going to war. But exactly four years later, the Confederacy was on the verge of losing the war that Lincoln had hoped so desperately to avoid.[9]

"The progress of our arms, upon which all else chiefly depends, is as well known to public as to myself; and it is, I trust, reasonably satisfactory and encouraging to all. With high hope for the future, no prediction in regard to it is ventured." The progress of Federal arms certainly was encouraging. By the spring of 1865, it was evident to anyone with a realistic eye to the future that the end of the war was in sight. Congress had already begun making plans for peacetime activities, discussing items that included the completion of the Pacific railroad, the resettlement of Indian tribes, and the availability of land for settlement in the West. The end of the war definitely seemed to be within reach. The phrase "after the war" began entering into conversations.

Lincoln next returned to another subject from his first inaugural address, reminding the audience that "four years ago, all thoughts were anxiously directed to an impending civil-war. All dreaded it—all sought to avert it." The first address was "devoted altogether to *saving the Union without war*." Preserving the Union was the first priority. "Both parties deprecated war; but one of them would *make* war rather than let the nation survive; and the other would *accept* war rather than let it perish. And the war came." Now the war was almost over, and the president had other things to talk about.

The next paragraph of the speech addressed one of the most important items on the president's agenda for the future of the country: the subject of slavery. "One eighth of the whole population were colored slaves, not distributed generally over the Union, but localized in the Southern part of it. These slaves constituted a peculiar and powerful interest." President Lincoln elected not to mention the economic reasons for the split behind the North and South, which were just as responsible for the war as slavery. The two sides had treated each other as separate countries long before Fort Sumter—the industrial North and the agricultural South disagreed with each other over taxes and tariffs and imports since the beginning of the republic. The differences of opinion between North and South were not just over slavery.

"All knew that this interest was, somehow, the cause of the war. To strengthen, perpetuate, and extend this interest was the object for which the insurgents would rend the Union, even by war; while the government claimed no right to do more than to restrict the territorial enlargement of it." This section of the address referred to Lincoln's own expressed interest to prohibit the expansion of slavery in the territories and in other sections of the country, but not to abolish it in the South. Lincoln was well aware that his Emancipation Proclamation had not freed any slaves. The "colored slaves" who lived in the seceded Southern states were beyond his jurisdiction and were still being bought and sold as if the Emancipation Proclamation did not exist.

"Neither party expected for the war, the magnitude, or the duration, which it has already attained. Neither anticipated that the *cause* of the conflict might cease with, or even before, the conflict itself should cease." This was absolutely true. In the days immediately following Fort Sumter, both sides thought that the fighting would be over by Christmas. "Both read the same Bible, and pray to the same God; and each invokes His aid against the other. It may seem strange that any men should dare to ask a just God's assistance in wringing their bread from the sweat of other men's faces; but let us judge not that we be not judged."

The president used the same Bible image of eating bread earned by the toil and sweat of others—which is based on a passage from the book of Genesis—in a debate with Stephen Douglas in 1858. It was just as effective in 1865 as it had been seven years earlier.

Lincoln continued with the use of Bible imagery, this time quoting from the book of Matthew: "Woe unto the world because of offences! for it must needs be that offences come; but woe to that man by whom the offence cometh!" A good many blacks were in the audience, including members of a lodge that called itself the African American Odd Fellows. They repeated "'bress de Lord' in a low murmur at the end of every sentence," according to the *New York Herald*.[10]

"If we shall suppose that American Slavery is one of those offences which, in the providence of God, must needs come, but which, having continued through His appointed time, He now wills to remove, and that He gives to both North and South, this terrible war, as the woe due to those by whom the offence came, shall we discern therein any departure from those divine attributes which the believers in a Living God always ascribe to Him?" Slavery was one of the offences committed by the country, and God punished the entire country, North and South, for this offence. The Civil War was nothing less than a scourge from God. "Fondly do we hope—fervently do we pray—that this mighty scourge of war may speedily pass away. Yet, if God wills that it continue, until all the wealth piled by the bond-man's two hundred and fifty years of unrequited toil shall be sunk, and until every drop of blood drawn with the lash, shall be paid by another drawn with the sword, as was said three thousand years ago, so still it must be said 'the judgments of the Lord, are true and righteous altogether.'" This quote was also from the Bible, from Psalm 19, which produced a long and enthusiastic round of applause, along with another chorus of "Bless the Lord."

The crux of the speech, Lincoln's main point, did not come until the end: "With malice toward none; with charity for all; with firmness in the right, as God gives us to see the right, let us strive on to finish the work we are in; to bind up the nation's wounds; to care for him who shall have borne the battle, and for his widow, and his orphan—to do all which may achieve and cherish a just, and a lasting peace, among ourselves, and with all nations." This is the best remembered section of the address, as well as the most eloquent.

This was not just political rhetoric—Lincoln meant what he was saying. He really did hope that the United States would be united for the first time in its history, with no more hostility or resentment between North and South when the fighting ended. "Neither party expected for the war, the magnitude, or the duration, which it has already attained." But if the peace turned out to be generous and magnanimous, maybe the four terrible years that just passed would produce a "just and lasting peace," along with a unified country and an end to slavery.

Photographer Alexander Gardner had set himself and his camera in the audience, in a position to the left of the rostrum, where he could record the event on film. His photo shows Lincoln with an intense expression on his face as he reads his address, which he holds with both hands. It is anything but a technical marvel, even for its time, but it is the only photo taken of Lincoln while he is speaking. Also in the audience, above and behind the president, standing to his left, John Wilkes Booth listened to the speech from a part of the building overlooking the rostrum. Booth would later claim that he could have shot the president from where he was standing. He was certainly within the range of a pistol shot while the president was giving his speech.

"After the delivery of the address, a national salute was fired by a battery stationed east of the Capitol," according to a reporter who covered the event.[11] People in the audience were as startled by the artillery salute as they were by the brevity of the president's speech—it was only 703 words long, and only lasted six or seven minutes. Everyone expected it to go on for some time, like most political speeches, especially most inaugural speeches. One of Lincoln's biographers reflected, "Seldom had a President been so short-spoken about the issues of so grave an hour."[12]

When the crowd realized that the speech actually had ended, and after the artillery had fired its salute, everyone burst into cheers and applause. The noise from the crowd drifted away after a minute or so, along with the smoke from the saluting batteries, and Chief Justice Salmon P. Chase stepped forward to administer the oath of office. President Lincoln had appointed Chase as chief justice only three months earlier, after the death of eighty-seven-year-old chief justice Roger B. Taney. In 1861, Chase had been one of Lincoln's opponents for the Republican Party's presidential nomination. Now, Chief Justice Chase turned toward the Supreme Court clerk, who handed him a Bible.

Lincoln placed his right hand on the book, which had been opened to the book of Isaiah, chapter five. The president repeated the oath after Chief Justice Chase and ended with a ringing "So help me God!" Lincoln then stooped slightly to kiss the Bible. Chase presented it to Mrs. Lincoln. With that, the inauguration ceremony was over—at 12:17 p.m.[13] The president's part in the proceedings, including delivering his speech, lasted less than fifteen minutes—one of the most memorable quarter hours in the country's history.

The president left the Capitol by way of the basement. Outside the basement exit, he shifted his lanky six-foot, four-inch frame into a waiting carriage and was driven back to the White House with his son Tad. All along the way, onlookers cheered and shouted and waved at Lincoln as he passed by. The president waved right back. Now that the inauguration ceremony was over, and he had been sworn in as president, he could afford to relax—at least for a while. But he would not be able to relax for very long. The day might have been over, but the night, and the public reception that was to be held at the White House in a few hours, was still ahead of him.

A crowd had been gathering outside the White House since late afternoon—several thousand people, according to most accounts. The gates were finally opened at 8:00 p.m., and the public began filing into the White House grounds. According to observers who were on hand for the event, the events that took place during the next three hours sound like a cross between a cattle stampede, a mob scene, and a madhouse.

President Lincoln spent most of his time during the reception in the East Room, shaking hands with guests—reporters estimate that he shook hands with more than six thousand visitors. One of the guests was Frederick Douglass, the outspoken black abolitionist. The president caught sight of Douglass as soon as he walked into the East Room. Since he was the only black person in the room, he was very easy to spot.

"Here comes my friend Douglass," Lincoln announced in a loud voice, loud enough so that everyone in the vicinity could hear him. He walked up to Douglass, shook his hand, and said, "I am glad to see you. I saw you in the crowd today, listening to my inaugural address. How did you like it?"

This was a risky question. Douglass had been present at Lincoln's first inaugural address, as well, and did not think very much of it. His main objection was that the president had been much too lenient regarding the South and, especially, regarding slavery.

Encouraging leniency for the South was the entire purpose of Lincoln's first inaugural address. He wanted to placate the Southern states, not to threaten or alienate them. Mentioning slavery would have been certain to do both. "We are not enemies, but friends," he said. "We must not be enemies." He urged the Southern people not to secede, and instead to be touched by the mystic chords of memory and the better angels of their nature and to return to the Union.[14] But Douglass only saw that the president had not taken Southerners to task over the question of slavery.

But slavery, "a peculiar and powerful interest," occupied a major part of the second inaugural address. President Lincoln was anxious to hear what Frederick Douglass had to say about it. Lincoln had a high regard for both Douglass and his opinion, and was disappointed that Douglass considered Lincoln's position on abolition lacking in dedication and forcefulness.

Douglass tried to evade the question. He told the president that he did not want to detain the president "with my poor opinion," when there were thousands of visitors waiting to shake hands with him. But Lincoln persisted—"I want to know what you think of it."

"Mr. Lincoln," Douglass replied, "it was a sacred effort."[15] The president was more than satisfied with his opinion. According to one writer's account, Lincoln "positively beamed" when he heard Douglass's verdict.[16]

By midnight, the reception had finally come to an end and the crowd had disappeared into the Washington night. Some visitors took souvenirs with them, unauthorized souvenirs—pieces of curtains from the East Room, flowers from the floral designs. One of the guards remarked that it looked as though a regiment from the Confederate army, with permission to forage, had taken up residence. President Lincoln was upset by the vandalism and could not understand how anyone could have caused such willful damage.

But the big day was finally over, and he had other things to worry about. He had just begun his second term of office as president, and the most pressing thing in his mind was the war—more specifically, with winning the war. Spring had arrived, and the fighting in Virginia would begin as soon as the roads dried out from the winter rains. After the Confederacy surrendered, and the fighting had stopped, he would be able to concentrate on other things. This included rebuilding the war-ravaged Southern states, dealing with Jefferson Davis and other Confederate political leaders, and ending slavery.

MARCH 5, 1865, SUNDAY
A WELCOME RELIEF

After all the pomp and ceremony of Inauguration Day, and its accompanying activity and busyness, the inactivity of Sunday, March 5, came as a welcome relief. The president desperately needed some time off, time to recover and to collect himself. He had clearly been overworking—everyone close to him, including his wife, could see that. The war may have been winding down, but nobody could say how many battles still had to be fought before the Confederates decided to give up. The coming weeks would be wearing, and Lincoln needed to conserve his strength. Taking Sunday off, especially after the pressure of the previous day, would not only be welcome but necessary.

The president and Mrs. Lincoln attended religious services that Sunday morning at the Methodist Episcopal Church. Bishop Matthew Simpson delivered the sermon—"a masterly effort and very touching."[1] Bishop Simpson made a point of mentioning the sudden burst of sunshine that occurred just as Lincoln stepped forward to begin his inauguration address on the previous day. Just as the sun had broken through the overcast, Bishop Simpson told the "large and attentive" congregation, peace would burst upon the divided country and dispel the clouds of war. It was a very nice allusion, but Lincoln was well aware that peace was not going to come that quickly or easily.

Abraham Lincoln was not a religious man. He never gave any indication that he ever belonged to any particular church or denomination, although he attended the local Baptist church when he lived with his parents in Pigeon Creek, Indiana. But young Abe never actually joined the church, in spite of his father's urging—"nagging" is probably a more accurate word—and he acquired a reputation as a rebel and a religious dissenter. One account said that he was considered "a village atheist" by his neighbors.[2]

Being an atheist, or a dissenter, or anything resembling a freethinker was a liability to anyone with any political ambitions in the orthodox Midwest, as Abraham Lincoln found out the hard way. In 1846, he ran for a seat in Congress against a Methodist preacher named Peter Cartwright. Cartwright accused Lincoln of ridiculing and looking down at Christianity, a charge that Lincoln considered serious enough to answer with a formal denial. "That I am not a member of any Christian church is true," he said, "but I have never denied the truth of the Scriptures; and I have never spoken with intentional disrespect of religion in general, or of any denomination of Christianity in particular."[3] Lincoln's defense must have been effective enough to satisfy the voters—he was elected to Congress by a considerable margin.

Even though Lincoln did not belong to any church and did not seem to have very much interest in organized religion in general, he did have an in-depth knowledge of the Bible. Along with most other families in that part of the country, the Bible would have been one of the few books the Lincolns had in their household, and it was read thoroughly and avidly by young Abraham. He seems to have compensated for his lack of interest in religion with an intense interest in the Bible. "In regard to the Great Book, I have but to say. It is the best gift God has given to man," he would write. "All things desirable for man's welfare, here and hereafter, are to be found portrayed in it."[4]

Over the years, Lincoln read and re-read the Bible many times over. This gave him the depth of knowledge and the ability to quote from scripture whenever he wanted to emphasize a subject or a remark, either in a debate or in one of his speeches—he made a point of using

Bible quotes in his second inaugural address. He could also use a biblical quotation as a joke when the situation presented itself.

The British ambassador, Lord Lyons, once made an official visit to
the White House to deliver a handwritten message from Queen Vic-
toria. The queen sent the note to inform the president that her son, the
Prince of Wales, was betrothed to the Princess Alexandra of Denmark.
Lord Lyons was a stuffy and pompous old bachelor who tended to take
himself too seriously. He made a formal speech "appropriate to the
occasion;" Lincoln replied in the "usual conventional manner."[5] When
the requisite formalities were safely out of the way, and the impending
marriage had been announced, Lincoln took the ambassador by the
hand and said, "And now, Lord Lyons, go thou and do likewise."

Lyons did not have a very high opinion of Lincoln to begin with—
in 1860, he reported to London that Lincoln was a rough farmer of
low origins, which was probably putting his thoughts politely. The joke
did not improve his opinion, especially since it had been made at his
expense. But Lincoln would have had a good laugh over the incident,
and from sticking a pin in the ambassador's overdeveloped sense of
self-importance.

After church services were over, the president and Mrs. Lincoln
were driven back to the White House. Lincoln had several administrative chores to attend to, including inviting Congressman Schuyler
Colfax to accompany his family to the Inauguration Ball, which would
be held on the following evening. Lincoln was on the verge of exhaustion, but he still had to attend to his official duties and responsibili-
ties. Sunday was another working day, just as Inauguration Day had
been. And he still had to get ready for the Inauguration Ball, which was
another chore for him to deal with.

MARCH 6, 1865, MONDAY
INAUGURATION BALL

The day's main activity, for both the president and Mrs. Lincoln, was the Inauguration Ball, which would be held that evening at the Patent Office. But there was a great deal to be done before the president could leave for the party. He met with the diplomatic corps around noon, posed for a photographer later in the afternoon, received members of the Perseverance Fire Company of Philadelphia in East Room at 4:00 p.m., and tended to several other official functions while his wife was preparing for the evening's events.

But the most important event of the day took place several hundred miles from Washington, DC, and had nothing to do with the president's activities. About 60,000 men commanded by General William Tecumseh Sherman crossed from South Carolina into North Carolina, moving north to join forces with General Ulysses S. Grant's army, just south of Petersburg, Virginia. Even though the roads in Virginia were still far too muddy to allow an army to move out of its winter camp, let alone mobilize for the coming spring campaign—the mud was more than a foot deep in some places—the campaign was already beginning.

President Lincoln both dreaded and anticipated the fighting that would soon occupy so much of his time. He hoped that the coming operations between the Army of the Potomac and Robert E. Lee's Army of Northern Virginia would be the final campaign of the war, and that General Grant would be able to bring about the surrender of General Lee and his army. He wanted to end the war quickly and, if at all possible, without another major battle between the two armies. There had already been too much killing.

But the main focus of Monday morning's headlines was not General Sherman and his march through the Carolinas. The newspapers of March 6 were mostly occupied with editorial opinions of the president's Inauguration Address. Papers from all across the country gave their views of the address, both pro and con. The *New York Times* thought that Lincoln had written a flop and a disappointment of a speech. "All that he does is simply to advert to the cause of the war," the *Times* complained, "and to drop an earnest exhortation that all will now stand by the right and strive for a peace that shall be just and lasting."[1] Another New York paper, the *World*, hated the speech—which was understandable, since the *World* was anti-Lincoln as well as outspoken in its support of Confederate independence. "The pity of it, that a divided nation should neither be sustained in this crisis of agony by words of wisdom nor cheered with words of hope."[2] Philadelphia's *Inquirer* had nothing but praise for the address, as well as for the president himself: "The address is characteristic of Mr. Lincoln. It exhibits afresh the kindness of heart, and the large charity which has ever marked his actions toward those who are his personal enemies as well as enemies of his country."[3]

The newspaper that came closest to grasping exactly what Lincoln had in mind with his speech was not from New York or Philadelphia or anywhere else in the United States. London's *Spectator* praised the Inauguration Address not only because of its content, but also because it showed how far Abraham Lincoln had matured and evolved as president during his four years in the White House. "Mr. Lincoln has persevered through all," the editor wrote, "visibly growing in force of character, in self-possession, and in magnanimity during his first term as president." In his address, "We can detect no longer the rude and illiterate mould of a village lawyer's thought, but find it replaced by a grasp of principle, the dignity of manner, and solemnity of purpose."[4]

President Lincoln certainly had been changed by the war since 1861. He seemed a lot older and more dignified, as well as a lot sadder and more reflective, than he had been four years earlier. "Poor Mr. Lincoln is looking so brokenhearted, so completely worn out," Mary Lincoln confided to her dressmaker. "I fear he will not get through the next four years."[5] And he was fully aware that the fighting was far from over. There would be more battles to come, with more slaughter and dying, before the war finally came to an end. For the president, the war could not end soon enough.

The Inauguration Ball had already been in progress for some time before the president and Mrs. Lincoln arrived at around 10:30 p.m. The Patent Office was filled "with many of the most distinguished men and women of the country." It was "a glorious spectacle, such has not been seen in Washington for years."[6]

Abraham Lincoln had visited the Patent Office once before. On May 22, 1849, when he was still a congressman, Lincoln registered a patent for a mechanical device that would move boats over sandbars and other river obstructions. It is the only patent ever to be registered to an American president.[7]

The Patent Office was one of Washington's landmarks. *The Stranger's Guide-Book to Washington City* says, "The Patent Office Building is one of superior finish and elegance."[8] It housed models for all the patented inventions, along with curiosities from the country's past, including a printing press that is reported to have belonged to Benjamin Franklin and personal possessions of George Washington. Since the beginning of the war, the building was also used as temporary barracks, and store for articles captured from the Confederacy.

Mrs. Lincoln was the center of attention at the ball, not President Lincoln—at least as far as the women in the room were concerned. Her ball gown attracted more attention than all the ornaments and decorations in the room put together: "Mrs. Lincoln is most richly dressed in a white moire antique, profusely ornamented with exquisite lace."[9] One news reporter wrote, "Mrs. Lincoln . . . wore a white silk skirt and bodice, an elaborately-worked white lace dress over a silk skirt."[10]

The president was mentioned, as well, but almost as an after-thought: "The president was dressed in black, with white kid gloves."[11] Four years earlier, at his first inauguration ball, the president also seemed ill at ease in his black suit, and especially with his kid gloves. An observer noted that Lincoln cut "an awkward figure" and had "a mind, absent in part, and in part evidently worked by white kid gloves."[12] He was probably just as uncomfortable at his second inauguration ball but was determined not to let it show.

The president and his wife were escorted from the ballroom to the dining room shortly after midnight. After dinner, the Lincolns left the ball and returned to the White House. Mary Lincoln enjoyed the evening's activities much more than her husband, but the ball was a nice change of pace for the president. At least the "glorious spectacle" took his mind off the problems and the pressures of his office for a few hours, which must have given him some relief. With the coming of the spring offensive, which could only be two or three weeks away at most, Lincoln knew that the pressures would increase even further.

OFFICE ROUTINE

The president spent much of Tuesday, March 7, endorsing applications for jobs: Philip C. Schuyler was recommended for a position as Indian agent for the Sac and Fox tribes; Charles C. Coffenberry had a similar recommendation as agent for the Otoe tribe; and M. R. Dutton received an endorsement as agent for the Kickapoo tribe, with the note, "This application assumes that the incumbent is wholly incompetent," which was initialed by Lincoln.[1]

President Lincoln also issued orders for five people who owned unspecified "products of the insurrectionary states" to bring these products "within military lines for sale to agents of government."[2] But in addition to these fairly mundane details, President Lincoln also sent a special communiqué to General U. S. Grant: "In accordance with a Joint Resolution of Congress, approved December 17, 1863," the president awarded a gold medal and an engrossed parchment copy of the resolution. Lincoln went on to say, "Please accept, for yourself and all under your command, the renewed expression of my gratitude."[3]

President Lincoln had appointed General Grant general-in-chief of all Union armies a year before, in March 1864, and also promoted him to the rank of lieutenant general. Grant was the hero of Vicksburg—he not only captured the city, but also forced the surrender of Confederate general John Pemberton's army of thirty thousand—and was one of the few generals whom Lincoln had faith in. Lincoln had gone through three other generals-in-chief before Grant—Winfield Scott, Henry Halleck, and George McClellan. All of them had either been too old—Winfield Scott was an overweight and infirm seventy-five-year-old—or just plain incompetent. In the year since Grant had taken command, he had driven Robert E. Lee and his army south through the Wilderness and Spotsylvania and Cold Harbor to Petersburg, where he kept the entire Army of Northern Virginia bottled up in their trenches all through the winter of 1864–65. None of his predecessors would have had either the determination or the ability to outfight General Lee, or to bring his fabled army to the brink of surrender.

"Grant has stamped a new character on the tactics of the Federals," the *Times* of London declared. This was certainly a remarkable reversal of opinion—the *Times* had always been deliberately antagonistic toward Lincoln, as well as his generals, every one of them. Now the editors were saying flattering and complimentary things, not only about Grant but also about his general strategy. "No other general would either have advanced upon the Wilderness . . . or followed up an almost victorious though retiring enemy. Under his command the Army of the Potomac has achieved in invading Virginia an amount of success never achieved before except in repelling invasion."[4]

Lincoln was more straightforward in his letter to General Grant. He just expressed his appreciation "for yourself and all under your command," his gratitude "for yourself and their arduous and well-performed public service"[5]

General Grant was too practical and down-to-earth to have his head turned by anything as flashy and transient as a gold medal, even if it was from Congress. He did not even mention the medal, or the engrossed parchment scroll, or the president's letter, in his *Memoirs*—that would have been completely out of character for the truly modest tanner's son from Ohio. He was certainly touched by the president's—and Congress's—gesture, but he was too unassuming to let his feelings show.

General Grant probably would also have said that the reason for his reticence was that he had more important things on his mind, namely the Army of Northern Virginia, Robert E. Lee, and exactly what General Lee intended to do with his army in the very near future. He was especially anxious that General Lee and his army would slip out of their Petersburg trenches and escape to North Carolina where they would join forces with General Joseph E. Johnston's army. He had done the same thing to General Lee the previous June—evacuated his entrenchments at Cold Harbor and escaped from General Lee—so he knew that it could be done.

"I felt that the situation of the Confederate army was such that they would try to make an escape at the earliest practicable moment," Grant would write many years later, "and I was afraid, every morning, that I would awake from my sleep to hear that Lee had gone, and that nothing was left but a picket line."[6] General Lee had the railroad at Danville, which was about 135 miles from Petersburg, to take his army south. He might just decide to load everything aboard a train— men, artillery, equipment, tents, and baggage—and simply disappear, leaving Grant stuck in his trenches south of Petersburg.

"I knew that he could move much more lightly and rapidly than I, and that, if he got this start, he would leave me behind so that we would have the same army to fight again further south—and the war might be prolonged another year." General Grant said that he was "naturally very impatient" to start his spring campaign against General Lee, "which I thoroughly believed would close the war."[7]

President Lincoln had the same hopes and the same fears—he hoped that the war would end in the spring, but was afraid that some-thing might happen that would prolong the fighting. Grant instructed his troops around Petersburg "to keep a sharp lookout to see that such a movement should not escape their notice."[8] The president was in full agreement with General Grant's orders, and dreaded the escape of General Lee and his army as much as Grant.

MARCH 8, 1865, WEDNESDAY
POLITICAL AFFAIRS

Among the president's activities on this Wednesday was a meeting with Secretary of State William Seward about a suitable appointment for former postmaster Montgomery Blair.

In September 1864, President Lincoln had asked Postmaster Blair to resign his position. The president's request had been a purely political move, which had been made to bolster his chances of winning the election. The candidate of the third-party Radical Democracy Party, John C. Fremont, was threatening to split the Republican vote in November. The Radical Democracy was made up mainly of dissatisfied and disgruntled Republicans who still held a good many of the same views as the Republicans, except that the Radicals were a lot more extreme in their outlook regarding slavery—they wanted to abolish slavery immediately and did not have the patience to wait until the end of the war. Fremont was popular enough that he might very well have taken enough votes away from Lincoln and Andrew Johnson to give the election to the Democrats and their candidate, George B. McClellan. Fremont agreed to withdraw from the race in exchange for Montgomery Blair's resignation.

Fremont and the Radicals wanted Blair out of politics, or at least out of the immediate political picture—among other things that alienated Fremont and his fellow Radicals, Blair had opposed the Emancipation Proclamation and was not an extreme abolitionist. So Lincoln asked for Blair's resignation in exchange for Fremont's dropping out of the presidential race.

As far as Lincoln was concerned, this was a more than fair exchange. He might have been president as well as commander in chief, but above

47

all he was a professional politician, and a very practical and hard-headed politician at that. Now that Blair had resigned as postmaster, Lincoln offered him a post as ambassador to either Spain or Austria. Blair considered Lincoln's offer and decided to reject both appointments.

The president also nominated a Commander John J. Young promotion to the rank of captain on the Navy's reserve list. Commander Young had been passed over for promotion "in consequence of physical disability, this disability having occurred in the discharge of his duties." The Senate confirmed Young's promotion two days later, on March 10, 1865.[1] One of Lincoln's more enjoyable duties as president included doing a good deed from time to time, including speaking up for a naval officer who had been slighted by government officials.

The time had not yet come when General Grant could "commence the spring campaign," as he would write,[2] but fighting had already started in North Carolina. On March 8, Federal troops under Jacob D. Cox were attacked by Confederates commanded by Braxton Bragg near the town of Kinston. Some of the Union troops broke and ran, but the line held and the Confederates were beaten off. In spite of this initial setback, Bragg continued his attack against the Union position. The battle was another indication that it would only be a matter of time before fighting began in Virginia—Kinston, North Carolina, is only 161 miles away from Petersburg, Virginia.

General Grant and President Lincoln were not the only ones who hoped that the impending battles would be the final campaign of the war. Every soldier in the trenches south of Petersburg was hoping for the same thing. "It rained hard all day and everything looks desolate, and I feel very lonely and homesick," Lieutenant Colonel Elisha Hunt Rhodes scribbled in his diary. "No news of a move yet, but it cannot be delayed long. If Lee stays in Petersburg General Grant will catch him from the south. I hope so, for I am tired of fighting and want the war to end."[3]

COMMUNICATIONS WITH GENERAL GRANT

The president spent much of the day in his office, seeing to endorsements and appointments. Among them was an endorsement for Corporal Hayden De Lany, of the Thirteenth Ohio Volunteers, to attend the US Military Academy at West Point. (De Lany entered West Point in July 1865, and received his commission as a second lieutenant in September 1867.) It was certainly the type of endorsement that Lincoln enjoyed making.[1]

The president also replied to a telegraph that General Grant had sent to Secretary of War Edwin M. Stanton. "I understand that rebel prisoners in the North are allowed to take the oath of allegiance and go free," the general said. "I think this is wrong. No one should be liberated on taking the oath . . . who has been captured while bearing arms against us except where persons of known loyalty vouch for them."[2]

Any Confederate prisoner who took the oath of allegiance also promised to obey and support the Constitution of the United States. General Grant did not trust either the rebel soldiers who took the oath or their motives. He strongly suspected that the prisoners were taking the oath only as an expedient—after swearing allegiance to the United States, they would cross the Confederate lines and rejoin their regiments. Confederate soldiers did not change sides unless they had an ulterior motive, at least not as far as Grant was concerned. If any rebel wanted to take the oath, they could always "come into our lines if they do not wish to fight."[3]

Lincoln intercepted Grant's telegram to Secretary of War Stanton—the president frequently visited the War Department's telegraph office to read the latest communiques from his generals, including General Grant. "I see your dispatch to the Sec. of War, objecting to rebel prisoners being allowed to take the oath and go free," Lincoln responded. "What has been done is that Members of Congress come to me from time to time with lists of names alleging that from personal knowledge," he went on to explain, "and evidence of reliable persons they are satisfied that it is safe to discharge the particular persons named on the list, and I have ordered their discharge."[4]

He went on to say that most of the released Confederate prisoners came from the border states, not the seceded Confederate states, and that only two of the "liberated" persons rejoined the army instead of returning home. "Doubtless some more have proven false; but on the whole I believe what I have done in this way has done good rather than harm." Those who agreed with Lincoln's point of view present this as evidence of his compassion for Confederate prisoners of war, too many of whom were suffering dreadfully in Northern prisoner of war camps. Critics complained that Lincoln was not behaving wisely, and that he was more soft-headed than soft-hearted in his dealings with the rebels.

General Grant was more than satisfied with the president's explanation. "Your dispatch of this morning shows that prisoners of war are being exchanged only in accordance with the rule I proposed," he replied on the afternoon of March 9. He went on to say that officers from Camp Morton and Rock Island prisoner of war camps had misinformed him that "great numbers were being discharged on taking the oath of allegiance." These officers were under the impression that any and all persons "who desired to do so" were being allowed to take the oath and immediately were being sent home, which is how Grant received the mistaken impression that anyone who took the oath could "go free." The president corrected Grant's misinformation, and also put his mind at rest.[5]

Fighting continued in North Carolina. Confederate troops under Braxton Bragg kept trying to break the Federal line held by Jacob Cox and his men near Kinton. At Monroe Crossroads, Confederate cavalry under Wade Hampton attacked Union forces commanded by General Hugh Kilpatrick. The Federals were taken completely by surprise, and ran from the field in confusion. According to myth, Kilpatrick was still in bed when the attack began—with a young woman from Columbia, in some versions—and was so flummoxed that he did not have time to put his trousers on before he ran out of his tent. Trousers or not, Kilpatrick managed to rally his men, turn them around, and counterattack. This time, it was Wade Hampton's turn to be surprised— Kilpatrick's unexpected charge drove them back in a full retreat. The episode is known historically as the Battle of Monroe's Crossroads, but in legend it is the Battle of Kilpatrick's Drawers.[6]

General Sherman was on the move from Randalsville, North Carolina, toward Fayetteville. He was impatient to make contact with forces under John M. Schofield, which were said to be at Wilmington, but was only able to move at a snail's pace because of bad roads. But his most immediate goal was Fayetteville, with its arsenal and its factories for making weapons and ammunition. When he reached Fayetteville, Sherman planned to destroy everything—the factories and machine shops, along with all the muskets and cannon in the arsenal and anything else he could put his hands on.

DAY OF REST

This turned out to be a much-needed day of rest for the president, a quiet day of relaxation and not much in the way of activity. He did discuss the possibility of offering a cabinet post to his former vice-president, Hannibal Hamlin, and also attended a meeting with his cabinet. But he sent no communiques on March 10, wrote no letters, and does not appear to have made any nominations or endorsements.

Abraham Lincoln was worn out by the spring of 1865, almost on the brink of exhaustion, and often complained about being tired. He had also lost weight, and appeared to be still losing weight; his face was heavily lined from anxiety and fatigue. An officer on General George Gordon Meade's staff took one look at the president and said that he was "the ugliest man I ever put my eyes on," and also that he had an "expression of plebeian vulgarity in his face."[1] Lincoln's secretary John Hay had a great deal more sympathy regarding the president's appearance, along with more understanding on the subject of what made him appear so old and worn-out.

John Hay had known the president for the past four years and was well aware that it had been the pressures and worries of the war—"the great conflict in which he was engaged and which he could not evade," is the way Hay put it—that had ground Lincoln down and made him an old man while he was still in his fifties. "Under this frightful ordeal his demeanour and disposition changed," Hay would write, "so gradually that it would be impossible to say when the change began; but he was in mind, body, and nerves a very different man" at the end of the four years that produced Gettysburg, Vicksburg, Antietam, Shiloh, and a score of other battles that cost horrible numbers of lives.[2]

The war, which Lincoln feared would produce additional battles and even more loss of life, was moving toward Virginia, but was not moving very quickly. General Sherman and his army made their way toward Fayetteville but were slowed dramatically, sometimes to a full stop in places, by the weather and especially by the mud that turned all the roads into bogs and swamps. None of the roads were paved, which meant they had to be covered by fence rails and felled trees—called corduroying—to make them even halfway safe for the horses and wagons and artillery that had to pass over them. The mud was so deep and so cloying that sometimes the logs would disappear into it after the army had driven over that section of road. It was very slow going, but General Sherman was determined to get to Fayetteville and was not about to let anything as insignificant as a sea of mud get in his way.[3]

At Kinston, about eighty miles away from Fayetteville, Jacob Cox's men managed to hold their line against Braxton Bragg's repeated attacks. Finally, on March 10, Bragg decided that enough was enough and broke off his attack. He marched his men off to join Joseph E. Johnston's Army of Tennessee. General Johnston was hoping to link up with Robert E. Lee's army, if and when Lee was able to slip away from Grant at Petersburg and escape to North Carolina, and he would be needing all the men he could find.

The atmosphere was becoming noticeably warmer as the month of March went on, and not just in the meteorological sense.

MARCH 11 AND 12, 1865, SATURDAY AND SUNDAY
LIFE AND DEATH DECISIONS

President Lincoln addressed another matter that was causing him no small amount of distress, namely the execution of deserters from the army. He had been able to save individual soldiers from the firing squad, but on March 11 the president signed a proclamation that all deserters "shall be pardoned." There was a condition, though: in order to earn the president's pardon, a deserter would have to return to the army and finish his enlistment.

According to the proclamation, "all deserters returning within sixty days . . . shall be pardoned on condition of returning to their regiments and companies or such other organizations as they may be assigned to until they shall have served for a period of time equal to their original term of enlistment."[1] Lincoln once claimed that he made more life and death decisions than all of his predecessors put together. He had just made another one.

On Sunday, March 11, Confederate cavalry left Fayetteville, North Carolina, riding over the bridges across the Cape Fear River. General Sherman's troops occupied the town as soon as the enemy left and began systematically destroying the arsenal and everything in it, along with anything else that might be useful to the Confederates.[2]

The men had a personal incentive for wanting to wreck the Fayetteville Arsenal—the factory turned out well over one million .58 caliber minié balls per year, lead bullets that were the infantryman's primary ammunition. Breaking up the arsenal meant that the Confederate army, including Joe Johnston's men, would be receiving at least a million fewer bullets to shoot at them. The destruction went on all day Sunday.

MARCH 13, 1865, MONDAY
NOT SICK, JUST TIRED

The pressures of office, added to the preparations for Inauguration Day and all of the other activities of recent weeks, had finally taken their toll on the president. By the middle of March, he was so exhausted that he decided to stay in bed for a few days. There was nothing physically wrong with him; he did not have a cold or a virus or any sort of illness. He was just worn-out, and needed some time off. The *New York Herald* said, "Mr. Lincoln is reported quite sick to-day, and has denied himself to all visitors."[1] But the *Herald* did not get its facts straight. Mr. Lincoln was not sick, just tired.

On the day before, March 12, General William Tecumseh Sherman had contacted General Grant from Fayetteville, North Carolina, to give him an update. "The army is in splendid health, condition, and spirits" Sherman wrote, "though we have had foul weather, and roads that would have stopped travel to almost any other body of men I ever heard of." General Sherman was obviously in splendid spirits himself. His men continued to wreck the arsenal—to smash it beyond recognition would probably be a more accurate description. "I shall therefore destroy this valuable arsenal so the enemy shall not have its use," he went on to say.[2] He was certainly doing his best to carry out his agenda.

In Richmond, Congress passed legislation allowing black troops to join the Confederate army. This revolutionary statute had been requested by General Robert E. Lee, who would be needing all the able-bodied men he could get for the battles that he knew were to come—he was as aware as General Grant and President Lincoln that renewed fighting would begin within the next week or ten days. Hundreds of men were deserting his army every day, and General Lee was desperate to find replacements for them.

Black men had been put to work as laborers for the army, digging trenches and preparing earthworks, but had never been recruited as soldiers. General Lee had expressed a low opinion of blacks as soldiers earlier in the war, but the current crisis in manpower made him change his mind. At the beginning of 1865, General Lee said that he was now in favor of having black troops in the Confederate army, along with an unspecified program of "gradual emancipation." As Lee now saw the situation, "The services of these men are now necessary to enable us to oppose the enemy."[3]

On March 10, General Lee wrote to Confederate president Jefferson Davis, "I do not know whether the law authorizing the use of negro troops has received your sanction, but if it has, I respectfully recommend that measures be taken to carry it into effect as soon as practicable." Later in the same communiqué, he reported, "I have received letters from persons offering to select the most suitable among their slaves, as soon as Congress should give the authority," and asked that President Davis take the necessary steps to "raise some negro companies" as soon as possible.[4]

A week after the Confederate Congress passed its legislation, on March 21, the Richmond *Sentinel* reported that "the company of colored troops under Captain Grimes" would parade in one of the city's squares dressed in Confederate gray. Black units were issued new uniforms and marched through Richmond's streets to encourage other blacks to enlist. Southern blacks did fight for the Confederacy, a fact that has been overlooked by a good many writers and historians. "I had as much right to fight for my native state as you had to fight for yours," a captured black soldier told a Union officer, "and a blame sight more than your foreigners what's got no homes."[5]

CABINET MEETING

"The President was some indisposed and in bed, but not seriously ill," Gideon Welles noted on his diary. "The [cabinet] members met in his bedroom."[1] Lincoln was still recuperating from stress and strain and overwork, and was also preparing himself mentally for the fighting that would soon begin again. The cabinet meeting was fairly short; the president does not appear to have written any letters or communiques.

In North Carolina, General William Tecumseh Sherman was also getting ready for the coming battles. Or, as he put it, he was preparing "for the next and last stage of the war." Sherman knew that General Joseph E. Johnston was organizing his army in the vicinity of Raleigh. "I was determined, however, to give him as little time for organization as possible," Sherman said, and began moving his army away from Fayetteville except for one division. This division was to stay at Fayetteville until the arsenal was completely destroyed. The arsenal "was deliberately and completely levelled on the 14th," General Sherman recounted, "when fire was applied to the wreck." He intended to leave nothing behind that might be of any use at all to the enemy, not even any standing walls.[2]

General Philip Sheridan had been moving north from the Shenandoah Valley for the past several days, heading toward General Grant's army at Petersburg. At Petersburg, Grant's men were expecting to receive orders to move at any time. "Well, I am ready," Colonel Elisha Hunt Rhodes reflected, "and may God give us victory."[3]

EVENING AT GROVER'S THEATRE

President Lincoln felt fit enough to return to his office after two days of recuperation. It was a fairly routine day: he made several endorsements and appointments, received the Austrian minister, Count Wydenbruck, and sent him a very cordial note wishing him an enjoyable residence in the United States. The president also wrote to Thurlow Weed, who was one of New York State's most influential Republican bosses. Thurlow Weed had praised a recent speech Lincoln made to the Congressional Notification Committee as well as his inaugural address.

The letter is surprisingly cheerful and upbeat, considering the tension and anxiety the president had been under. "Everyone likes a compliment," Lincoln wrote. "Thank you for yours on my little notification speech, and on the recent Inaugural Address." He agreed with Weed that the inaugural speech will "wear as well as—perhaps better than—anything I have produced," even though it was not immediately popular. "Men are not flattered by being shown that there has been a difference of purpose between the Almighty and them."[1]

That evening, the president and Mrs. Lincoln, along with Colonel James G. Wilson and Clara Harris, attended a performance of Mozart's opera *The Magic Flute* at Grover's Theatre. The opera "was performed in excellent style by the German company last night," according to the Washington *Evening Star*.[2]

"Mr. Lincoln's life was almost devoid of recreation," according to his secretary, John Hay.[3] Actually, the president's life was not all that lacking for either recreation or amusement. Lincoln enjoyed the theater, everything from opera to Shakespeare to minstrel shows, and went as often as he could—for relaxation as much as for entertainment. But because of his current frame of mind, he was not always able to enjoy the performance.

During the performance of *The Magic Flute*, the president "sat in the rear of the box leaning his head against the partition, paying no attention to the play and looking . . . worn and weary." Colonel Wilson asked Lincoln if he was enjoying the performance, and was told that he had not come to the theater to see the opera—he had come for some rest: "I am being hounded to death by office seekers, who pursue me early and late, and it is simply to get two or three hours relief that I am here." Attending the opera was just an excuse for getting away from the White House and all of its worries.[4]

John Wilkes Booth had also been to the theater on March 15. He was in Washington to work out a plan for the abduction of President Abraham Lincoln; his visit to the theater was part of that plan. He had gone to Ford's Theatre to watch a performance of *The Tragedy of Jane Shore*, by Nicholas Rowe, along with two friends, John Surratt and Lewis Powell.

Booth was not all that interested in the play, which has been described as an imitation of one of Shakespeare's history plays. He bought his guests tickets for the box above the stage, where president and Mrs. Lincoln sat when they attended plays at Ford's Theatre. His main object in going to Ford's Theatre was for John Surratt and Lewis Powell to see the inside of the box, to familiarize themselves with it, while Booth himself watched the play from backstage, along with members of the cast.

After the performance, Booth and Lewis Powell went to Gautier's Restaurant to wait for four other men: Samuel Arnold, George Atzerodt, David Herold, and Michael O'Laughlen. Booth had reserved one of the restaurant's private rooms. All the men smoked, drank, and played cards until about 1:30 on the morning of March 16, when the waiters and other members of Gautier's staff finally locked the building and went home.

None of Booth's guests had any idea why they had been invited to Gautier's. None of the men knew each other very well; David Herold did not know Samuel Arnold or Michael O'Laughlen at all. After the restaurant staff left for the night, Booth finally announced the reason for the meeting—he had called everyone together because he had concocted an idea to kidnap President Lincoln, and he needed their help to carry out his plan.

His scheme involved handcuffing Lincoln and lowering him to the stage during one of the president's visits to Ford's Theatre. The president and his wife frequently went to Ford's, and always sat in the box above the stage. Since Powell was familiar with the layout of the presidential, this should help facilitate the abduction.

According to his arrangement, Booth and one other man would handcuff Lincoln and lower him down to the stage, where he would be seized by the others and carried out of the theater. A carriage would be waiting just outside of the stage entrance. All of the men, including Booth, would then gallop across Washington and escape out of the city, where they would make contact with Confederate agents. The president would then be held hostage in exchange for Confederate prisoners of war.

John Wilkes Booth thought his plan was perfect—not only foolproof but brilliant. By holding President Lincoln for ransom, the South would not only have the ultimate bargaining chip for carrying out a prisoner of war exchange, but Booth would also be dealing a severe blow to the morale of the North. He was certain that everyone present would agree that his kidnapping scheme was nothing less than outstanding.

The reaction to Booth's scheme came as a rude shock. Everyone in the room reached a unanimous agreement, but it was not the agreement that Booth was expecting—his cronies thought that the plan was ludicrous, foolhardy, and, above all else, suicidal. They pointed out that the president was not just going to sit still and let himself be tied up and manhandled out of the theater. Also, Lincoln was sure to be surrounded by guards, who would also have something to say about kidnapping the president. And Samuel Arnold pointed that the idea of using Lincoln as a hostage for exchanging Confederate prisoners was totally unfeasible—General Ulysses S. Grant had already reinstated a prisoner of war exchange two months earlier, in January 1865. Booth's plan was completely impractical, everyone said, and had absolutely no chance of succeeding.

Booth tried to argue with Sam Arnold and the others, and did his best to convince everyone that his plan would succeed if they would only give it a chance. But no one would listen. Booth's would-be conspirators wanted no part of his proposal; they refused to risk their lives by taking part in such an insane scheme.

John Wilkes Booth was angered and disappointed by the reaction. But he was determined to do something that would put an end to Lincoln and his presidency—Booth considered Lincoln to be one of the great tyrants in history, as well as the South's principal enemy. The idea for kidnapping Lincoln had fallen through, but there would be other plans and other opportunities. As far as Booth was concerned, anything, including assassination, would be more than justified when done to stop a tyrant.[5]

MARCH 16, 1865, THURSDAY
TAD

President Lincoln indulged in another one of his favorite forms of relaxation: he went for a ride. He usually went with Mary Lincoln, but on this particular day he decided to go with his eleven-year-old son, Thomas "Tad" Lincoln. Tad Lincoln spent a good deal of time with his father. He frequently accompanied Lincoln on trips, often attended cabinet meetings, and stayed with the president in his office for hours on end. People frequently told stories about how close Tad and his father were, and about the boy's many and various pranks. One of these pranks took place during a visit to Grover's Theatre. During the performance, Tad managed to slip out of the president's box unnoticed. President Lincoln had no idea that his son was missing until he saw the boy down on the stage, singing "The Battle Cry of Freedom" with the chorus. Tad was wearing a Union army blouse about three sizes too large for him, and was almost unrecognizable in the oversized uniform top.

Tad Lincoln had his mother's nervous temperament. He was also on the hyperactive side, and did not show much interest in learning—he was considered a slow learner by a succession of tutors—and also had a speech impediment. President Lincoln's bodyguard William Crook said, "Taddie could never speak very plainly." His impairment sometimes made it seem like he had his own language, especially when he was speaking of other people. Tad called his father "papa-day," which everyone supposed meant "papa dear." In Tad's lingo, Crook became "Took." But the president enjoyed Tad's company and spent as much time with the boy as he could—the boy's very presence seemed to take the president's mind off the pressures of Washington. "I believe he was the best companion Mr. Lincoln ever had," Crook observed, "one who always understood him, and whom he always understood."[1]

Most people were touched by the relationship between the president and his son, but there were those who complained that Tad was completely undisciplined and was allowed to get away with too much mischief. But Lincoln had lost one son, William Wallace "Willie" Lincoln, most likely due to typhoid fever, when the boy was eleven years old. Because of this, Lincoln was more inclined to let Tad get away with his pranks. Lincoln might have been even more lenient if he had known that Tad would die at the age of eighteen, in 1871.

"On the 15th of March the whole army was across Cape Fear River," General William Tecumseh Sherman wrote, "and at once began its march for Goldsboro."[2] The army encountered "pretty stubborn resistance" from Confederate General William J. Hardee's infantry, cavalry, and artillery. Heavy rain helped to curtail the fighting, but on Thursday March 16, "the opposition continued stubborn." Near the village of Averysboro, General Hardee's men dug themselves into a strong defensive position. General Sherman ordered one of his brigades to outflank Hardee's trenches. The maneuver succeeded—217 Confederates were captured, and another 108 were killed in the course of the flanking move.

By the following morning, General Hardee's force had disappeared, "in full retreat toward Smithfield." The Battle of Averysboro, as General Sherman called it, was not exactly a rout, but it did allow Sherman's army to continue its move northward, toward Petersburg and Grant's army. "From Averysboro the left wing turned east, toward Goldsboro, the Fourteenth Corps leading," General Sherman would write.[3]

THE PRESIDENT THINKS AHEAD

Although President Lincoln's thoughts were never very far away from the coming campaign in Virginia, he was also beginning to think ahead toward what would happen to the country after the war had ended. On March 17, Lincoln looked away from Virginia long enough to see and appreciate what was taking place in the West. He issued a proclamation calling for the court martial of anyone supplying weapons to Indian tribes in the lands west of the Mississippi. "Whereas reliable information has been received that hostile Indians within the limits of the United States have been furnished with arms and munitions of war," which is enabling them "to prosecute their savage warfare upon the exposed and sparse settlements of the frontier."

The president went on to proclaim that "all persons detected in that nefarious traffic" will be arrested and tried by court martial and, if convicted, "shall receive the punishment due to their deserts."[1]

During his first term in office, the president was fully preoccupied with the war and how it was being conducted—with the performance of General George B. McClellan and his less-than-successful campaign against Robert E. Lee in 1862; with General Grant's siege of Vicksburg in 1863; with the course of the US Navy's blockade of Southern ports; and his own chances of being reelected in 1864. But now all those problems were safely behind him. The war looked to be nearing its end.

If everything went the way Lincoln hoped, the fighting might be over by early summer or even before that. He now had the time to focus on items that would occupy his time and his thoughts during the remainder of his second term, beyond the war. One of these matters was the settling of the West, which meant creating new states and protecting settlers from "hostile Indians." His concern was no longer centered on the North and the South. He could now afford to consider the future of all the states, and the entire reunified country. Lincoln's proclamation of March 17, 1865, was a step in that direction.

On the same day, President Lincoln made a speech to the 140th Indiana Regiment, during which he presented the regiment with a flag that it had captured a Fort Anderson, North Carolina, that past February. After making his presentation, the president turned to the main point of his remarks—the recruitment of black soldiers into the Confederate army. Or, as Lincoln put it, "the recent attempt of our erring brethren," as he called the Confederates, "to employ the negro to fight for them."[2]

As far as Lincoln was concerned, any black man who agreed "to fight for those who would keep them in slavery" deserved to be a slave.[3] But recruiting slaves was also another indication that the Confederacy was on its last legs, and that it would not be very long before the rebellion collapsed. "We must now see the bottom of the enemy's resources," he told his audience. "They have drawn upon their last branch of resources. And we can now see the bottom."

The speech was good-natured, and was interrupted several times by applause and laughter. But the president's message was clear enough— the war was almost over, the end was in sight, and he "could see the bottom." He ended with, "I am glad to see the end so near at hand," which was received with another round of applause. "I have now said more than I intended, and I will therefore bid you goodbye."[4] But he was also afraid that there would be one more big battle before it all ended, possibly something on the scale of Gettysburg or Antietam/ Sharpsburg, and he feared for the resulting loss of life during that battle.

MARCH 18 AND 19, 1865, SATURDAY AND SUNDAY
EXECUTIVE DECISIONS

The president spent most of the weekend tending to administrative duties. He authorized General Edward R. S. Canby to assist in raising funds for the Orphans' Home of the State of Mississippi, discharged a Private Charles T. Dorsett from the army at the request of the soldier's father, and annulled the sentences of two contractors named Benjamin G. Smith and Franklin W. Smith, both of whom were convicted of committing fraud against the government. Lincoln did not believe that the two had willfully defrauded the government and declared that "the judgement and sentence are disapproved and declared null."[1]

Secretary of the Navy Gideon Welles, who was well acquainted with the details of this particular case, thought that Lincoln's famous charity was misplaced in this instance, and that he never should have overturned the conviction. "It is, I regret to say, a discreditable endorsement," Welles reflected, "and would, if made public, be likely to injure the president."[2] Secretary Welles did not think Lincoln was being charitable or compassionate, only unwise.

On Sunday, March 19, Lincoln approved General John Pope's "plan of action for Missouri," which the general had sent earlier in the month.[3] Missouri was a border state that supplied men to both sides, and also had had a history of vicious guerilla fighting since the beginning of the war. General Pope's proposal was to remove all "United States troops" from the state, unless they were needed "to defend it against an armed invasion." As long as Federal troops remained, Pope explained, "they will be a constant source of embarrassment and a difficult obstacle to the renewal of the civil administration." General Pope recommended that the troops be withdrawn, so that Missouri could form its own state government. The president agreed with Pope's recommendation and sent his approval.

This is another instance of President Lincoln looking beyond the war, and of taking the postwar development of the country into consideration. Most of his second term would be concerned with reconciling and reunifying the country. Approving General Pope's endorsement was another step toward reunification.

General Sherman was still doing his best to join with General Grant at Petersburg, but, as ever, was being slowed by bad roads, bad maps, and General Joseph E. Johnston. "The country was very obscure," General Sherman complained, "and the maps extremely defective."[4] All the roads were basically rivers of mud, and Joe Johnston always seemed to be somewhere nearby, just waiting for the chance to strike.

On March 19, cannon fire came from the direction of Bentonville. "Johnston's army struck the head of Slocum's columns," Sherman would write.[5] The heaviest day of fighting was March 19, but the battle went on for several more days—Sherman considered the fighting of March 20 and 21 nothing more than "mere skirmishing." By March 23, every one of Sherman's corps had reached Goldsboro, in spite of all opposition and inconveniences, "thus effecting a perfect junction of all the army at that point, as originally contemplated."

Now that Sherman's army had arrived at its goal, the next step was to move north into Virginia—"to resume our march," according to General Sherman, "and come within the theatre of General Grant's field of operations."[6] At this point in time, Sherman thought his army could do absolutely anything he asked it to do. It had just made "one of the longest and most important marches ever made by any organized army in a civilized country"—from Savannah to Goldsboro, 425 miles in fifty days, had destroyed Columbia and Fayetteville, forced the evacuation of Charleston, had "utterly broken up" all the railroads in South Carolina, and had accomplished all of this "with the army in superb order."

Now that he had done all of these impressive things, what General Sherman wanted most of all was to finish up the war with his old friend Grant. He would rest his army at Goldsboro, refit, reequip, pick up some rations, and march to Petersburg. In Sherman's own words, his men were "ragged, dirty, and saucy, and we must rest and fix up a little."[7] Sherman had the idea that Grant should wait for him and his army to arrive, so that they could begin their spring offensive against General Lee together. The two armies, teamed up and fighting together, would make an unbeatable combination and would be able to achieve anything: capture Richmond, overwhelm General Lee, or whatever General Grant might have in mind—at least in General Sherman's considered opinion.

But General Grant did not share his friend's enthusiasm. "Sherman was anxious that I should stay where I was until he could come up, and make a sure thing of it," he later would write, "but I had determined to move as soon as the roads and weather would admit my doing so." He would have to wait until Philip Sheridan arrived with his cavalry, "as both his presence and that of his cavalry were necessary to the execution of the plans which I had in mind."[8]

General Grant was not inclined to stay in Petersburg until General Sherman showed up. His main anxiety was still that General Lee and his army would get away from him and escape to North Carolina. He intended to begin operations against Lee around March 28, and did not have the time to wait for Sherman. "Every possible precaution was taken meanwhile to prevent Lee from withdrawing his army," General Grant's aide, Colonel Horace Porter, recalled. "Scouts and spies were more active than ever before; about 30,000 men were kept virtually on the picket line, and all the troops were equipped and supplied, ready to make a forced march at a moment's notice in case Lee should be found moving."[9]

Although Grant was nervous about General Lee and what he had planned for the immediate future, just about everyone in Washington seemed to be optimistic about the war and its impending outcome. "The news from the army continues favorable," Gideon Welles wrote, "and it seems impossible for the Rebel leaders to continue much longer to hold out."[10] But President Lincoln did not agree with this point of view. If anything, he was even more anxious than Grant. Lincoln wanted to end the war as quickly as possible, and with as little additional loss of life as possible. He did not want Lee to escape from Petersburg, which would extend the fighting for another three to six months, and possibly longer.

MARCH 20, 1865, MONDAY
CITY POINT

At about 10:00 a.m., General Grant telegraphed President Lincoln, "Can you not visit City Point for a day or two? I would like very much to see you, and I think the rest would do you good."[1]

The president did not need much coaxing. He replied to General Grant later that day: "Your kind invitation received," Lincoln wrote. "Had already thought of going immediately after the next rain. Will go sooner if any reason for it. Mrs. L. and a few others will probably accompany me. Will notify you of exact time, once it shall be fixed upon."[2]

Lincoln had been looking for an excuse to get away from Washington and everything—and everybody—that went with it for quite some time. This was his excuse. He realized that this would be a working vacation, at best, but at least it would be a change.

City Point was General Grant's headquarters, and was also the main supply depot for the Army of the Potomac. Since 1861, it had evolved from a small riverside village to a burgeoning seaport on the James River, about ten miles northeast of Petersburg. The base was dirty and overcrowded, with wharves and docks that stretched all along the riverfront for over a mile. All these wharves and warehouses kept the army supplied with everything it needed, from artillery ammunition to fresh bread. City Point was nobody's idea of a vacation resort, but at least the trip would get Lincoln away from the White House for a while.

But the trip would not be all rest and relaxation. While he was at City Point, the president would also meet with General Grant to discuss the end of the war and what to do about the Army of Northern

73

Virginia. Specifically, he wanted to make certain that Grant did not discuss any subjects with General Lee except purely military matters. Grant was forbidden to make any mention at all regarding peace negotiations, or any subject outside the surrender of Lee's army.

But before the president did anything else, he had to make arrangements for the journey to City Point. It was decided he would sail from Washington aboard the USS *Bat*, a side-wheeled steamer that has been described as fast and well-armed. The *Bat*'s captain, Lieutenant Commander John S. Barnes, reported to the White House on this particular Monday to meet with President Lincoln regarding the trip. The president was very friendly and approachable, but Commander Barnes noted that Lincoln had a general look of sadness that upset him. After a few minutes of casual conversation, Lincoln mentioned that Mrs. Lincoln would be joining him on the trip. He asked Commander Barnes if the *Bat* would be able to accommodate his wife and her personal servant and dresser, Mrs. Elizabeth Keckley.

Commander Barnes also spoke with Mrs. Lincoln about the coming trip. He was introduced to the president's wife, who also was very cordial and friendly. She explained that she would be accompanying her husband to City Point and wanted Barnes to make arrangements to take herself, Mrs. Keckley, and a bodyguard aboard his ship along with the president.

This presented a problem. USS *Bat* was a warship. It was built in Liverpool, England, and had been purchased by the Confederate government as a blockade runner. In October 1864, the ship was captured by Union warships off the North Carolina coast and became part of the US Navy's blockade squadron in January 1865. It had not been designed for luxury, and did not have any amenities for women. The *Bat* would have been fine if the president was going to City Point by himself. He would have been quite comfortable aboard the small, fast boat. But having women on board brought another set of circumstances into the picture. Commander Barnes would discuss the situation with Assistant Secretary of the Navy Gustavus Fox. Between the two of them, they would decide exactly what arrangements would have to be made.

At City Point, General Ulysses S. Grant was glad that President Lincoln had taken him up on his invitation, but he had more urgent and immediate things on his mind than a presidential visit. General Grant's main concern was still General Robert E. Lee and exactly what Lee was planning for the immediate future of his army. He later found out that General Lee and Confederate president Jefferson Davis had met to discuss "the situation of affairs in and about Richmond and Petersburg," and also that the two of them had reached the decision that "these places were no longer tenable for them, and that they must get away as soon as possible."[3] Lee and Davis were just waiting for the first opportunity to slip out of the trenches south of Petersburg, which Grant realized would be as soon as the weather and the roads allowed the army to travel. "They, too, were waiting for dry roads," Grant remembered, "or a condition of the roads which would make it possible for them to move."

MARCH 21, 1865, TUESDAY
LINCOLN DECIDES TO TAKE A TRIP

Lieutenant Commander John S. Barnes returned to the White House with some disappointing news for President Lincoln: USS *Bat* would not be suitable as transport for his wife to City Point. The *Bat* was a steel-hulled warship, designed as a blockade runner. It was one of the fastest ships afloat—it was certainly capable of out-running anything the Confederates sent to challenge her—but it did not have the toilet facilities or any of the amenities that Mrs. Lincoln would require. The president seemed more amused than annoyed by this report. Commander Barnes remembered that Lincoln "translated our difficulties" with accommodating women aboard a warship in "very funny terms."[1]

But Commander Barnes and Assistant Secretary Fox had another idea. Instead of traveling to City Point aboard the *Bat*, the side-wheeled passenger boat *River Queen* would be put at the president's disposal. The *River Queen* was unarmed and was manned by a civilian crew, but was also larger, much more luxurious, and would be much more comfortable for Mrs. Lincoln. In other words, the *River Queen* was not as safe as the *Bat* but was much more spacious. The president gave his consent—he and his wife would travel to City Point aboard the *River Queen*, with the *Bat* as an armed escort.

The president may have been satisfied to be traveling aboard the *River Queen*, but Assistant Secretary Fox, along with Secretary of the Navy Gideon Welles, were apprehensive, to put it mildly. Both Fox and Welles were very concerned over the president's safety and were also well aware that Lincoln was under threat of assassination by Confederate fanatics. From the time of his election in November 1860 and all throughout his four years as president, he had received a steady influx of threatening letters.

The secretary of war, Edwin M. Stanton, had been against the trip from the beginning. As far as Stanton was concerned, City Point was no place to be visiting as a vacation stop—it was a military base, not a holiday resort, and was also on the edge of a war zone. He was afraid that the Confederates would somehow find out that the president was visiting Grant's headquarters and stage some sort of guerrilla raid to either kill or capture Lincoln. A bomb had recently exploded at one of the base's docks, damaging at least one ship, blowing up stores and equipment, and making a wreck of dockside facilities. Taking Lincoln prisoner, or killing him, would not give the South any sort of military advantage, but it would certainly give a boost to Confederate morale. And the South was just desperate enough to resort to such a plot.

Both Commander Barnes and Assistant Secretary Fox were just as alarmed as Stanton. They also agreed that Lincoln would be putting himself in danger just by going to City Point. Traveling aboard the unarmed *River Queen* would increase the danger. The large passenger ship would make a very inviting target for enemy gunners.

The problem of the president's safety was at least partially solved by assigning the USS *Bat* as an escort. The president and his wife would be aboard the *River Queen*, but the *Bat* and her guns would be right beside her. Fox and Stanton were still anxious about the president's trip, but giving him an armed naval escort helped to put everyone's mind at least slightly more at ease.

President Lincoln had no anxieties at all over his impending trip. He was looking forward to it and could not wait to get out of Washington. As far as he was concerned, assassination plots and kidnapping conspiracies were not worth worrying about. If Fox and Welles and

Stanton wanted to wring their hands in anxiety, that was up to them. He was determined to enjoy himself, or at least to do his best.

The president never paid much attention to his own personal safety. Some referred to this trait as physical courage, others thought that it was fatalism on Lincoln's part, and some people put it down to stupidity. Whatever his reason, he never gave any thought to the possibility that he might be shot, in spite of the fact that there were Southern fanatics in Washington who would have thought nothing of sacrificing their own lives for the chance to kill the president.

In July 1864, Lincoln had decided to visit Fort Stevens, one of the installations defending Washington, during Confederate general Jubal A. Early's raid on the capital. He arrived unannounced, riding in a carriage with his wife. His main reason for the visit was to see the situation at Fort Stevens for himself—the fort was under attack at the time—as well as to raise the morale of its defenders.

Lincoln was met by the commander of the Sixth Corps, General Horatio Wright, who asked the president if he would like to see some of the fighting. To General Wright's surprise, Lincoln said yes. The president then proceeded to climb up on one of the fort's ramparts, where he could get a good view of the shooting that was going on just outside.

Jubal Early's sharpshooters could see the president a lot better than he could see them. Lincoln was very tall—six feet, four inches tall, with a few extra inches added by his boots and his stovepipe hat. Confederate snipers occupied the upper stories of houses near the fort and were routinely picking off any Union soldiers who showed themselves. A medical officer standing only a few feet from Lincoln was hit in the leg (some sources say the ankle) by a sharpshooter's bullet. But in spite of this, knowing that he had placed himself in danger, the president continued to stand where he was.

Soldiers and officers around Lincoln did their best to persuade the president to get down off the wall—including surgeon C. C. V. A. Crawford, the officer who had been shot a few minutes earlier. According to legend, Captain Oliver Wendell Holmes—who would one day become a US Supreme Court justice—shouted at Lincoln to get down before he got himself shot, and also called the president a damn fool. But Lincoln was apparently enjoying the view, and refused to be persuaded.

Finally, in exasperation, General Wright resorted to threats. "He still maintained his ground," the general said many years later. "till I told him I would have to remove him forcibly."[2] Watching General Wright wrestle with the tall, rangy president certainly would have raised the morale of everyone present, but the general did not get the chance to carry out his threat. Lincoln was finally persuaded to climb down from the rampart; Secretary of the Navy Gideon Welles saw him sitting with his back to it. But even after this rebuke, Lincoln did not stay under cover for very long. General Wright complained that the president kept on standing up to get a look at the fighting—Lincoln insisted upon "standing up from time to time, thus exposing nearly one-half his tall form."[3]

President Lincoln and his wife, who had insisted upon accompanying the president, finally left Fort Stevens later in the afternoon. Units of General Wright's Sixth Corps reinforced the fort's garrison, and Fort Stevens held. Abraham Lincoln could truthfully claim to be the only sitting president to come under fire in combat.

Over the years, a good many people have tried to explain exactly why Lincoln decided to put his life at risk for no apparent reason. There was no political or publicity advantage for him; most newspapers hardly mentioned his visit to Fort Stevens. Some have speculated that he was so tired and depressed at the time that he really did not care if anyone shot him or not, a viewpoint that seems a bit extreme and more than just slightly lurid. It was more than possible that he just wanted to see what a battle actually looked like, and that his curiosity got the better of him. Whatever the reason, he certainly gave everyone at Fort Stevens a fit of anxiety.

By March 1865, everyone who saw President Lincoln mentioned how unhappy and nervous he seemed. His attitude toward any assassination attempts was either pure fatalism or the result of depression, depending upon a person's point of view. Lincoln's own attitude was that if anyone wanted to shoot him, there was not very much that anybody could do about it. He seemed content to let his bodyguards worry about his safety; Lincoln himself did not seem concerned at all. This was the main reason why he would not allow himself to be talked out of visiting City Point.

"We now think of starting to you about One P.M. Thursday," the president telegraphed his son, Captain Robert Lincoln. "Don't make public."[4] Captain Lincoln was a member of General Grant's staff. The president wanted his son to be on hand when he arrived at City Point two days later.

Robert Lincoln, the president's eldest son, had been the center of a fairly intense family dispute for quite some time. The cause of the dispute was Robert's desire to join the army and take part in the war. Neither of his parents shared young Robert's enthusiasm for the army, but Mrs. Lincoln was almost violently opposed to his joining up. She had already had lost one son, Willie, who died of an illness, probably typhoid fever, in 1862. Mrs. Lincoln was desperately afraid that if Robert enlisted he would be killed.

To soothe Mary's fears and satisfy Robert's enthusiasm at the same time, the president made arrangements for his son to join General Grant's staff. In January 1865, he wrote to the general, "Please read and answer this letter as though I was not President, but only a friend."[5] Lincoln went on to explain that Robert was now twenty-two years old, had graduated from Harvard, and "wishes to see something of the war before it ends." After explaining that he did not want to put his son in the ranks, or to give him a commission ahead of those soldiers who were better qualified, Lincoln finally came to the point. "Could he, without embarrassment to you, or detriment to the service, go into your Military family with some nominal rank?" He ended his letter with a note of consideration that not many chief executives would have shown: "If no, say so without the least hesitation, because I am anxious, and as deeply interested, that you shall not be encumbered."

Two days later, General Grant responded that he would be more than happy to have Robert Lincoln in his "Military family" with the rank of captain. On February 23, Robert Lincoln joined General Grant's staff. "The new acquisition to the company at headquarters soon became exceedingly popular," Charles Porter recalled. "He had inherited many of the genial traits of his father," and "never expected to be treated differently from any other officer." Colonel Porter went on to say that Robert Lincoln's experience on General Grant's staff "did much to fit him for the position of Secretary of War," which he held from 1881 to 1885.[6]

And so President Lincoln managed to solve three problems at the same time with the help of General Grant. He satisfied his son's ambition to join the army, he quieted news reporters and other critics who had accused Robert of shirking his duty by not enlisting, and he placated his wife by the fact that Robert had been assigned to General Grant's staff instead of a combat unit. But Mary Lincoln was of a mental condition that can be most diplomatically described as delicate. Her condition would make itself known again in the very near future.

That evening, the president and Mrs. Lincoln went to Grover's Theatre to attend a performance of François-Adrien Boieldieu's opera *La Dame Blanche.*[7] Because of his impending trip to City Point, Lincoln was probably in a more relaxed frame of mind than usual. This actually might have allowed him to enjoy the performance, instead of just using a night at the theater as an excuse to get a few hours of escape from the pressures of the White House.

MARCH 22, 1865, WEDNESDAY
A FLATTERING LETTER

President Lincoln received a visit from Senator Charles Sumner, who brought an unusual piece of correspondence. The senator showed Lincoln a letter from the Duchess of Argyll, which was dated March 2, 1865. Elizabeth Georgiana Campbell Granville, Duchess of Argyll, was a prominent and outspoken opponent of slavery in Britain, and was also a friend of Harriet Beecher Stowe, the author of *Uncle Tom's Cabin*. Because the president was featured so prominently in the duchess's letter, Senator Sumner thought Lincoln would be interested in reading it.

Because she was a dedicated abolitionist, the duchess's primary concern was with the slaves in the South, along with what would become of them. "I do not know what your opinion is as to giving the Franchise to the negroes in the Slave States," she wrote. "One wd. be inclined to think that that [*sic*] that there ought to be some realization first of their new condition."[1] In other words, before any freed slaves were given the right to vote, they should first be given at least some fundamentals of education.

"We feel great confidence in the President," she went on to say, referring to her friends in England. The duchess also commented that "the speech at the Gettysburg Cemetery will live."[2]

It was certainly a flattering letter, as well as highly unusual, at least from Lincoln's point of view. Members of the British upper class were not always as complimentary toward President Lincoln and rarely admitted to having "great confidence" in him. Most British aristocrats found themselves in agreement with Lieutenant Colonel Garnet Wolseley, a future field marshal and viscount, who referred to Abraham Lincoln's presidency as "the dictatorship of an insignificant lawyer."[3]

Lincoln was also happy to hear that his Gettysburg Address "must live." Not everyone had been so generous in their opinion of the speech. Immediately after delivering "the speech at the Gettysburg Cemetery," Lincoln himself told his friend and bodyguard Ward Lamon, "Lamon, that speech won't *scour*," using a phrase from his prairie years.[4] Failing to scour meant that the heavy soil had built up on the blade of a plow, making it unable to turn the earth. He had changed his mind during the past fourteen months, and was glad that there was somebody who agreed with him.

General Grant sent a long letter to General William Tecumseh Sherman on March 22. The Richmond newspapers made mention of the fact that General Sherman had arrived in Goldsboro, North Carolina, and Grant sent his letter to Sherman at Goldsboro. Much of its contents concerned the movements of General Philip Sheridan's cavalry, along with Grant's instructions that Sheridan should continue to destroy the rail lines around Petersburg and then advance along the Danville road "as near to the Appomattox as he can get."[5] But Grant's main worry was still Robert E. Lee. "It is most difficult to understand what the rebels intend to do; so far but few troops have been detached from Lee's army," he wrote to General Sherman. "If Lee detaches, I will attack; if he comes out of his lines, I will endeavor to repulse him, and follow it up to the best advantage." General Grant did not mention anything about President Lincoln's impending visit.

At Petersburg, Colonel Elisha Hunt Rhodes had celebrated his twenty-third birthday the day before. "Twenty-three years and have been in service nearly four years," he reflected. "God has been very good to me, and I am grateful for his protecting care."[6] Colonel Rhodes's diary entry for March 22 was more straightforward: "All quiet and nothing to do but drill and watch the enemy, but business will soon be brisk enough to suit us all. This siege must end soon."

HEADING FOR CITY POINT

"We start to you at One P.M. to-day," President Lincoln telegraphed General Grant at City Point. "May lie over during the dark hours of the night. Very small party of us."[1] The president's party consisted of the Lincolns; their son Tad; Mrs. Lincoln's maid, Elizabeth Keckley; William H. Crook, the bodyguard; and Captain Charles Penrose, who had been assigned by Secretary of War Stanton to protect the president. "The *River Queen*, closely followed by the *Bat*, left Washington on March 23, 1865," Commander John S. Barnes noted with crisp naval efficiency.[2]

Secretary of War Stanton was so concerned with President Lincoln's safety that he decided to go to the Sixth Street Wharf to see the president off himself. He had not been feeling very well for the past several days and went to the wharf against the advice of his wife, Ellen. The secretary's anxieties were not helped any when he arrived at Sixth Street just in time to watch the *River Queen* steaming off toward City Point—the president was already on his way.

An hour or so later, Stanton's worries increased even further. An intense thunderstorm, accompanied by strong gusts of wind, erupted over Washington while the *River Queen* was out on the Potomac River. A reporter with the Washington bureau of the *New York Herald* reported that "terrific squalls of wind, accompanied by thunder and lightning, did considerable damage here."[3] The storm was called, among other things, a squall and a gale. A Washington newspaper insisted that it was a hurricane. Whatever it was, it did its share of damage—uprooting trees, destroying houses, and blowing boats out on the Potomac off their course. "The roof of a factory on Sixth Street was blown off into the street, and fell upon a hack," the *Herald* stated.

Secretary Stanton was so alarmed that he roused himself out of bed and made his way to the War Department's telegraph office to contact the president. At 8:45 p.m., he sent Lincoln an urgent telegram: "I hope you have reached Point Lookout safely not-withstanding the furious gale that came on soon after you started."[4] He went on to request that Lincoln inform him of his safe arrival as soon as he reached Point Lookout.

Actually, Secretary Stanton's panic was completely misplaced. The *River Queen* apparently left for City Point just in time to miss the storm. Lincoln was thoroughly enjoying the trip. He stood on deck and watched as Washington receded into the distance, relieved that he would not have to look at it again for a while. Afterward, he went belowdecks and had a long conversation with the *River Queen*'s captain, Captain Bradford, who had been involved with chasing down Confederate blockade runners earlier in the war. For several hours, Captain Bradford regaled the president with stories of his adventures off the Confederate coast. Lincoln did not go to bed until nearly midnight.

Tad Lincoln was enjoying the trip as much as his father, if not more so. The Lincolns' bodyguard, William Crook, noted that young Tad roamed all over the ship, studying every screw of the engine and every rivet in the boiler room. He also made friends with just about every member of the *River Queen*'s crew and was treated as the ship's mascot by everyone on board.

During the night, while the president and his party were asleep, the *River Queen* steamed out of the Potomac and into the deeper waters of Chesapeake Bay. As soon as she entered the bay, the temperature began to drop and the water became choppy and turbulent. William Crook shared a stateroom with Tad Lincoln. He was startled out of a sound sleep when Mary Lincoln entered the cabin to check on Tad. "It is growing colder, and I came to see if my little boy has enough covers on him," she explained. Crook managed to drift off to sleep again after Mrs. Lincoln left but was reawakened by the tossing of the *River Queen* in the wind and weather. He felt as though the ship was "slowly climbing up one side of a high hill and then rushing down the other."[5] The pitching apparently did not disturb Tad, who slept right through the wind and weather, but it gave Crook a long, restless night.

MARCH 24, 1865, FRIDAY
ARRIVAL

William Crook was not the only one aboard the *River Queen* who was having an unpleasant voyage. The president was suffering from an upset stomach, which he blamed on the *Queen's* supply of drinking water. He requested that a supply of fresh water be taken aboard when the ship docked at Fortress Monroe, on the Virginia coast. His request was seen to as quickly as could be arranged; casks of water were loaded aboard the ship around noon. But apparently the job was not done quickly or efficiently enough to suit the fort's acting quartermaster, Major William L. James. "I am exceedingly mortified at the delay which you have experienced in obtaining the water you desire," Major James wrote to the president. "I have sent several messengers already to the officer [in charge of the water detail] to make all possible haste, and that he should have delayed so is exceedingly annoying to me. I shall certainly call him to account for his bad management."[1]

Major James was a lot more annoyed than President Lincoln, who shrugged off the whole matter. "I am not at all impatient, and hope Major James will not reproach himself or deal harshly with the officer having the matter in charge," he responded to the major's letter. "Doubtless he, too, has met some unexpected difficulty."[2]

Mary Lincoln's difficulties were more emotional than physical. She was highly nervous to begin with. During the night of March 23/24, her husband dreamed that the White House was on fire and, in the way of conversation, told Mary about his dream. The story only served to increase her anxiety. During the day on Friday, Mary sent two telegrams to the White House to ask the staff if everything was alright. It was not a favorable omen for what was to come during the Lincolns' visit to City Point.

The *River Queen* anchored off City Point "very late" on the evening of March 24, according to Commander Barnes of the USS *Bat*.[3] William Crook stood on deck and enjoyed the view—the many colored lights of the ships nearby, along with the lights of City Point itself. The ships were mostly warships, small freighters, and colliers, and the lights on shore came from offices and warehouses and barracks, but it was a surprisingly peaceful scene, considering that General Lee and his army were only a few miles away.

General Grant did not even mention President Lincoln's arrival in his memoirs, but the president's coming ashore seems to have been quite an occasion for his wife, Julia. They had both been informed of the event by none other than Captain Robert Lincoln—"a noble, handsome young fellow" in Julia Grant's opinion—who escorted the general and his wife to the *River Queen*. The Grants were aboard a smaller steamship, the *Mary Martin*, which was tied up alongside. "Our gracious president met us at the gangplank, greeted the General most heartily, and, giving me his arm, conducted us to where Mrs. Lincoln was awaiting us," Julia Grant remembered.[4] Mary Lincoln received General and Mrs. Grant "most cordially." After the greetings and handshakes, the president announced that he was "going to leave you two ladies together" while he went off with General Grant to have "a little talk."

When the president and General Grant left the cabin, Mrs. Lincoln asked Julia Grant to sit down. Mrs. Grant assumed that Mary Lincoln meant for her to sit beside her on a small sofa, so "I seated myself beside her." But "seeing a look of surprise from Mrs. Lincoln," she immediately got up and excused herself, saying "I crowd you, I fear." Mrs. Lincoln "kindly extended her hand to deter me," and said, "Not at all." After a moment, Julia Dent quietly sat down in a nearby chair and normal conversation between the two women began.[5]

When Julia Dent was asked about her visit with Mrs. Lincoln, she noted "the very awkward mistake on my part," and said that if there was any blame to be placed for the incident, she was to blame. "I was a trifle embarrassed, and I would not have taken the seat," is the way she explained it.[6] Mrs. Grant also mentioned "the sensational story," referring to the way the incident had been described by Adam Badeau in his book *Grant in Peace*, who quoted Mrs. Lincoln as scolding, "How dare you be seated until I invite you."[7]

While Mrs. Lincoln and Mrs. Grant were together, the president and General Grant had their own conversation in the president's room. The general assured Lincoln that the war was winding down and that the end was finally in sight. This report certainly satisfied the president—bodyguard William Crook noticed that Lincoln seemed to be particularly happy. It was just what he wanted to hear.

After the Grants took their leave and left the *River Queen*, the president and Mary Lincoln talked for quite a while. Both of them were in very good spirits. After a while, they decided to call it a night and go to bed—they would have a long day ahead of them in the morning.

VISITING A BATTLEFIELD

The president telegraphed his anxious secretary of war, Edwin M. Stanton, on Saturday morning: "Arrived here, all safe, about 9 A.M. yesterday. No war news."[1] Secretary Stanton's mind must have been put at ease by Lincoln's communiqué. He responded, "I would be glad to receive a telegram from you dated at Richmond before you return" to Washington. This was apparently the straight-laced Mr. Stanton's attempt at making a joke.[2]

Commander John S. Barnes came aboard the *River Queen* for breakfast. His first activity was to escort Mary Lincoln to the dining room. When Commander Barnes and Mrs. Lincoln arrived, they found that the president was already there, not looking very well, still suffering the effects of yesterday's illness. "Mr. Lincoln ate very little," Commander Barnes wrote, "but was very jolly and pleasant."[3] Tad Lincoln was also present for breakfast, along with Captain Penrose.

While everyone except the president was having their sausages and eggs, they were joined by Captain Robert Lincoln. It was an unexpected visit but was not entirely a social call—Captain Lincoln explained that he had come with a message from General Grant. "Robert just now tells me that there was a little rumpus up the line, and ended about where it began," is how the president reported the contents of his son's communiqué.[4]

The message that Robert Lincoln had delivered was a lot more significant than the president's cheerful tone indicated. It meant that General Grant's long-awaited spring offensive had finally begun, only it had not been begun by General Grant. Early that morning, General Lee had attacked the Federal lines south of Petersburg at Fort Stedman. The fort was about two hundred yards south of the Confederate trenches. Lee's attack surprised everyone, including General Grant. Only a week earlier, he had written to his father, "I am anxious to have Lee hold on where he is a short time longer so that I can get him in a position where he must lose a great portion of his army."[5]

But General Lee seldom did what anyone expected. His predawn attack was not just a "little rumpus;" it was a major assault that had broken a hole in Grant's lines. "The charge, however, was successful and almost without loss," the general wrote in his usual straightforward manner, "the enemy passing through our lines between Fort Stedman and Battery No. 10."[6] The fort itself was also captured, and its guns were turned against the Federal troops. Besides the element of surprise, the attackers also had darkness on their side—in the predawn haze, it was just about impossible to tell friend from foe, which also made it impossible to bring up any artillery to use against the Confederates.

As soon as the sun rose above the horizon, and the gunners were able to distinguish Union troops from Confederate, heavy artillery fire was brought down on the attackers. This made all the difference. At about 7:45, a Federal counterattack stopped General Lee's assault and also recaptured Fort Stedman. The Union artillery had prevented any reinforcements from reaching the Confederates, who lost all the ground they had captured just a few hours earlier. "This effort of Lee's cost him about four thousand men and resulted in their killing, wounding, and capturing about two thousand of ours," General Grant would later report.[7]

The surprise attack on Fort Stedman had been a desperate attempt by General Lee to break through the Federal lines. The purpose of his assault was to upset and delay General Grant, which would allow the Confederates a head start on their run toward North Carolina. "The movement was well planned and carried out," Colonel Horace Porter reflected, "but it proved a signal failure."[8]

After the president had finished his breakfast, and after Robert Lincoln had delivered his message about Fort Stedman, several officers came to see President Lincoln and pay their respects. Among those present were Admiral David Dixon Porter, General Grant's old friend from Vicksburg, and Commander John S. Barnes from the USS *Bat*. During the course of their conversation, it was decided to visit the scene of that morning's fighting. No one actually had any real news regarding the battle, and the president wanted to have a first-hand look at the battleground himself.

At around noon, the president and a "large party" boarded a train and rode from City Point to General Meade's headquarters. As the train approached Meade's office, it quickly became apparent to everyone on board that the fighting at Fort Stedman had been a lot more serious, and a lot more costly in lives, than Captain Lincoln had indicated—it had not been just "a little rumpus up the line." As Commander Barnes described, "The ground immediately around us was still strewn with dead and wounded men, Federal and Confederate."[9] Some of the wounded were still sprawled over the railroad tracks that led to Meade's headquarters, and had to be removed before the train could proceed.

Once the president arrived at headquarters, "Mr. Lincoln was taken in charge by General Meade," and the visitors were escorted to a spot where the entire battlefield could be seen. "We passed through the spot where the fighting had been most severe," Commander Barnes recalled, "and where great numbers of dead were lying, with burial parties at their dreadful work."[10]

The president rode one of General Grant's horses, a little black pony named Jeff Davis. The pony may have been just the right size for General Grant, who was five feet eight inches tall. But the sight of

President Lincoln on Jeff Davis was anything but distinguished; the president's feet nearly touched the ground. "Mr. Lincoln was a good horseman," at least in the opinion of William Crook, "but always rather an ungainly sight on horseback."[11] Everybody laughed at the president, including Lincoln himself. "Well, he may be Jeff Davis and a little too small for me," Lincoln said, "but he is a good horse."

This turned out to be one of the few light moments of the afternoon. After observing the burial parties at work, the president passed several hundred Confederate prisoners who had been captured that morning. Lincoln did not say very much as he watched them shamble past, but he was obviously affected by this "dirty lot of humanity" being herded off to a prison camp. "He remarked that he had seen enough of the horrors of war, that he hoped this was the beginning of the end, and that there would be no more bloodshed or the ruin of homes."[12]

The president also had another look at some actual fighting— "some lively skirmishing," artillery fire that had broken out "between the picket-lines of the two forces."[13] He had a very good vantage point, on a hill not more than a quarter mile from where the shooting had broken out. "We could see the shells as they were fired," William Crook wrote, "but while we were there they burst in the air and did no damage." Lincoln asked if he might be standing "too close for comfort of his party" to the cannon fire. When he was assured that there was no danger, the president stayed at that position for two more hours. He did not move until the fighting had ended.

Lincoln carried a map with him, which he took out of his pocket and looked at several times during the afternoon. "He had the exact location of the troops marked on it," Colonel Horace Porter noted, "and he exhibited a singularly accurate knowledge of the various positions."[14] The president wanted to get as much first-hand information of actual fighting conditions as possible, without actually putting himself in danger. Reading combat dispatches in the War Office gave him a good overview, but there was no substitute for observing the situation himself.

The afternoon's activities left the president in a serious and reflective mood. When he returned to City Point later in the day, he sat by the campfire and spoke with General Grant and several members of the staff. "At first, his manner was grave and his language much more serious than usual."[15] Among other things, he talked about "the appalling difficulties encountered by the administration, the losses in the field, the perplexing financial problems, and the foreign complications."

But after a while, the president's tone of voice changed and his manner became much more cheerful. He told one of his famous stories, this one was about a barber who gave one of his customers such a close shave that he also succeeded in cutting his own finger. After finishing his story, Lincoln compared the barber with England, and her "inimical attitude" toward the North. Along with most of the Northern population, he resented Britain's support of the Confederacy, as well as her supplying the Confederate navy with commerce raiders, including the *Alabama* and the *Shenandoah*. "And so England will discover that she has got the South into a pretty bad scrape by trying to administer to her," Lincoln explained, "and in the end she will find that she has only cut her own finger."[16] (President Lincoln usually said "England" when he meant "Britain.")

The president's audience laughed at the story, including General Grant. When the laughter died away, Grant asked Lincoln a pointed question: "Mr. President, did you at any time doubt the final success of the cause?" The president instantly replied, "Never for a moment."[17] Everyone present, including Grant, was impressed by the quickness and sincerity of Lincoln's response.

Returning to the subject of the relationship with Britain, Lincoln mentioned the *Trent* affair, which had happened over three years earlier and was another point of conflict between Britain and the United

States. In 1861, the American warship USS *San Jacinto* stopped the British steamer *Trent,* which was sailing from Cuba to Europe with two Confederate officials aboard. The two representatives were forcibly removed from the *Trent* in international waters, and were taken to Boston as prisoners. Britain angrily demanded their immediate release, and Lincoln complied with the demands. Lincoln was not happy about giving up the two Confederate ministers, but he was certain that "after ending our war successfully, we would be so powerful that we could call her to account."[18]

Colonel Horace Porter thought it was more than appropriate for General Grant to hear the president's remarks regarding Britain, because President Ulysses S. Grant would preside over what would become known as the "*Alabama* claims." These claims would result in compensation from Britain, in the amount of $15,500,000, for damages inflicted upon the American merchant navy by British-built commerce raiders during the Civil War. These claims resulted in "the payment from England of fifteen and a half millions of dollars as compensation for damages inflicted upon our commerce."[19]

Earlier in the day, the president had sent a telegram to Secretary of War Edwin M. Stanton from General Meade's headquarters. "I am here within five miles of the scene of this morning's action," he wrote. "I have nothing to add to what Gen. Meade reports, except that I have seen the prisoners myself and they look like there might be the number he states—1,600."[20] He wanted to keep Secretary Stanton informed of his activities before he became so involved in the day's activities that he would forget.

Now that the day was finally over, President Lincoln wanted nothing more than to get back to the *River Queen* and go to bed. He politely declined General Grant's invitation to have dinner with him at his headquarters and went aboard the *River Queen* to spend the night.

THE PRESIDENTRESS

I n the morning, President Lincoln seemed to be in excellent spirits after a good night's sleep. He "wandered into the tent of the headquarters telegraph operator," where Colonel Horace Porter and a few other members of General Grant's staff were spending some time. He proceeded to take a telegram from Secretary of War Stanton out of his pocket and said, with a broad smile, "Well, the serious Stanton is actually becoming facetious. Just listen to what he says in his dispatch: 'Your telegram and Parke's report of the scrimmage this morning are received.'"[1] General John G. Parke commanded the Ninth Corps, which had been manning the Fort Stedman sector of the Petersburg lines. "The rebel rooster looks a little the worse, as he could not hold the fence. We have nothing new here. Now you are away, everything is quiet and the tormentors vanished. I hope you will remember General Harrison's advice to his men at Tippecanoe, that they can 'see as well a little farther off.'"[2] Secretary Stanton was still as worried as ever about President Lincoln's safety and was sending him a humorous warning not to put himself in danger again, as he had done at Fort Stedman.

After breakfast, the president made his way over to General Grant's headquarters; this was the beginning of a day of military reviews. General Grant told Colonel Porter, "I shall accompany the President, who is to ride 'Cincinnati,' as he seems to have taken a fancy to him."[3] The general rarely allowed anyone else to ride his big black horse. But since Jeff Davis was much too small to accommodate Lincoln's six-foot, four-inch frame, Grant thought it best that the president rode Cincinnati. It was a matter of comfort and convenience for the president, as well as a gesture of courtesy.

General Grant also had some instructions for Colonel Porter: "I wish you would take Mrs. Lincoln and Mrs. Grant to the reviewing ground in our headquarters ambulance," he told the colonel.[4] Although it has been designed as medical transport, the "ambulance" was frequently used as an ordinary carriage throughout the war. This particular "headquarters ambulance" had been fitted with springs, to give a smoother ride for its passengers, but it was still anything but a luxury vehicle. Colonel Porter expressed his pleasure "at bring selected for so pleasant a mission" as serving as escort for the president's wife. His pleasure would turn to something a great deal more disagreeable and unpleasant before the day was over.

The second major event of the day, after the president's visit, was the arrival of General Philip Sheridan. "Sheridan reached City Point on the 26th day of March," General Grant reported in his usual straightforward manner.[5] General Sheridan's army had just reached Harrison's Landing and his cavalry would be riding north to join with General Grant's forces.

Before setting off on his review of troops with President Lincoln, Grant took a few minutes to have a private conversation with General Sheridan regarding the activities of his army. Grant had already met with Sheridan, and had advised him to return to North Carolina to join forces with William Tecumseh Sherman against Confederate general Joseph E. Johnston's army. But in this second conversation, when there would be no one else present, General Grant informed Sheridan, "General, this portion of your instructions I have put in merely as a bind"—in other words, he did not want his actual plans to be made public.[6] Grant was using this meeting, in private, to inform General Sheridan of his actual plans: he intended to keep General Sheridan with him as part of the Army of the Potomac; Sheridan would not be going south to join General Sherman; and Grant was planning to bring the war to an end as soon as possible right there in Virginia—"I intend to close the war right here," is the way he put it. General Sheridan had not been happy about leaving Grant for North Carolina; his face "at once brightened up" when he heard Grant's change of plan. "I'm glad to hear it," he said, slapping his leg, "and we can do it."

General Sheridan was invited to join President Lincoln and his party on their trip to review his own troops. The *River Queen* cast off at eleven o'clock, carrying the Lincolns and their guests—the Grants, General Sheridan, Admiral Porter, Lieutenant Commander Barnes, Colonel Horace Porter, and General Grant's secretary Adam Badeau—up the James River. Horses and Grant's headquarters ambulance were also loaded aboard. "The president was in a more gloomy mood than usual on the trip up the James," Colonel Porter observed. "He spoke with much seriousness about the situation, and did not attempt to tell a single anecdote."[7]

It did not take long for the *River Queen* to reach the place where Sheridan's troops were making their way across the river. The cavalry was in the process of crossing a pontoon bridge, which had been built by army engineers for the occasion. While the rest of the men waited for their turn to cross, they washed themselves in the river, watered their horses, and generally enjoyed themselves, "laughing and shouting to each other and having a fine time." When they found out that the president was watching them, the cavalrymen "cheered vociferously."[8]

The *River Queen* left Sheridan's cavalry behind and steamed past Admiral Porter's flotilla of warships, which were a short distance upriver, giving President Lincoln another spectacle. It was quite an array of naval power—the ships were "dressed with flags, the crews on deck cheering as the *River Queen* passed by."[9] The president returned the salute—"as he passed each vessel, [he] waved his high hat as if saluting old friends in his native town, and seemed as happy as a schoolboy."

President Lincoln's mood certainly had changed since he left City Point. His entire attitude had improved completely, almost miraculously. When the *River Queen* tied up alongside Admiral Porter's flagship, the USS *Malvern*, the president and his entourage discovered that they were the admiral's guests for lunch. Lincoln was clearly delighted by the "grand luncheon" and by the quantity and variety of the food that was being served.[10] "It was the cause of funny comments and remarks by the President," including jokes about the difference between life in the army, with its hardtack and mud marches and dismal unpalatable rations, and life aboard ship, which featured appetizing lunches. Everybody laughed at Lincoln's remarks, and he visibly enjoyed being "the moving spirit" of the occasion as much as he enjoyed lunch.

After lunch, the *River Queen* left Admiral Porter's flotilla and proceeded to take the president and his guests to Aitken's Landing. General Grant had planned a presidential review of troops under General Edward O. C. Ord, commander of the Army of the James. All the horses, along with the headquarters ambulance, were put ashore for the trip inland to the reviewing ground.

When the *River Queen* arrived at Aitken's Landing, several officers were on hand to escort the president and all the other visitors to the review. General Ord wanted to make a favorable impression with both the president and General Grant and spared no effort in his attempt to show his troops to their best possible advantage. "There were probably twenty or thirty officers and a few orderlies in the party," Commander Barnes wrote, "all in their best uniforms, and as brilliant a squadron as could be expected from an army in the field."[11]

After the presidential group had come ashore, the party traveled the four miles to the parade ground in two groups. The president, General Grant, Commander Barnes, and General Ord rode to the review on horseback, accompanied by some of General Ord's officers. Mary Lincoln, Julia Grant, Colonel Horace Porter, and Colonel Adam Badeau followed behind in the ambulance.

Mrs. Lincoln was upset and more than slightly annoyed when she discovered that her husband would not be riding in the ambulance with her. The reason that the president rode ahead with the officers was simple enough: as commander in chief, the president's place was to be with General Grant and General Ord as they inspected the troops, not to ride in a carriage with his wife. But Mary Lincoln was not interested in the reason behind the president's absence. She did not like being separated from her husband, and she was extremely unhappy that he would not be traveling to the parade ground with her.

As he rode off toward General Ord's encampment, Lincoln had no inkling of the trouble that was developing back on the riverbank: "The President was in high spirits, laughing and chatting first to General Grant and then to General Ord as they rode forward through the woods and over the swamps."[12] His horse was gentle, "gentle with an easy pacing," according to Commander Barnes, which allowed the president to enjoy both the ride and the company of Grant and the other officers.

Even though President Lincoln would be appearing in front of hundreds of soldiers and officers under General Ord's command, he did not seem to have given very much thought to his appearance. This was not unusual—Lincoln seldom paid very much attention to the way he looked: "The President was dressed in a long-tailed black frock coat, not buttoned, black vest, low cut, with a considerable expanse of a rather rumpled shirt front, a black carelessly tied necktie, black trousers without straps, which, as he ambled along, gradually worked up uncomfortably and displayed some inches of white socks."[13]

Lincoln might not exactly have been a total sartorial horror, but he was anything but a fashion plate. The commander went on to say that the president also wore "a high silk hat, rather out of fashion," and that had probably never been brushed. At least his costume did not interfere with his riding. He galloped along "with some ease;" although the stirrups were adjusted to their extreme length "to suit his extraordinarily long limbs."[14]

President Lincoln and the officers in his group covered the distance between Aitken's Landing and General Ord's parade ground in good time. But because of the delay caused by Admiral Porter's elaborate lunch, they arrived much later than expected. When they reached the reviewing grounds, Mrs. Lincoln and Mrs. Grant were nowhere to be seen—nobody knew if they had taken the wrong road and were lost, or if they had gotten off to a late start, or exactly what had happened to them.

General Ord's troops had been waiting for the review to begin for the past several hours, "drawn up in a wide field at parade rest," and also had not eaten anything since breakfast.[15] General Ord asked General Grant if he wanted to delay the start of the review until Mrs. Lincoln and Mrs. Grant arrived. General Grant asked President Lincoln—as commander in chief, he had the final say. The president did not want any additional postponement, and the review finally began—without Mrs. Lincoln and Mrs. Grant.

The two ladies, accompanied by Colonel Porter and Colonel Badeau, were on their way, but were being slowed by both the roads and by the ungainliness of their ambulance/carriage. Colonel Porter would later remark, "as the road was swampy, and part of it corduroyed with the trunks of small trees . . . the ambulance could make but slow progress."[16] As far as the vehicle itself was concerned, the additional springs that had been installed for the comfort of the passengers actually turned out to be a liability. When one of the wheels struck an obstacle, or ran over an oversized tree trunk in the corduroyed road, the new springs bounced the four people out of their seats with more force than before the springs were fitted. It was turning out to be a jarring and uncomfortable trip.

At this point in time, Mary Lincoln's primary concern was not with her own personal comfort. Her main concern was that she would be late for the review, and she wanted to go faster. Colonel Porter heard what she said and reluctantly ordered the driver to increase speed. This only served to make the ride even more uncomfortable—"when the horses trotted, the mud flew in all directions, and a sudden jolt lifted the party clear off the seats."[17]

The jolt slammed Mrs. Lincoln's head against the ambulance roof; the impact was forceful enough to trigger a severe headache. (Some sources insist that it was a migraine.) This put her in an even worse mood than before, which increased her anger and impatience. She took her antagonism out on everybody around her. According to one of her biographers, "Mary Lincoln berated horses, driver, aides, and Julia Grant."[18] In her anger, she even insisted on getting out of the vehicle and walking, but was soon talked out of this—the road was literally knee-deep in mud. "I persuaded her that we had better stick to the wagon as our only ark of refuge," is the way Colonel Porter put it.[19]

By the time that Mrs. Lincoln and the others arrived at the parade ground, the review had already begun. She immediately spotted her husband among the generals and the soldiers—at six-foot-four, wearing a tall black hat, he would have been difficult to miss. She also could not help but notice that the president was accompanied by General Ord's wife, Mary Ord, who has been described as "a remarkably handsome woman and a most accomplished equestrienne," who handled her horse expertly and with "extreme grace."[20]

Mrs. Ord saw the ambulance at about the same time, and rode across the field with Commander Barnes to join Mrs. Lincoln, with the president not far behind. Mary Lincoln was not glad to see Mary Ord, to put it mildly—she was outraged by the fact that this "remarkably handsome woman" had been allowed to ride at the side of her husband, as well as by the fact that her husband seemed to be enjoying her company. She began calling Mrs. Ord any number of unflattering names, loud enough so that everyone within earshot could hear everything she said. Mrs. Ord was stunned by this outburst. Bystanders saw her burst into tears and ask Mrs. Lincoln exactly what she had done wrong. Julia Grant did everything she could to calm the president's wife and defuse the situation, but Mary Lincoln was in a frenzy and was in no mood to be placated.

After venting her anger and resentment at Mary Ord, Mrs. Lincoln next turned on her husband. She climbed down out of the ambulance and strode toward him in an obvious bad temper. As soon as she reached the president, she began scolding him and berating him for allowing Mary Ord on the parade ground. She was very jealous of her status as First Lady—the *New York Herald* had used the term "Presidentress" to describe her position, which Mary Lincoln clearly enjoyed[21]—and was also jealous of Mrs. Ord. "Mrs. Lincoln repeatedly attacked her husband in the presence of officers," according to Colonel Badeau.[22]

President Lincoln did his best to retain a trace of dignity through all this: "He bore it as Christ might have done with an expression of pain and sadness that cut one to the heart, but with supreme calmness and dignity."[23] Like Julia Grant, he tried his best to calm his wife. Nothing he said seemed to have any effect. "He called her 'mother,' with his old-time plainness. He pleaded with his eyes and tones, till she turned on him like a tigress, and then he walked away hiding his noble ugly face that we might not catch the full expression of its misery." Apparently, he had given up on any further attempts to placate his wife.

But Mrs. Lincoln's display of temper had not yet run its course. That night, aboard the *River Queen*, President and Mrs. Lincoln entertained General and Mrs. Grant, along with members of the general's staff. During dinner, Mary Lincoln once again scolded her husband for flirting with Mrs. Ord, and urged him to remove General Ord from his command. General Ord was unfit, she insisted, to say nothing of his wife. General Grant spoke up on General Ord's defense, in spite of Mrs. Lincoln's tirade. His words did not seem to have any effect on Mrs. Lincoln, any more than the president's did that afternoon.

Julia Grant gives a much more diplomatic account of Mary Lincoln's activities than Colonel Badeau. According to Mrs. Grant's version, Mrs. Lincoln was growing "more and more indignant" regarding Mrs. Ord, and lashed out at General Ord when he suggested that Mrs. Lincoln should get a "finely-trained" horse that "will not let the lady leave her husband's side."[24] The general was trying to make a joke that would soothe the president's wife, but his remark only served to make a bad situation even worse.

Seeing that Mary Lincoln was in a highly agitated frame of mind, Mrs. Grant tried her best to act as peacemaker. "Dear Mrs. Lincoln, he does not mean anything," she said quietly, placing her hand on Mary Lincoln's hand. "He has only made an unfortunate speech." Mrs. Dent also requested that General Ord stop presenting any more of his officers to Mrs. Lincoln, "gallant fellows who dashed past," because the president's wife was so out of sorts.[25] Mary Lincoln then turned on Mrs. Grant, making cutting remarks, asking if she supposed that she would get to the White House herself someday, but Mrs. Grant makes no mention of this in her account.

Colonel Horace Porter does not mention anything at all about Mrs. Lincoln's behavior. He only says that Mrs. Ord and the wives of several of the officers "appeared on horseback as a mounted escort to Mrs. Lincoln and Mrs. Grant."[26] As far as the review itself is concerned, Colonel Porter does note that Mrs. Grant "enjoyed the day with zest," but goes on to say that Mrs. Lincoln was so tired and stressed that "she was not in a mood to derive much pleasure from the occasion." This statement represents either the height of diplomacy or else was an attempt to raise understatement to a new level. He ends his account by advising that in future ambulances should never be used "as vehicles for driving distinguished ladies to military reviews," but should only be "confined to their legitimate uses of transporting the wounded and attending funerals."

Commander John S. Barnes did not witness the commotion that had been caused by Mrs. Lincoln—he had been riding with the president and his group at the time. But when he galloped across the parade ground to meet the two women later in the day, he immediately could tell that something was wrong. "Our reception was not cordial," he stated, "it was evident that some unpleasantness had occurred."[27] Porter and Badeau looked unhappy, and Mrs. Grant sat there silent and embarrassed. The best course of action, at least as far as he was concerned, was to ride away from the ambulance and its inhabitants—"it was a painful situation for which the only solution was to retire." Along with Mrs. Ord and a few officers, Commander Barnes rode back to headquarters at City Point.

The cause of Mary Lincoln's "erratic" behavior, as it has been frequently described, had been the subject of argument and speculation even before Mrs. Lincoln became First Lady. She had always been nervous, impulsive, and prone to mood swings. "Hints of Mary's erratic personality appeared early in her adult life," according to one source; she was subject to "lavish spending sprees and grandiose thinking."[28] But no one, from historians to psychologists, has been able to agree over what made Mary Lincoln's behavior so erratic.

One explanation, probably the most frequent, is mental illness. "Three of her four kids didn't live to adulthood, and her husband was shot as he held her hand," is another opinion.[29] "If anyone ever deserved to go crazy, it was Mary Todd Lincoln." But mental illness is only one justification. "It is hard enough to diagnose mental illness when a patient is alive," stated one expert. "You might be able to attach it"—Mrs. Lincoln's behavior—"to mental illness. You can also explain it according to events and circumstances. It doesn't have to be mental illness."

Some physicians have attributed her bizarre conduct to bipolar disorder; others have blamed a brain disorder caused by syphilis. Other possible causes included diabetes, chronic fatigue disorder, and Lyme disease. A cardiologist wrote that Mary Lincoln may have suffered from pernicious anemia, which is caused by vitamin B-12 deficiency.[30]

The most persistent reason remains mental illness, largely because Mary Lincoln was committed to a mental institution in 1875. Her son Robert, who was a practicing attorney in the State of Illinois at the time, arranged an insanity trial for his mother. During the trial, Robert testified, "I have no doubt my mother is insane. She has long been a source of great anxiety to me."[31] The finding of the court agreed with Robert Lincoln. Mary Lincoln was committed to a private mental institution, Bellevue Palace, in Batavia, Illinois, on May 20, 1875. Less than four months later, on September 11, 1875, she was released into the custody of her sister and brother-in-law, Ninian and Elizabeth Edwards. On June 15, 1876, Mary was declared legally sane by a Chicago court.

Mary Lincoln may or may not have been insane, but she certainly was persistent. After the stress and strain caused by the unpleasant events of March 26, Commander John S. Barnes decided to go to bed early. But at about eleven o'clock, an orderly interrupted his sleep with a message from the president—Lincoln wanted to see him aboard the *River Queen*. Commander Barnes dressed as quickly as possible and reported to the *River Queen*, where he found Mr. and Mrs. Lincoln waiting for him in the upper saloon.

The president seemed "weary and greatly distressed."[32] He was in the middle of an uncomfortable discussion on the subject of Mrs. Ord—it seemed to Commander Barnes that the exchange more of an interrogation than a discussion. Mary Lincoln was continuing with her argument of earlier in the day. She insisted that Mrs. Ord had been "too prominent" during the review that day, and that her husband had "distinguished her with too much attention." The president "very gently suggested" that he had "hardly remarked to the presence of the lady." But Mrs. Lincoln was not satisfied with her husband's explanation, "and appealed to me to support her views." Even several hours after the review had finished, Mrs. Lincoln would not let the matter of Mrs. Ord come to an end.

Commander Barnes was embarrassed by the argument, as well as by the fact that he had been called in to take part in it. Actually, the president did not have much to say—he seemed almost as embarrassed as Commander Barnes. The commander later said that he was not in any position to answer Mrs. Lincoln's question—"I could not umpire such a question," is the way he put it.[33] He "could only state why Mrs. Ord and myself found ourselves in the reviewing column," and that they immediately withdrew from it as soon as Mrs. Lincoln and Mrs. Grant appeared in the ambulance. In other words, he tried to calm Mrs. Lincoln without causing any additional embarrassment to President Lincoln or to himself.

"It was a very unhappy experience," Commander Barnes recalled. "I extricated myself as well as I could, but with difficulty," he went on, "and asked permission to retire."[34] The president said good night, "sadly and gently." The commander set out for City Point on horseback.

Commander Barnes does not mention exactly when he arrived back at City Point. He only states that he was "rather tired, with my unwonted horseback experience."[35] But the *River Queen*, accompanied by the USS *Bat*, returned to her City Point dock at about 8:15 p.m. Probably sometime after dinner, and following Mrs. Lincoln's tirade against General Ord, the president and General Grant retreated to the after part of the boat to talk. "Neither the President not General Grant joined even in a square dance, but sat in the after part of the boat conversing," according to Colonel Horace Porter.[36]

According to Colonel Porter, the main topic of conversation was the campaign against General Lee's army and how to put a stop to the battles and the fighting and the killing as soon as possible. The president was anxious to avoid another prolonged operation, which would not only result in thousands of additional killed and wounded but would also put an additional financial strain on the Federal treasury—the war was costing about four million dollars a day. The general did his best to answer all the president's questions, and to put his mind at rest.

"General Grant now confided in the President his determination to move against Lee as soon as the roads were dry enough," Colonel Porter would later write, "and to make what was intended to be the final campaign."[37] His immediate plans were to accomplish two things: to dislodge General Lee's army from its Petersburg trenches; and to make certain that General Philip Sheridan's cavalry would reach the rail station at Danville, down near the North Carolina border, in time to stop General Lee from escaping to join General Joseph E. Johnston. He also assured President Lincoln that his aim was exactly the same as the president's—to put an end to the fighting quickly and to force the surrender Lee and his army.

The discussion went on for quite some time. Neither the president nor General Grant paid any attention to the festivities that were taking place aboard the *River Queen*; the music and all the activity did not distract them at all. At about 10:00 p.m., the conversation finally ended—by that time, General Grant had successfully replied to all of the president's questions and concerns. He unceremoniously took his leave from the man he referred to as "Mr. Lincoln," and returned to his headquarters.

In the trenches south of Petersburg, about ten miles southwest of City Point, Colonel Elisha Hunt Rhodes had no idea what President Lincoln and General Grant had in mind for his own immediate future. His diary entry for March 26 was mainly concerned with the fighting at

111

Fort Stedman the day before. "We had a very exciting day yesterday," he wrote. It was also a very long day, which began with a five-mile march in relief of the Ninth Corps, included "a good shelling" from Confederate artillery, and ended when the sun finally went down and it was too dark to see the enemy. "We had neither breakfast nor dinner and were half starved when we reached camp at 3 o'clock this morning."[38]

There would be many more such days for Colonel Rhodes and his men in the very near future. The offensive that Rhodes had anticipated for the past several weeks had finally begun.

MARCH 27, 1865, MONDAY
ABOARD THE *RIVER QUEEN*

The most important development of the day, at least as far as President Lincoln was concerned, was the arrival of General William Tecumseh Sherman at City Point. General Sherman arrived aboard the small steamer *Russia*; he had set out on his journey from Goldsboro, North Carolina, two days earlier. After a day on a train and another on the steamer, he finally reached his destination. The general described City Point as "a pretty group of huts on the bank of the James River, overlooking the harbor."[1] Other visitors were not nearly as complimentary in their description.

The main purpose of General Sherman's visit was to report to his immediate superior, General Ulysses S. Grant. Talking to the president was a secondary consideration. As soon as the *Russia* docked, and even before General Grant had time to reach the wharf, "Sherman had jumped ashore and was hurrying forward with long strides to meet his chief."[2] Colonel Horace Porter was with Grant when the two old friends met each other. They shook hands "in a cordial grasp," and shouted "'How d'you do, Sherman!'" and "'How are you, Grant!'" to one another. "Their encounter was more like that of two school-boys coming together after a vacation than the meeting of the chief actors in a great war tragedy."

Sherman and Grant walked up to headquarters, where Julia Grant met Sherman with a "cordial greeting." The three of them proceeded to talk for about an hour. Mostly, they talked about Sherman's march through Georgia—more exactly, Sherman talked and the Grants listened. Sherman was of a very nervous and edgy disposition; he rattled on about crossing rivers and destroying telegraph wires and other things he had seen for himself during his expedition from Atlanta to the sea. "The story, told as he alone could tell it, was a graphic epic related with Homeric power."[3]

After listening to Sherman and his account of the Georgia campaign, General Grant informed his old friend that President Lincoln was on board the *River Queen*, which was tied up at the pier. He went on to suggest that the two of them pay Lincoln a visit before dinner— the president would certainly be very glad to see him, especially since the capture of Atlanta had virtually assured his reelection in 1864. It was a suggestion that suited General Sherman. The two generals—the tall, red-headed Sherman and the shorter, round-shouldered Grant— started off for the *River Queen* without any further discussion.

"We walked down to the wharf, went on board, and found Mr. Lincoln alone in the after-cabin," General Sherman recalled. "He remembered me perfectly, and at once engaged in a most interesting conversation."[4] Sherman had met Lincoln once before, at the White House in March 1861—a few days after Lincoln had been sworn in for his first term as president, and before Sherman had received his commission as colonel assigned to inspect Washington, DC's defenses. At the time, Sherman came away from the meeting with an opinion of the new president that was anything but complimentary.

When they boarded the *River Queen*, the two generals discovered that the president "was full of curiosity about the many incidents of our great march."[5] Sherman told General Grant all about his activities in Georgia, and was more than glad to repeat them for Lincoln's benefit. From the dispatches he read in the War Office telegraph office and from newspaper accounts, President Lincoln knew the general overview of the campaign, but he appreciated hearing a first-hand account from the commanding general. Lincoln "seemed to enjoy very much the more ludicrous parts" of his story, including anecdotes that described the "bummers," the foragers who collected food and provisions from the countryside.

Sherman mentioned an incident to General Grant that involved a bummer who cut down a Federal telegraph line. When he was scolded, the soldier responded that he was one of "Billy Sherman's Bummers," and that Billy Sherman had instructed him, "Be sure and cut down all the telegraph-wires you come across, and don't go foolin' away time askin' who they belong to."[6] This was just the sort of story that Lincoln relished.

But President Lincoln was not just interested in hearing funny stories and anecdotes. During his meeting with General Sherman, Lincoln "expressed a good deal of anxiety" that "some accident" would take place with the army in North Carolina while Sherman was absent. Specifically, he was afraid that Joseph E. Johnston's army might slip away and move into Virginia, where he would be in position to join with General Lee. But General Sherman reassured the president. "I explained that the army was snug and comfortable, in good camps at Goldsboro," he wrote. He went on to say that "General [John] Schofield was fully competent to command it in my absence."[7] But President Lincoln's mind was set on ending the war at the earliest possible date and was only partially calmed by Sherman's reassurances.

The conversation lasted about an hour, according to Colonel Porter, but General Sherman himself thought it was "a good long social call."[8] When Sherman left the *River Queen*, he returned to Grant's headquarters along with General Grant. (In his memoirs, Sherman does not mention that Grant took part in his conversation with Lincoln.) When the two of them arrived, they found Julia Grant talking to Colonel Porter and also discovered that Mrs. Grant had prepared tea for the four of them.

She asked the two generals if they had paid their respects to Mrs.

THE LAST WEEKS OF ABRAHAM LINCOLN

Lincoln while they were on board the *River Queen*. Grant said no, they had not, and explained that they had gone "rather on a business errand."[9] Sherman added that he did not even know that Mrs. Lincoln was on board. "Well, you are a pretty pair," Mrs. Grant scolded, and took them to task for being so neglectful. Neither of the two men seemed very upset over their neglect of the First Lady. "Well, Julia," her husband offered in the way of an apology, "we are going to pay another visit in the morning, and we'll take good care then to make amends for our conduct to-day."

It would not have made very much difference if either of them had inquired regarding Mary Lincoln's health. They would have been informed that Mrs. Lincoln was indisposed. When Commander John S. Barnes reported to President Lincoln on board the *River Queen* on the morning of March 27, he made a point of asking about Mrs. Lincoln. He was "hoping that she had recovered from the fatigue of the previous day," as he diplomatically phrased it.[10]

Commander Barnes's diplomacy was not lost on the president. He received the commander "with marked kindness," and said that his wife was "not at all well."[11] Lincoln also "expressed the fear that the excitements of the surroundings were too great for her, or for any woman."

One of Mary Lincoln's biographers was a good deal less diplomatic. According to this source, Mrs. Lincoln's embarrassing behavior of the day before "had incapacitated Mary Lincoln with a bad case of self-inflicted shame."[12] Anyone who asked for her was informed that she was "indisposed," "as indeed she was." Mrs. Lincoln was, literally, ashamed to show her face. "Mortified and apologetic, she stayed in her cabin on the *River Queen* and was only seen walking along the bank near Point of Rocks with Tad or Robert" on the following day, "or sitting on a chair on the ship's stern." But Mrs. Lincoln would cause another embarrassing scene with Commander Barnes before the day had ended.

116

Julia Grant was also on board the *River Queen*. After leaving the president, Commander Barnes joined Mrs. Grant in the forward cabin, and asked about the president's wife. Mrs. Grant pointed out the window to Mary Lincoln standing on deck, near the pilot house, and suggested that he bring a chair out to her. He pushed "a large upholstered armchair" out on deck, said good morning to Mrs. Lincoln, and offered her the chair. Mrs. Lincoln declined the offer.

A bit nonplussed by Mary Lincoln's conduct, Commander Barnes returned to the forward cabin. Mrs. Grant had been watching through the window and had seen what had just happened. A few minutes later, Mrs. Lincoln came to the window and gestured for Mrs. Grant to join her on deck. Through the same window, Commander Barnes watched the "animated conversation" that took place. Mrs. Lincoln was obviously agitated, while Mrs. Grant spoke in a calm, soothing manner.

After the conversation ended, Mrs. Grant returned to the cabin to let Commander Barnes know exactly why Mrs. Lincoln had wanted to speak to her—Mrs. Lincoln objected to the commander's presence aboard the *River Queen* and wanted him to know all about her objections. Apparently, she was upset because he did not take her side during the argument with her husband on the night before.

Commander Barnes was on board expressly because he had been invited to accompany the Lincolns on a trip up the Appomattox River to a place called Point of Rocks. It was meant to be a combination pleasure trip and sightseeing tour. According to legend, Point of Rocks is where Pocahontas saved the life of Captain John Smith. But Mary Lincoln's attitude toward him made his presence aboard the *River Queen* untenable. "This made things rather uncomfortable for a pleasure party," Commander Barnes drily remarked.[13] After tactfully conferring with Mrs. Grant about the correctness of such an action, the commander decided to leave the *River Queen* as quickly and as discreetly as possible.

When the boat docked at Point of Rocks, Barnes deliberately stayed on board while the Lincolns went ashore. Before they returned, the commander asked the *River Queen*'s captain to put him ashore on the other side of the Appomattox River, where the boat's quartermaster loaned him a horse. From there, "somewhat discomfited" and for the second day in a row, Commander Barnes rode back to City Point.

Strangely enough, Commander Barnes did not seem to be offended. Instead of being annoyed with Mary Lincoln, he felt sorry for her. He realized that she was not well, "the mental strain upon her was great," which brought about "extreme nervousness approaching hysteria," along with "extreme sensitiveness as to slights" and "want of politeness or consideration."[14]

"I had the greatest sympathy for her," Commander Barnes later wrote, "and for Mr. Lincoln, who I am sure felt deep anxiety for her."[15] Not very many people shared the commander's sympathy for Mrs. Lincoln. Friends and acquaintances of the president tended to share the commander's consideration for him and felt sorry for anyone who happened to be married to anyone as eccentric—some would have said crazy—as Mary Lincoln. Very few people had anything but negative feelings, ranging from contempt to ridicule, for Mary Lincoln.

While they were at Point of Rocks, the Lincolns were shown the facilities of the nearby military hospital. The president toured the hospital grounds with his wife and two sons but did not go inside the building and did not visit any of the wards. Mary Lincoln went inside the hospital to visit the soldiers with Tad and Robert. Lincoln walked down to the river and sat under an oak tree, while the rest of his family made the rounds with senior members of the hospital staff.

The visit came as a tonic to the recuperating patients. It not only broke the monotonous grind of their daily routine, which usually consisted of nothing more than reading and playing endless games of cards, but also raised the morale of everyone in the hospital. For convalescing patients, morale was every bit as vital to their well-being as anything any doctor or surgeon could do for them. By the time the Lincolns were ready to leave, hundreds of soldiers, probably everyone who could walk, came out to catch a glimpse of the president. They waved and cheered and applauded; they appreciated the Lincolns' visit and wanted them to know how much. In response, President Lincoln raised his hat in salute.

Even though the war was not over yet, and there was still a possibility that General Lee might escape to North Carolina, President Lincoln was making preparations to celebrate the end of the fighting. Specifically, he was planning a flag-raising ceremony at Fort Sumter in April, which would commemorate the surrender of the fort to Confederate troops, and the beginning of the war, four years earlier. Secretary of War Edwin M. Stanton telegraphed the president on March 25: "I have invited Henry Ward Beecher [celebrated writer and speaker] to deliver an address on raising the flag upon Fort Sumter and will give directions . . . to make all suitable arrangements for the occasion and fire a salute of five hundred guns. The flag will be raised by [General Robert] Anderson"—Anderson was in command of the fort when it surrendered to Confederate forces in 1861. "Please let me know if these arrangements have your approval."[16]

President Lincoln certainly did approve of Secretary Stanton's idea—commemorating the end of the war with such a patriotic observance would be fitting and appropriate, exactly what Lincoln had in mind. There was only one problem—the president could not remember if the fort surrendered on April 13 or April 14. "Yours inclosing Fort-Sumter [*sic*] order received," the president replied by telegraph on March 27. I think of but one suggestion. I feel quite confident that Sumter fell on the thirteenth (13th) and not on the fourteenth (14th) of April as you have it." He went on to explain that the fort fell on Saturday the thirteenth, that the first call for troops was "got up" on the fourteenth, and the order itself was issued on Monday the 15th. "Look it up in the old Almanac & other data and see if I am not right."[17]

Secretary Stanton responded to Lincoln's good-natured inquiry at 6:30 that evening. He said that his own recollections agreed with the president's—that Fort Sumter surrendered on April 13.

But the official report, which had been made by Anderson and submitted to Stanton in April 1861, stated that Anderson "marched out of the fort on Sunday afternoon the 14th inst with colors flying and Drums beating bringing away private property and saluting my flag with fifty guns."[18] The secretary of war went on to remind Lincoln that the attack began "on the 12th at 4:30, continued the next day & during the afternoon of the 13th." The actual evacuation took place on the afternoon of April fourteenth.

In a verbal shrug of the shoulders, Lincoln telegraphed Secretary Stanton on March 28, "After your explanation I think it is little or no difference whether the Fort-Sumpter ceremony takes place on the 13th or 14th."[19] As long as there was a ceremony, Lincoln did not really care if it was held on a Thursday or a Friday. This exchange of telegrams shows that President Lincoln was convinced that the war was nearly over, and also that he hoped that it would end soon, with any luck within the next few weeks.

MARCH 28, 1865, TUESDAY
"LET THEM ALL GO"

The main activity on President Lincoln's agenda for March 28 was a conference aboard the *River Queen* with General William Tecumseh Sherman and General Ulysses S. Grant, along with Admiral David Dixon Porter. The main topic of the discussion would be the end of the war—how to end the fighting as quickly as possible, and how to rebuild and restore the South when the war was over. "It was in no sense a council of war," Colonel Horace Porter commented, "but was only an informal interchange of views between the four men who, more than any others, held the destiny of the nation in their hands."[1]

The two generals and Admiral Porter were taken by what is usually described as a small tug out to the *River Queen*, which was lying at anchor in mid-river. They were met by President Lincoln as soon as they stepped on board, and were immediately escorted to the upper saloon, which General Sherman referred to as the after cabin. No arrangements had been made to convert the cabin into a meeting room—there was no conference table, there were no maps on the walls, and nothing special had been done to renovate the room for the occasion. Everyone sat in whatever chairs happened to be on hand. The atmosphere of the meeting would be just as relaxed and informal as the cabin's furnishings, which was exactly what Lincoln had in mind.

General Grant immediately began the proceedings by asking about Mary Lincoln—according to General Sherman, he "inquired after *Mrs.* Lincoln" (General Sherman's emphasis).[2] Grant remembered his wife's scolding of the day before and intended to make amends for "the unintended slight." The president appreciated Grant's tactful gesture, and went to his wife's stateroom to deliver the general's greetings. He returned a few minutes later with word that Mrs. Lincoln "was not well" and did not want to leave her room. Whether Mary Lincoln's illness was physical or mental, or whether she was still just suffering from a case of acute embarrassment over her behavior involving Mrs. Ord, has never been determined.

With the pleasantries and preliminaries safely out of the way, the meeting finally began. General Grant informed the president that General Sheridan was crossing the James River from the north at that very moment, "by pontoon-bridge below City Point."[3] Actually, General Sheridan had crossed the James about thirty-six hours earlier. Grant also informed Lincoln that, in his opinion, "matters were drawing to a crisis." His only fear continued to be that General Lee "would not wait long enough," and might attempt an escape to North Carolina. President Lincoln shared this same fear, which he had stated several times before and would express again before the meeting ended.

General Sherman then gave the president a report on his own army's capabilities. He explained that "my army at Goldsboro was strong enough to fight [General] Lee's army and [General] Johnston's combined, provided that General Grant could come within a day or so."[4] He went on to state that "if Lee would only remain at Richmond another fortnight"—he meant Petersburg—he would be able to move his army into a position where Lee "would have to starve inside his own lines," or else would be forced to "come out from his intrenchments and fight us on equal terms." General Grant had been trying to accomplish just this for the past ten months.

President Lincoln had not said very much up to that point. Admiral Porter noted that Lincoln "was then wrought up to a high state of excitement" from listening to what Grant and Sherman had to say.[5] "His heart was tenderness throughout," according to Admiral Porter; the president wanted to end the war as quickly as possible, and "as long as the rebels laid down their arms, he did not care how it was done."

The president was also not happy to hear that either Grant or Sherman would have to fight one more major battle before the war ended—"one or the other of us would have to fight one more bloody battle," is what General Sherman said to him.[6] Lincoln asked if it would be at all possible to avoid another pitched battle because, as he phrased it, "there had been blood enough shed." Sherman explained that such an event was beyond the control of Grant and himself, but that, in his opinion, "both Jeff. Davis and General Lee would be forced to fight one more desperate and bloody battle." Sherman guessed that the battle he was predicting would be fought "somewhere near Raleigh" between himself and Joe Johnston. General Grant added that "if Lee would only wait a few more days," Union forces would be in position to "be on his heels" in the event of a breakout toward North Carolina.

Another continuing point of anxiety for the president was the fact that General Sherman was not with his army at Goldsboro. Putting this particular fear to rest turned out to be fairly easy. Sherman once again assured Lincoln "that General Schofield was fully competent to command in my absence." He went on to say that he planned to start back for North Carolina that very day, and also that Admiral Porter had been kind enough to put the USS *Bat* at his disposal for the trip. The USS *Bat* was a faster boat than the *Russia*, which had brought him to City Point. General Sherman did not indicate whether or not this news helped to calm the president's nerves.

After all the reports to the president, and questions from the president regarding troop movements and impending battles, General Sherman had a question of his own: he wanted to know if Lincoln "was all ready for the end of the war." Specifically, Sherman wanted to know what should be done about the thousands of Confederate soldiers, the rebels who had taken up arms against the United States Government, after the war ended. He also wanted to know how the Southern political leaders, including Jefferson Davis, should be treated. These were two pointed questions. Lincoln's answers would have a far-reaching effect on the future of the country for many years to come.

The president did not seem to be either upset or agitated by General Sherman's questions. "He said he was all ready," according to the general. "All he wanted from his generals was to defeat the opposing armies and to get the men comprising the Confederate armies back to their homes, at work on their farms and in their shops."[7]

As far as what should be done about Jefferson Davis, the president dropped a broad hint that Davis should be allowed to "escape the country," although he did not say this in so many words. Instead, the president made his point with one of his famous humorous stories. He told everyone an anecdote about a man who had taken the pledge never to touch a drop of alcohol but was invited by a friend to have a drink. Rather than risk being thought of as unfriendly by turning down the invitation, he agreed to have a glass of lemonade. His friend agreed to pour him a glass of lemonade, but added that a shot of brandy would make it taste a lot better. The man replied that he would not object if a dram of brandy was added, provided that it was done "unbeknown" to him.

Lincoln was trying to make the point that he would not object if Jefferson Davis left the country, as long as it was done "unbeknown" to him—he would discreetly look the other way if the president of the Confederacy should happen to escape to Canada or Cuba or some other foreign country.

At this late stage of the war, President Lincoln had three goals: to bring about the surrender of Robert E. Lee's and Joseph E. Johnston's armies, to allow the former Confederate soldiers go home and start new lives, and to bring the seceded states back into the Union. When the Confederate armies were no longer a threat, the Confederate government would cease to exist. Whatever Jefferson David did, or wherever he went, was beside the point, at least as far as Lincoln was concerned.[8]

Admiral Porter was impressed by the fact that President Lincoln wanted to end the war as soon as possible, and that he would be willing to accept peace on almost any terms. According to Admiral Porter, Lincoln insisted upon only two conditions from the former Confederate states: they would be required to rejoin the Union, and they must agree to abolish slavery. He was not adamant about anything else. "Let them all go, officers and all," Lincoln said. "I want submission, and no more bloodshed. . . . I want no one punished; treat them liberally all round. We want those people to return to their allegiance to the Union and submit to the laws."[9]

After about an hour and a half of talk and deliberation—Admiral Porter noted that the "interview between the two generals and the President lasted about an hour and a half"—the meeting finally wound down.[10] All four men stood up, with the tall and angular Lincoln towering over the others, and shook hands as they prepared to leave. No formal minutes of the meeting were taken. Admiral Porter said that he "jotted down what I remembered of the conversation . . . when anything interesting occurred."

Before everyone went their separate ways, the president took General Sherman aside to have a private word. "Sherman, do you know why I took a shine to Grant and you?"[11]

The general was slightly taken aback by the question. "I don't know, Mr. Lincoln," he replied. "You have been extremely kind to me, Mr. Lincoln, far more than my deserts."

"Well," the president said, "you have never found fault with me."

Lincoln was almost certainly thinking of General George B. McClellan when he said this, the same George B. McClellan that Lincoln had removed from command after the Battle of Antietam/

Sharpsburg in September 1862, when he would not pursue the retreating Army of Northern Virginia, and also the same George B. McClellan who had been Lincoln's opponent in the 1864 presidential election. McClellan despised Lincoln and never missed an opportunity to criticize him or ridicule him—among other things, he called Lincoln as a baboon and a gorilla. It must have been a great relief to discover that neither Grant nor Sherman were anything like George B. McClellan, and he wanted to take a minute to let Sherman know how much he appreciated his loyalty.

For his own part, General Sherman had a few complimentary things to say about the president, as well. The Abraham Lincoln that Sherman met at City Point was not the same Abraham Lincoln he had known a few years earlier. The war had changed Lincoln, just as it had changed the country itself. The Abraham Lincoln of 1865 was no longer the ruthless and sometimes arbitrary politician of earlier in the war, who had suspended habeas corpus and had about 13,000 people put in jail without a trial. General Sherman was well aware of the change that had taken place. "We parted on the gangway of the River Queen, about noon of March 28th, and I never saw him again," Sherman would remember. "Of all the men I ever met, he seemed to possess more of the elements of greatness, combined with goodness, than any other."[12]

The ninety-minute conference between the four men was to have had far-reaching effects on the future of the reunited country—"They were hammering out a national fate," according to one of Lincoln's biographers.[13] No one could have known that in two and a half weeks an event would take place that would also change the nation's fate, and would undo everything that had been approved and agreed upon during the course of the meeting.

Later that afternoon, General Sherman left City Point for his own headquarters aboard the USS *Bat*. After the *Bat* had cast off and was underway, Commander Barnes thanked the general for making the journey on his ship instead of the *Russia*, which had brought him to City Point. He explained that Admiral Porter had given him the job of escorting and attending the *River Queen*; this assignment also gave Commander Barnes the "special duty" of looking after Mrs. Lincoln as long as she was at City Point and until she returned to Washington.

Because of Mary Lincoln's attitude toward him after the incident involving Mrs. Ord and the president, Commander Barnes was not happy about being made her special caretaker. The assignment made Barnes's position "very unpleasant," according to General Sherman.[14] But the change of duty had absolved the commander from having to look after Mrs. Lincoln; "he felt much relieved when he was sent with me to North Carolina," General Sherman observed. Commander Barnes was apparently not aware that the job of taking General Sherman back to North Carolina had also come from Admiral Porter.

President Lincoln would be staying behind at City Point, aboard the *River Queen*, with his wife. He could see that the war's final campaign would be starting very soon. General Sherman had already departed to join his army, and General Grant would be off for Petersburg the next day. It did not take very much in the way of foresight to realize that the battle between Grant and General Lee, the "one more bloody battle" that Lincoln was dreading and anticipating, was imminent. The president decided not to return to Washington until the fighting along the Petersburg line had ended, which, for all intents and purposes, would also mean the end of the war.

Colonel Elisha Hunt Rhodes, writing in his diary in the Petersburg trenches, was having the same thoughts as President Lincoln. "We are still under orders to be ready to move, and no doubt a few days more will settle the fate of Petersburg."[15] Colonel Rhodes also shared the president's view on the outcome of the impending battle: "I shall be glad to welcome the dawn of peace, for I am tired of bloodshed."

MARCH 29, 1865, WEDNESDAY
"YOUR SUCCESS IS MY SUCCESS"

At about 8:30 in the morning, President Lincoln went ashore from the *River Queen* to say goodbye to General Grant, who was in the process of moving his headquarters to the Petersburg front. When the president arrived, horses were being put aboard the train that would take the general and his staff the ten or so miles to Petersburg. General Grant livened up the occasion with a funny story—he regaled the president with one of the "numerous ingenious and impracticable suggestions" on how to win the war that were sent to him on an almost daily basis.[1] The latest idea was to equip the Union army with bayonets that were exactly one foot longer than the enemy's. When the two armies met in battle, "our bayonets would go clear through the enemy, while theirs would not reach far enough to touch our men, and the war would be ended."

The president laughed at the story, and reciprocated with a story of his own about the "terror of cold steel."[2] When he was a young man visiting Louisville, a "very tough-looking citizen" blocked his way and waved a bowie knife in front of his face. After a few minutes, the knife-wielding "citizen" asked, "Stranger, kin you lend me five dollars on that?" Lincoln quickly reached into his pocket and handed the man a bank note. "There's ten, neighbor; now put up your scythe."

These jokes provided one of the few light moments for the president that morning. General Grant had already said goodbye to his wife. Colonel Horace Porter thought that Julia Grant looked sad and sorrowful, but Mrs. Grant said that she felt nothing but admiration as her husband "mounted and rode away to victory and peace."[3] But as President Lincoln walked toward the train with General Grant, Colonel Porter remarked that the president seemed more serious than at any other time since he had been at City Point—"The lines on his face seemed deeper and the rings under his eyes were of a darker hue."[4]

Just before the general and his staff boarded the train, the president shook hands with Grant and with every officer on the platform. Once on board, everyone raised their hats "respectfully" to the president. President Lincoln returned the salute and said, in a voice choked with emotion, "Good-by, gentlemen. God bless you all."[5] And in a remark that was typical Lincoln, he added, "Remember, your success is my success." He was fully aware that he would never had been reelected in 1864 if it had not been for the accomplishments of the army in the field, especially the capture of Atlanta by General Sherman.

General Grant recognized the president's uneasy state of mind. "He intends to remain at City Point for the present, and will be the most anxious man in the country to hear from us, his heart is so wrapped up in our success," he told Colonel Porter and other staff members on board the train.[6] Grant did not seem very concerned about the immediate future, and predicted, "but I think we can send him some good news in a day or two."

The general wasted no time in communicating with President Lincoln—he sent the president three telegrams within hours of leaving City Point. In his first communiqué, Grant informed Lincoln that he had arrived at the front at 11:15 a.m., and that there was "No firing."[7] His second message stated that all troops were in their assigned positions for the coming offensive, and that there still had not been any enemy opposition. But it was the general's third telegram, sent from Gravelley Creek and received at 5:10 p.m., that immediately captured Lincoln's attention. Grant wired that General Charles Griffin's division had been attacked at about 4:00 p.m.—"The enemy were repulsed leaving about 60 prisoners in our hands," and added that both sides had suffered casualties.

President Lincoln immediately wired back—"Your three dispatches received. From what direction did the enemy come that attacked Griffin? How do things look now?"[8] As General Grant had pointed out, the president was the most anxious man in the country to hear from him, and he was especially anxious to hear some good news.

Grant replied that Griffin had been attacked near the intersection of the Quaker Road and the Boydton Plank Road, and also updated his earlier account. "Warren [General Gouverneur K. Warren] reports the fighting pretty severe but the enemy repulsed leaving one hundred prisoners in our hands."[9] Grant's main point was that the enemy had been driven back, and there was no need for any anxiety. Union forces had cut the Boydton Plank Road in two places, and were now in position to move against the Confederate right flank.

The president also sent a message to General Godfrey Weitzel, near Richmond. Lincoln telegraphed this short communiqué: "What, if any thing, have you observed on your front to-day?"[10] General Weitzel replied that the most recent intelligence informed him that Fitz Hugh Lee's cavalry passed through Richmond the day before, and was seen moving toward Petersburg "at a fast gait." He ended by saying, "as soon as I hear anything new I will telegraph you."

This was the most up-to-date information available, but it is doubtful that it helped to put the president at ease. He knew that a major battle was about to begin, probably the last significant battle of the war, and Lincoln would not be able to relax until it was over.

The army was in position to move out as soon as the order came through from General Grant. General Weitzel waited in front of Richmond; General Sheridan was in place at Dinwiddie Court House, about twelve miles southwest of Petersburg; General Ord's position was a few miles east of Sheridan, at the intersection of Hatcher's Run and the Vaughan Road. Altogether, five infantry corps, along with Sheridan's cavalry, were standing by. Colonel Elisha Hunt Rhodes noted, "I feel that the enemy are about to leave Petersburg, and we are held in readiness to pursue them."[11]

All that was needed to begin the attack was several days of dry weather. The weather had been cooperating with all the troop movements during the past several days. Julia Grant wrote that it had been a "glorious bright morning" when her husband left for Petersburg.[12] But the weather changed abruptly later in the day—clouds started forming up during the afternoon, and changed to a heavy rain that night. General Grant feared that the rain would make the roads impassable for any large-scale troop movements, especially for Sheridan's cavalry. As the rain continued into the next day, Grant could see that he would have to delay the start of his offensive against General Lee. The sudden change in the weather, along with the resulting change in plans, increased everyone's anxieties, including President Lincoln's.

While President Lincoln was aboard the *River Queen*, a man came on board and asked to see the president. The stranger was referred to William H. Crook, Lincoln's bodyguard. Crook did not give the exact date of the stranger's visit; he only mentioned that it took place not long before the final assault on Petersburg. The president had given instructions not to admit anyone except General Grant or Admiral Porter; Crook informed the visitor that Lincoln was busy and could not be disturbed.

When he heard what Crook had to say, the visitor became "very much excited."[13] He explained that he had known "Mr. Lincoln" when they were both living in Illinois, and that he had rendered "valuable services during his campaign for the presidency," and also that he had spent large sums of money on Lincoln's behalf. Now he was in trouble, and needed to see the president; he insisted that he knew Lincoln personally. Crook asked the visitor for his name. At first, the man refused to give it, but finally said that it was Smith and that he used to live near Lincoln in Illinois.

Crook delivered Smith's message to the president, who laughed when he heard the name—"Smith is, of course, an uncommon name." But after thinking about it for a minute, Lincoln's entire demeanor changed. "If what he says is true, I would know," he said with a note of seriousness in his voice. "But I do not. The man is an impostor, and I won't see him."

Mr. Smith was "very much disturbed" when he heard the president's answer. He begged Crook to take him to see the president; when that failed, he resorted to bribery. Crook ordered Smith to leave the *River Queen*, and threatened to have him arrested if he refused. Before he left, Smith turned and said to the *River Queen*'s captain, "If Mr. Lincoln does not see me now, he will know me dammed soon after he does see me." With that, "Mr. Smith" stormed down the gangplank, walked onto the shore, and disappeared.

William Crook was convinced that "Mr. Smith" was actually John Surratt, one of John Wilkes Booth's co-conspirators. "I think 'Smith' and Surratt were the same man," he later recalled. Crook had lived in the same Maryland county as John Surratt, and knew what he looked like. Smith/Surratt had changed over the years—as Crook remembered him, John Surratt was pale and emaciated, while Smith "was ragged and dirty and very much sunburned"—but Crook thought the change in appearance might have been caused by a "change in circumstance," or by the passage of time, or by a disguise. Crook had no doubts that Smith and Surratt were the same man, and that he had come on board the *River Queen* to kill Lincoln. Long after the war ended, he would write, "I shall always believe that Surratt was seeking an opportunity to assassinate the President at this time." There would be other opportunities in the very near future.

WAR NERVES

President Lincoln seemed to be of two mindsets when he considered his stay at City Point. He sent a telegram to Secretary of War Edwin M. Stanton explaining his dilemma. "I have begun to feel that I ought to be at home," he cabled, "and yet I dislike to leave without seeing nearer to the end of General Grant's present movement."[1]

The president went on to say that Grant had "been out" from City Point since yesterday morning, but that "no considerable effect has yet been produced." His nerves were beginning to get the better of him—he was well aware that General Grant was planning a general advance against General Lee, and wished that he would begin his attack and get it over with. Waiting for news was making him tense and jittery.

There were at least some individuals back in Washington who were not sorry that the president was away. Gideon Welles spoke with Secretary of State Seward, who was under the impression that Lincoln should have returned by that time. But Secretary of War Stanton remarked "that it was quite as pleasant to have the President away, and that he (Stanton) was much less annoyed" when Lincoln was not present.[2] Not everyone missed Lincoln, at least not all of his cabinet members.

Actually, General Grant *had* telegraphed the president, but his communiqué had nothing to do with his pending general attack. He let Lincoln know that all of his troops were in position for the coming attack against General Lee—"our troops have all been pushed

135

forward" is the way that Grant phrased it—but this was sent just to keep the commander in chief informed.[3] Because of the torrential rain that came down all day long on Thursday, the troops were not able to go anywhere. Grant was not able to send any more definite information about his planned offensive.

As soon as the rain let up, General Grant knew exactly what he wanted to do. He had telegraphed General Philip Sheridan on the day before, and told him, "I feel now like ending the matter, if it is possible to do so, before going back."[4] He also instructed General Sheridan not to "cut loose and go after the enemy's roads." Instead, he wanted Sheridan to "push around the enemy, if you can, and get on his right rear. . . . We will all act together as one army until it is seen what can be done with the enemy."

Grant did not intend to capture the roads, the rail links, or any of the transportation links that had been keeping the Army of Northern Virginia fed and equipped. Instead, he was going to go after the army itself. He wanted to end the war as soon as it was possible, to end the matter, and the best way of accomplishing this would be to go right at the enemy.

The only problem was that it looked like it was never going to stop raining. As the downpour went on, the roads got worse. "Sometimes a horse or a mule would be standing apparently on firm ground," General Grant wrote, "when all at once one foot would sink, and as he commenced scrambling to catch himself all his feet would sink and he would have to be drawn by hand out of the quicksands."[5] If the roads could not support a single horse or a mule, they certainly would not be able to sustain a unit of cavalry.

General Grant ordered the construction of corduroy roads "every foot of the way as we advanced" toward the country southwest of Petersburg, which was also toward the farthest left flank of the Confederate lines. The general was fairly satisfied with the progress of the corduroying. "The army had become so acquainted to this kind of work," he said, "and were so well prepared for it, that it was done very rapidly."[6]

But even though Grant was satisfied with the road restoration, there were some who thought it might be advisable to postpone the coming assault. General John A. Rawlins, Grant's friend and confident, told the general that he had his doubts about the impending offensive. According to General Rawlins, the success of turning Lee's right flank depended upon quickness of movement, which would be impossible because of the bad weather and the bad roads. If the Federal forces did not move from their present position quickly, Joseph Johnston might attack from the rear. The bad roads would make it impossible to deliver forage to General Sheridan's cavalry, and the inability to move forward would give Lee more time to prepare his defenses. In short, "it might be better to fall back, and make a fresh start later on."[7]

General Grant was not impressed with General Rawlins's argument, even though he listened patiently until Rawlins finished. He replied that if Joe Johnston was able to move quickly enough to reach him in such foul weather, he would turn on Johnston with his entire command, annihilate his army, and then go after Lee. Grant was not about to let anything as trivial as bad weather or flooded roads get in his way or interfere with his plans.

No sooner had this conversation ended than General Sheridan rode into the headquarters camp on Breckinridge, his white horse, slowly through knee-deep mud. When he dismounted, the general was asked about "the situation" on the extreme left flank, out toward Dinwiddie Court House. General Sheridan was as forceful and as optimistic in his outlook as General Grant had been. "I can drive in the whole cavalry force of the enemy with ease," he informed the assembled staff officers—General Grant had retired to his tent—"and if an infantry force is added to my command, I can strike out for Lee's right, and either crush it of force him to so weaken his intrenched lines that our troops in front of him can break through and march into Petersburg."[8] Sheridan's entire manner almost bristled with confidence. If President Lincoln had been present, his many anxieties about the fighting to come would have been put to rest, or at least reduced to their proper perspective.

One of the staff officers brought up the subject of forage—food for the animals—one of General Rawlins's concerns. "Forage!" Sheridan shouted. "I'll get up all the forage I want. I'll haul it out, if I have to set every man in the command to corduroying roads, and corduroying every mile of them from the railroad to Dinwiddie. I tell you, I'm ready to strike out to-morrow and go to smashing things."[9]

Grant came over and spoke with General Sheridan in private, on the subject of Sheridan's immediate plans. After about twenty minutes, Sheridan said goodbye to Grant, mounted his horse, waved to the onlooking staff officers, and began riding off to the southwest, toward Dinwiddie. As he had predicted, he would very shortly go to smashing things.

President Lincoln's mind was still as preoccupied with the war as ever, but his view was basically that of an onlooker and spectator. Just standing by and waiting for news was not helping to calm his nerves. If anything, the anticipation of the coming campaign, and the accompanying loss of life, was only serving to make him even more tense and uneasy.

An incident that took place on the night of March 29 gives some idea of the state of the president's mood. Firing broke out in the vicinity of Petersburg at 10:15 p.m., and lasted for two hours. Lincoln described it as "a heavy musketry-fire," which lasted about two hours.[10] "The sound was very distinct here," in City Point, "as also were the flashes of the guns upon the clouds." The president was under the impression that "a great battle" had started, "but the older hands here scarcely noticed it, and, sure enough, this morning it was found that very little had been done."

General John G. Parke, in command of the Ninth Corps, solved the mystery behind all the firing and noise the next day. General Parke telegraphed that the enemy had driven in his picket lines near Fort Stedman—"Signal Rockets were thrown up by the enemy & general cannonading ensued accompanied with heavy musketry on both sides."[11] This is what the president had seen from City Point— not a "great battle" but only a local skirmish. "The main line was not touched," General Parke went on, "& the picket line re-established."

This had only been a skirmish, but the battle that the president was anticipating, and that was making him so tense and anxious, was not very far off.

MARCH 31, 1865, FRIDAY
MUCH HARD FIGHTING

At 12:30 p.m., General Grant sent President Lincoln the news he had been waiting for: "There has been much hard fighting this morning," the general telegraphed. "The enemy drove our left from near Dabney's house back well toward the Boydton plank road. We are now about to take the offensive at that point, and I hope will more than recover the lost ground."[1]

The final campaign, the battle that Lincoln hoped would be the last of the war, had started. The rain was still coming down in torrents, but General Grant's advance was underway. General Sheridan had assigned a division under General George Armstrong Custer to keep working on the roads to make them more passable. General Lee sent two infantry divisions, along with most of his cavalry, to stop Sheridan in the vicinity of Dinwiddie Court House.

The Confederates managed to push Sheridan back; two Federal divisions broke and ran when the enemy attacked. General Grant blamed General Gouverneur K. Warren for this setback. According to Grant, General Warren had moved his troops much too slowly and, when he finally did move forward to reinforce Sheridan, he was much too deliberate about it. If Warren's troops had been in position, and had been on hand to support General Sheridan, the reverse never would have taken place.

But the setback turned out to be minor and temporary. That afternoon, General Sheridan recovered from the morning's loss and set to strike out and go smashing things, as he phrased it, at the strategic crossroads of Five Forks, just a few miles away. General Lee had set his men to digging trenches and earthworks at Five Forks, which was the junction of five roads and a vitally important strategic location. Both Grant and Lee recognized this. General Lee knew that Five Forks was the key to protecting his right flank; he would not be able to stay in Petersburg if Grant took possession of this crossroads. General Grant also knew this, and realized that General Lee would do his best to protect Five Forks. He was not at all surprised when General Sheridan reported that Lee was hard at work fortifying the junction.

It had stopped raining by late afternoon, and the sun had actually broken through the clouds. General Sheridan ordered Custer and his cavalry to make a counterattack, a grand charge at the enemy. Custer did his best to comply, but the ground was too soft and soggy. The horses were barely able to walk through the quagmire or make any headway at all, let alone gallop. The grand charge Sheridan and Custer had planned got stuck in the mud.

But even though Custer's cavalry charge failed, infantry units managed push their way forward in spite of the mud, and drove the Confederates back to their own lines. The Federal troops not only reoccupied the ground they lost that morning, they even captured four of the enemy's flags. In a communiqué to Confederate Secretary of War John C. Breckinridge, General Lee summed up the day's activities. He wrote that "the enemy advanced and was firmly met by our troops and driven back" to the vicinity of Boydton Plank Road. "Our troops were then withdrawn and were followed by the enemy, who in turn drove us back to our lines."[2]

President Lincoln received a telegram from General Grant at about 7:00 p.m., which updated the general's earlier message and essentially said the same thing that Lee had told Breckinridge: "Our troops after being driven back on to Boydton plank road turned & drove the Enemy in turn & took the White Oak Road which we now have. This gives us the ground occupied by the Enemy this morning."[3] In what was probably an attempt to cheer up the president, Grant added, "I will send you a rebel flag captured by our troops in driving the Enemy back," and went on to say that four flags had been captured.

Although President Lincoln was clearly very nervous and apprehensive about the fighting that had finally begun, it might have encouraged him to know that General Grant and General Sheridan had no doubts at all. Colonel Horace Porter spoke with General Sheridan just north of Dinwiddie Court House and found the general happy and optimistic. A band from one of Sheridan's units was nearby, and was "playing 'Nellie Bly' as cheerfully as if furnishing music for a country picnic."[4]

The colonel found General Sherman in the same mood as his musicians. He was not at all upset by the day's events—he said that it had been "one of the liveliest days in his existence," and went on to say that he would hold his position at Dinwiddie "at all hazards."[5] As far as he was concerned, it was the enemy's troops that were in danger, not his: "We at last have drawn the enemy's infantry out of its trenches, and this is our chance to attack it."

The general's main concern was with the immediate future, for what was to come during the next few days, and with preparing for the attack on General Lee's infantry. Troops kept moving into position, but the roads were still knee-deep in mud. To complicate matters still further, a bridge had to be built over Gravelley Run in the middle of the night. "Staff-officers were rushing from one headquarters to another," Colonel Porter remembered, "making extraordinary efforts to hurry up the movement of troops."[6] Everyone from President Lincoln to every private in every regiment waited for the morning.

President Lincoln received a telegram from Secretary of War Edwin M. Stanton on the subject of the president's stay at City Point. "I hope you will stay to see it out, or for a few days at least," Secretary Stanton said, encouraging Lincoln to stay where he was. "I have strong faith that your presence will have great influence in inducing exertions that will bring Richmond; compared to that no other duty can weigh a feather."[7] Stanton assured Lincoln that there was nothing for him to do in Washington except "petty private ends that you should not be annoyed with," and ended with, "All well here."

As Secretary of War, Stanton's main interest over Lincoln's presence at City Point concerned the army—that he would help maintain the army's morale and would also have a "great influence" on its "exertions." But, as Gideon Welles pointed out, Stanton had also remarked "that it was quite as pleasant to have the President away," and also said that he was "much less annoyed" when Lincoln was not in Washington.[8]

ANXIETY AT CITY POINT

The most important event for President Lincoln, or at least the event that had the most immediate effect on his life at City Point, was the departure of Mary Lincoln for Washington. One of Lincoln's biographers wrote, "To her husband's undoubted relief, she went back to Washington, leaving Tad with his father."[1] The president telegraphed Edwin M. Stanton on Saturday afternoon, "Mrs. L. has started home; and I will thank you to see that our coachman is at the Arsenal wharf at eight (8) o'clock to-morrow morning, there wait until she arrives."[2]

Mary Lincoln, for her own part, seemed very glad to get away from everything and everyone connected with City Point. Secretary of State Seward, who had been visiting the president for the past two days, accompanied Mrs. Lincoln back to Washington aboard the steamer *Monohasset*. An associate of the president named Carl Schurz, who had campaigned for Lincoln in 1860, remarked that Mary Lincoln's spirits rose very quickly as soon as she was away from City Point. Carl Schurz also noted that she was "overwhelmingly charming to me," and that she "had me driven to my hotel in her own state carriage" as soon as the *Monohasset* docked.[3] Mrs. Lincoln felt more at home in the White House, where her role as First Lady was clearly defined, than in the man's world of an army base surrounded by troops and officers and munitions.

While his wife was on her way back to Washington, President Lincoln spent much of the day on Saturday at City Point's telegraph office. General Grant had promised to keep the president notified concerning activities southwest of Petersburg "because he was so much interested in the movements taking place that I wanted to relieve his mind as much as I could."[4]

The general telegraphed the president three times on April 1. The first two messages were mainly concerned with the fighting of the previous day, which moved Lincoln to complain that "they contain little additional except that Sheridan also had pretty hot work yesterday, that infantry was sent to his support during the night, and that he, Grant, has not since heard from Sheridan."[5] But Grant's third dispatch, which was received at 5:05 p.m., contained just the news that Lincoln had been waiting for. Federal cavalry under General Thomas C. Devin had "carried the barricade" at Five Forks that had been held by George E. Pickett's division, and "the whole 5th Corps" is now moving up toward Five Forks to attack the enemy.[6] "Our men have never fought better," the message goes on. "All are in excellent spirits and are anxious to go in. . . . The enemys loss yesterday was very heavy many of their dead are lying in the woods."

The telegram had actually been sent by Colonel Horace Porter, who had been expressly posted to Sheridan's command by General Grant. "I wish you would spend the day with Sheridan's command and send me a bulletin every half-hour or so," Grant told Porter, "advising me fully of the progress made."[7] Colonel Porter met General Sheridan at about 10:00 a.m. on the Five Forks road, and stayed with him throughout most of the day. As a result, he also had a first-hand view of the fighting throughout the day, because Sheridan was usually in the middle of it. His account of what he saw at Five Forks is vivid and colorful.

"Bullets were now humming like a swarm of bees around our heads, and shells were crashing through the ranks," he wrote. Several members of General Sheridan's staff were shot, including a sergeant who had been holding the general's personal battle flag. "All this time Sheridan was dashing from one point of the line to another, waving his flag, shaking his fist, encouraging, entreating, threatening, praying, swearing, the true personification of chivalry, the very incarnation of battle."[8]

Colonel Porter had been sending frequent dispatches to General Grant back at headquarters during this time, including the message that President Lincoln received at 5:05 p.m. At about 7:30, he started back to headquarters to report to General Grant in person. He covered the distance between Five Forks and Grant's headquarters as quickly as the muddy roads allowed and found the general and his staff sitting around a "blazing camp-fire." Grant wore a blue cavalry overcoat, and sat quietly smoking a cigar. As soon as he arrived, Colonel Porter started shouting the news—General Sheridan had broken General Lee's line, the way to the Confederate rear was now wide open, and thousands of prisoners had been taken.

The colonel was so excited that at least one onlooker thought he must be drunk. "Dignity was thrown to the winds," Porter remembered.[9] He became so carried away that he slapped General Grant on the back—much to the general's surprise, and everybody else's amusement. The general did not join in all the shouting and excitement. He just stood silently, watching the commotion with a cigar in his mouth, until he heard Porter mention prisoners. "How many prisoners were taken?" he wanted to know. Colonel Porter responded that over five thousand prisoners were now behind the Union lines, and noticed that the general's expression actually changed slightly when he heard the colonel's answer—Grant's "impassive features" gave way to a slight smile.

After listening to the account of what had happened at Five Forks that day—"to the description of Sheridan's day's work," as noted by Colonel Porter—General Grant walked into his tent to write several field dispatches, which were telegraphed to all commands. After handing his messages to an orderly, the general rejoined the group and calmly announced, "I have ordered a general assault along the lines."[10]

147

The attack was scheduled for four o'clock the next morning. Colonel Porter noted that Grant gave the order, "as coolly as if remarking about the weather."

General Grant's idea was to have all commands move against the Confederate lines as quickly as possible, to prevent General Lee from withdrawing troops from Petersburg and sending them against General Sherman. He sent another dispatch at 9:30 p.m., adding that he wanted the artillery to support the attack and that he would let the troops "attack in their own way."[11]

His commanders replied with enthusiasm. General Ord said that he would go into the enemy's works "as a hot knife goes through butter," and General Horatio Wright of the Sixth Corps responded that he would "make the fur fly."[12] General Grant was encouraged by the enthusiasm of his generals. He went to bed just after midnight— "the general soon tucked himself into his camp-bed, and was soon sleeping as peacefully as if the next day was to be devoted to a picnic instead of a decisive battle."

General Grant could afford a good night's sleep. Shortly before going to bed, he sent a report on General Philip Sheridan's activities. "He has carried everything before him," Grant telegraphed, "he has captured three brigades of infantry and a train of wagons and is now pushing up his success."[13] It looked as though the morning's coming general offensive would bring another day of triumph and achievement. "I have ordered everything else to advance and prevent a concentration of the enemy against Sheridan." There did not seem to be any reason for Grant to lose any sleep.

President Lincoln, on the other hand, did not have General Grant's calm and steady temperament. If Grant's planned offensive succeeded, it would mean the end of the war; he realized that, but it would also mean more dead and wounded and more killing. The fact that his son Robert was a member of Grant's staff probably added to the president's apprehensions. He spent most of the day at City Point's telegraph office, reading messages from the front and forwarding some of them along either to Secretary Stanton or Secretary Seward in Washington.

Toward the end of the day, Lincoln returned to the *River Queen*. "There his anxiety became more intense."[14] His bodyguard, William Crook, wrote that the president could hear cannon fire from "not many miles away," discharging their salvoes into the Confederate positions southwest of Petersburg. After the sun went down, he could also see the muzzle flashes.

The firing kept Lincoln awake all night. He refused to go to his cabin, and would not even consider getting some much-needed sleep. "Almost all night he walked up and down the deck, pausing now and then to listen or to look out into the darkness to see if he could see anything."[15] The president's nerves were even more on edge than usual. "I have never seen such suffering in the face of any man as was in his that night." And the morning promised to bring another full day of fighting.

MESSAGES FOR GENERAL GRANT

The very first telegram President Lincoln sent on this Sunday morning was to his wife Mary, which gives some idea of how concerned he must have been about her well-being. The message was mainly a summary of the fighting that had taken place during the past twenty-four or so hours. He summarized General Grant's telegraph of the night before, stating that General Sheridan had captured three brigades of infantry, and went on to quote the general's communiqué of earlier that morning: "The battle now rages furiously. Sheridan with his Cavalry, the 5th Corps & [Nelson A.] Miles Division of the 2nd Corps, which was sent to him since 1 this A.M. is now sweeping down from the West."[1] Lincoln ended on a personal note: "Robert yesterday wrote a little cheerful note to Capt. Penrose, which is all I have heard from him since you left."

Mary Lincoln arrived in Washington that morning, aboard the steamer *Monohasset*, and found her husband's message waiting for her. She was undoubtedly glad to be back "home," or at least to be away from City Point. But she also missed both her husband and her son Tad. Tad would turn twelve years old in a few days, on April 4, and Mary liked celebrating her children's birthdays with parties and gifts.

Later in the morning, the president sent word to Secretary of War Stanton: "Dispatches frequently coming in," including from Gen. Grant. Grant's message advised that forces under Horatio Wright had gone through the enemy's line, and that "I do not see how the portion of the rebel army south of where Wright broke through . . . are to escape."[2] Lincoln's telegraph to Stanton reflected Grant's enthusiasm. "All going finely. Parke, Wright, and Ord . . . have all broken through the enemy's intrenched lines, taking some forts, guns, and prisoners." Three hours later, he sent Secretary Stanton a few more details, which was also more good news. "Everything has been carried from the left of the Ninth Corps," he wrote. "We are now closing around the works of the line immediately enveloping Petersburg."

Grant's attack did not begin at 4:00 a.m., as had been originally planned. It had to be postponed because of darkness—the sun had not yet come up, and it was too dark to see. There were too many trenches, rifle pits, parapets, and other obstacles to be either gone through or gone around, and "a little daylight would be of material assistance."[3] But at 4:45, there was enough light in the sky for the charge to begin. "The thunder of hundreds of guns shook the ground like an earthquake, and soon the troops were engaged all along the lines," is how Colonel Horace Porter described the opening of the attack. General Grant was soon sending his own descriptions of what was happening, and President Lincoln devoured every word at City Point's telegraph office.

As soon as there was enough daylight for the men to see where they were going, the artillery stopped firing and the infantry began climbing out of their trenches. They did not advance very far before running head on into a solid line of Confederate musket fire. Muzzle flashes lit up the earthworks from end to end. General Horatio Wright's Sixth Corps lost over one thousand men in about fifteen minutes. John G. Parke's Ninth Corps lost about the same number of men in the same amount of time. Veterans remembered Cold Harbor during the previous June, when thousands of Federal troops had been shot down in a headlong charge against the enemy's fortifications.

But Petersburg was not Cold Harbor, and April 1865 was not June 1864. Federal troops moved forward so quickly that some Confederates only had time to fire one volley before abandoning their trenches and running toward the rear. The blue infantry overran the enemy's lines and kept going, chasing the enemy and taking prisoners. At least one unit captured a line of earthworks and remained in them, breaking the Confederate line.

Not very long after the attack began, Grant's headquarters received a communiqué from General Wright: his Sixth Corps had cracked the enemy's line of defenses and was moving forward. General Parke sent a similar message a short while later, reporting that he had captured eight hundred prisoners, twelve artillery pieces, and a line of enemy fortifications. But in spite of these losses, the defenders show no signs of giving up.

General Grant watched the battle from a nearby hill. He had a good view of the fighting, but Confederate artillerymen a short distance away also had a good view of him. The enemy gunners fired at him and his observation position, but Grant was so engrossed in watching the fighting that he did not notice—his famous single-mindedness was getting the better of him.

Several staff officers suggested that Grant move someplace else, someplace safer and a lot less conspicuous, but the general paid no attention. He kept on issuing orders and writing dispatches and running the battles from where he was. When he had finished, Grant seemed to notice the artillery fire for the first time. At that point, he finally decided to move off the hill and out of range of the enemy gunners. But he did not move until he was ready—his ability to concentrate on the problem at hand allowed him to ignore any and all distractions, including Confederate artillery fire.

General Grant was in a state of excitement and high spirits over what he had seen from his hilltop observation post, as well as over the progress of the day's fighting. He wrote to his wife to describe what was taking place—Julia Grant noted that "I had letters daily from the General, always hopeful."[4] The letter to Julia overflowed with confidence. He explained that he was writing from what had been a Confederate fortification a short time before, which was solidly built and had been heavily defended, and went on to say that he was highly impressed by the fact that his troops had been able to capture it. The general added that he might have more campaigning and fighting ahead of him, but that he hoped that this was not the case.

General Grant sent a telegram to Colonel Theodore S. Bowers, an officer on his staff, which was intercepted and read by President Lincoln at City Point's telegraph office. In his message, Grant said essentially the same thing as he had said to Julia Grant, but his tone was much more "official" and straightforward. "We are now up, and have a continuous line of troops, and in a few hours will be intrenched from the Appomattox, below Petersburg, to the river above."[5] The telegram was received by 4:30 p.m.

The general also explained that two Confederate divisions, Henry Heth's and Cadmus M. Wilcox's divisions, had been isolated—"such part of them as were not captured"—and went on to say that General Sheridan and the Fifth Corps' cavalry "is above them."

From President Lincoln's point of view, the second part of Grant's telegram was even better than the first. "The whole captures since the army started out will not amount to less than 12,000 men, and probably 50 pieces of artillery. I do not know the number of men and guns accurately, however."[6] Grant's numbers did not have to be one hundred percent accurate, at least not as far as Lincoln was concerned. The figures showed that the Confederates had suffered a significant setback, which was exactly what Lincoln wanted to hear from his general-in-chief.

"A portion of [Robert S.] Foster's division, Twenty-fourth Corps, made a most gallant charge this afternoon, and captured a very important fort from the enemy, with its entire garrison," General Grant went on. "All seems well with us, and everything quiet just now." The president certainly appreciated hearing that "all seems well." This was the best news that he ever could have hoped for.

Lincoln forwarded Grant's telegram along to Secretary of War Stanton, with an added note: "At 4:30 p.m. to-day General Grant telegraphed as follows." But the president did not include the last line of Grant's telegram: "I think the president might come out and pay us a visit to-morrow."[7]

At 8:15 p.m., Lincoln sent this message to General Grant: "Lieut. General Grant, Allow me to tender you, and all with you, the nations [sic] grateful thanks for this additional, and magnificent, success."[8] He completed his short message by advising the general, "At your kind suggestion, I think I will visit you tomorrow."

The president also sent another message to his wife later in the day, and was just as cheerful and optimistic as he had been in his earlier telegram. He addressed the wire to "Mrs. Lincoln," and reported that General Grant "has Petersburg completely enveloped."[9] The message went on to say, "He [General Grant] suggests that I shall go out and see him in the morning, which I think I will." Lincoln concluded on a personal note, "Tad and I are both well, and we will be glad to see you and your party here at the time you name." Apparently Mrs. Lincoln was planning to return to City Point, possibly for Tad's birthday, but these plans were not carried out.

General Robert E. Lee had been sending telegrams as well, but his were just the opposite of President Lincoln's enthusiastic messages. He sent this grim communiqué to President Jefferson Davis in Richmond: "I think it absolutely necessary that we should abandon our position tonight," he began, and went on to advise President Davis to evacuate Richmond.[10] He was sending an officer to Richmond "to explain the routes to you by which the troops will be moved to Amelia Court House, and furnish you with a guide and any assistance that you may require for yourself."

General Lee sent another telegram, this one to General John C. Breckenridge, the Confederate Secretary of War, that was even more stark and depressing. "I see no prospect of doing more than holding our position here till night," he began.[11] "I am not certain I can do that. . . . Enemy have broken through our lines." He did not even try to be tactful or diplomatic; he said exactly what was on his mind. "Our only chance, then, of concentrating our forces is to do so near Danville Railroad, which I shall endeavor to do at once. I advise that all preparations be made for leaving Richmond to-night."

For General Lee, the situation was every bit as bad as he had stated in his telegrams. The Petersburg lines had been captured, which made the Confederate position untenable. Colonel Horace Porter gave the Federal point of view in his own assessment, which was in total agreement with General Lee. "By noon all the outer works were in our possession, except two strong redoubts which occupied a commanding position," he wrote.[12] The two forts were taken later in the day.

As he had done at Fort Stedman in March, President Lincoln decided to ride out to the battlefield and see some of the fighting for himself. "We rode out to the intrenchments, close to the battleground," his bodyguard, William H. Crook, wrote.[13] "Mr. Lincoln watched the life-and-death struggle for some time, and then returned to City Point." Later in the day, the president received General Grant's telegram giving the number of prisoners and artillery pieces that had been captured. "The news made the President happy," Crook recalled. "He said to Captain Penrose that the end of the war was now in sight."

About twenty-four hours earlier, as the president watched artillery fire from the deck of the *River Queen*, Crook had been moved to comment on the suffering and the sadness he saw in Lincoln's face. But the results of this Sunday's fighting had brought the war a giant step closer to the end, and had also brought a substantial change in

Lincoln's outlook and demeanor: "He could go to bed and sleep now. I remember how cheerful was his 'Good-night, Crook.'"[14]

General Grant was just as optimistic concerning the results of the day's efforts. He also realized that the end of the war was now in sight. At the end of the day, several "prominent" officers suggested that he should order an attack of the Petersburg trenches immediately, to break through the inner defenses and capture the city before nightfall. But General Grant rejected the idea. "He said the city would undoubtedly be evacuated during the night," and that "he was firm in his resolve not to sacrifice the lives necessary to accomplish such a result."[15] Another attack, which would have meant another several thousand killed and wounded, would be unnecessary. President Lincoln would have been in full agreement with this line of thinking.

"GET THEM TO PLOWING ONCE"

President Lincoln was up early, and received the news that General Grant had guessed correctly—Petersburg had been evacuated during the night. General Parke had gone through the inner defenses at 4:00 a.m., and the city had surrendered at 4:38. In a communique that was typical of him, straightforward and to the point, Grant had immediately telegraphed the news to Colonel Theodore S. Bowers: "Petersburg was evacuated last night. Pursuit will be immediately made."[1]

The general sent another telegram to Colonel Bowers a short while afterward. This message was mainly concerned with President Lincoln's impending visit. "Say to the President that an officer and escort will attend him, but as to myself I start toward the Danville Road with the army." His explanation was, "I want to cut off as much of Lee's army as possible."[2] But Grant would change his mind and would decide to stay in Petersburg and wait for the president to arrive.

Lincoln wired Secretary of War Stanton at 8:00 a.m. to relay the good news regarding Petersburg, as well as to inform Stanton of his own plans. "This morning Gen. Grant reports Petersburg evacuated; and he is confident Richmond also is. He is pushing forward to cut off, if possible, the retreating army." He ended the message with, "I start to him in a few minutes."[3]

Secretary Stanton was very much taken by surprise to hear that President Lincoln would be joining Grant later that day. He congratulated the president on the "glorious news" regarding Petersburg, but also "respectfully" asked Lincoln to consider "whether you ought to expose the nation to the consequence of any disaster to yourself in the pursuit of a treacherous and dangerous enemy like the rebel army."[4] He reminded the president that "Commanding generals are in the line of their duty in running such risks. But is the political head of a nation in the same condition?"

President Lincoln did not pay any attention to Secretary Stanton's advice—he certainly did not think that he would get himself assassinated by visiting General Grant, which he had done before—and boarded a special train for Patrick Station, which was about a mile from Petersburg. Admiral David Dixon Porter, Tad Lincoln, and Commander John S. Barnes accompanied the president. Admiral Porter borrowed a horse from a cavalryman and rode from the rail station to Petersburg, while Lincoln and Tad rode by ambulance into the city.

Commander Barnes decided to walk the distance; as he approached the city on foot, he was greatly impressed by the trenches and barricades that had defended its approaches during the siege. He had heard about them, but this was the first time he had the chance to inspect them. The defenses were made up of a "labyrinth" of trenches, breastworks, rifle pits, and earthworks that went on for miles. "They were very elaborate with zigzag approaches and connections dug deep into the ground."[5] He wondered how anyone was able to capture such a line of elaborate and well-built fortifications.

When Commander Barnes finally made his way through the battlements and reached Petersburg itself, he discovered that the president, along with Tad and Admiral Porter, would soon be returning to the train. Because he was on foot, Commander Barnes decided to start back to the rail station right away. On his way out of the city, he picked up a "trophy bag" of tobacco. These bags were lying about on the street, and were being confiscated by every soldier who happened to pass by.[6]

General Grant had been in Petersburg since morning, and set

up a temporary headquarters at the home of Thomas Wallace at 21 Market Street. "Many of the citizens, panic-stricken, had escaped with the army."[7] Most of the white residents who decided to remain stayed indoors. A "few groups of negroes gave cheers," but the general atmosphere throughout the city "was one of complete desertion."

The president arrived at the Thomas Wallace house "soon after" General Grant, according to Colonel Horace Porter, accompanied by his son Robert, who had met his father at the railway station, along with Tad and Admiral Porter. He climbed out of the ambulance "and came in through the front gate with long and rapid strides, his face beaming with delight."[8] As General Grant stepped forward to meet the president, Lincoln took the general's hand and shook it with warmth and emotion. "I doubt whether Mr. Lincoln ever experienced a happier moment in his life."

After offering his "warm congratulations" for the victory, the president said, "Do you know, general, that I have had a sort of sneaking idea for some days that you intended to do something like this."[9] Colonel Porter remembered that the president added, "but I thought some time ago that you would so maneuver as to have Sherman come up and be near enough to cooperate with you."[10] In his memoirs, General Grant explains that he had political motives for not bringing Sherman north. If the "Western armies" operated against Richmond and Lee along with armies from the East, the situation "might lead to disagreeable bickerings between members of Congress of the East and those of the West in some of their debates."[11] Lincoln responded that he never thought of that. He was so anxious about the end of the war, and how soon it could be brought about, "that he did not care where the aid came from so the work was done."

President Lincoln and General Grant continued their conversation for about an hour and a half. Besides General Sherman and his Western army, they also talked about "civil complications" that might cause problems with reconciling the former Confederate states into the

Union after the war ended, as well as showing leniency toward them. Showing tolerance and clemency toward the South was a vitally important issue for the president, which he made very clear. "He intimated very plainly," Colonel Porter remembered, "that thoughts of leniency to the conquered were uppermost in his heart."[12]

General Grant shared the president's point of view regarding compassion and moderation toward the defeated enemy. When he entered Petersburg that morning, he could see that the ground in front of him was "packed with the Confederate army." But he did not order artillery to be brought up. "At all events, I had not the heart to turn the artillery upon such a mass of defeated and fleeing men," he reflected, "and I hoped to capture them soon."[13] A year earlier, in the spring of 1864, Grant would have lost no time in ordering his gunners to bring every available piece of artillery to bear on the enemy troops. But now Lee and his army were in full retreat, the end of the war was only a matter of weeks away, and President Lincoln had convinced him that leniency would be the best policy toward the fading Confederate army. Grant had battered his opponent for the past eleven months, from the Wilderness to Five Forks, and realized that it was now time to stop fighting and to begin looking forward toward peace and reconciliation.

While President Lincoln and General Grant were busy conferring and making plans for the future, young Tad Lincoln had a more immediate concern. General George H. Sharpe, another member of General Grant's staff, noticed that Tad was looking increasingly anxious and uncomfortable as the afternoon went by and guessed what was wrong—the boy had not had any lunch and was hungry. General Sharpe addressed the situation immediately and ordered some sandwiches to be sent up, which Tad devoured. Both the president and General Grant thought the scene was amusing and touching—a top-level conference between Lincoln and his general-in-chief had been brought to a stop because of lunch for an eleven-year-old boy.

When the conversation between the two men finally came to an end, General Grant excused himself. He had to ride to the front, he explained, and join General Ord's column before the army advanced too far. The president once again shook General Grant's hand and, "with great warmth of feeling," wished him every success.[14] The president clearly did not want to detain his general-in-chief. Within only a few minutes after saying goodbye to the president, Grant and his officers were well on their way toward the front.

General Grant and his staff had only ridden about nine miles, as far as Sutherland's Station, when they were overtaken by a dispatch rider from General Godfrey Weitzel. The message was not as direct and to the point as one General Grant would have written, but it certainly conveyed the same meaning: "We took Richmond at 8:15 this morning. I captured many guns. The enemy left in great haste. The city is on fire in two places. Am making every effort to put it out. The people received us with enthusiastic expressions of joy."[15]

General Grant read General Weitzel's message without showing any emotion at all. His only reaction was regret that the news had not arrived before President Lincoln left Petersburg. After reading what Weitzel had to say, General Grant ordered that "the news be circulated among the troops as rapidly as possible."[16]

The news certainly did circulate. When he received the report that Petersburg had been evacuated, Colonel Elisha Hunt Rhodes wrote, "Great is the rejoicing."[17] But when he learned that Richmond was occupied by Federal troops, and that the city was "in flames," he was not all that enthusiastic about it. "Well, let it burn, we do not want it," he said. "We are after Lee and are going to have him."

President Lincoln did not agree with Colonel Rhodes or with his point of view. Lincoln wanted to see Richmond. As he would explain to Admiral Porter, Richmond was not only the capital of the Confederacy, it was also the capital of the rebellion, and he very much wanted it and also planned to visit the city. He was well aware that Lee's army was General Grant's primary goal, and that the war would not be over until Lee surrendered. But he also realized that if Richmond fell the surrender of Lee's army and the end of the war would only be a matter of weeks, or possibly days.

In Washington, the news of Petersburg and Richmond triggered a celebration that all but shut down the city. "Intelligence of the evacuation of Petersburg and the capture of Richmond was received this A.M., and the city has been in an uproar through the day," Gideon Welles wrote in his diary.[18] "Most of the clerks and others left the Departments, and there were immense gatherings in the streets," he went on. "Flags were flying from every house and store that had them . . . and Washington appeared patriotic beyond anything ever witnessed."

Washington was not the only city that celebrated. Residents of New York and every other city throughout the North broke out all their flags and shouted and carried on like overexcited schoolboys all day long. The *New York Times* ran headlines that reflected the national mood: "Grant, Richmond, and Victory! The Union Army in the Rebel Capital."[19] The front page of the *Chicago Tribune* announced, "Richmond Is Ours. The Old Flag Floats over the Rebel Capital."[20]

One person who did not seem very excited by the day's triumphs and achievements was Lincoln's bodyguard, William H. Crook. He was more shaken and upset than excited. The sight of the dead on the field outside Petersburg dampened any enthusiasm he might have had for the day's fighting. One of the soldiers he saw had a bullet through his forehead; another had both arms blown off. When he finally arrived in the city, Crook was taken to see General Grant.

He found the general sitting on the piazza of a white frame house, and once again received a disappointment. Crook did not seem very impressed by what he saw, either by the setting for the scheduled meeting between the president and his general-in-chief or by General

Grant himself. From his account, Crook did not seem to think that "a white frame house" was either suitable or adequate for such an important conference, and he was totally unimpressed by General Grant. "Grant did not look like one's idea of a conquering hero," he commented.[21] Short, stubby, and round-shouldered, wearing the uniform of a private with the three stars of a lieutenant general sewn on, Ulysses S. Grant was not very imposing, and did not try to be. "He didn't appear exultant, and he was as quiet as he ever had been." General Grant was just too plain and unassuming to satisfy William Crook's idea of what a commanding general should look like.

Although he did not attend the meeting between the president and General Grant, Crook thought that Lincoln's attitude toward Grant before the meeting began was "almost affectionate."[22] While the two were having their conference, Crook decided to use the time to "stroll through Petersburg," and to see what was left of it. The city was almost deserted, but he did have the chance to talk with a few of its residents. "They said they were glad the Union army had taken possession; they were half starved," he later recounted. "They certainly looked so."

Like Commander Barnes, Crook managed to acquire some tobacco before he left the city, only he had to pay for his—a five-pound bale for twenty five cents. "The tobacco warehouses were on fire," he explained, "and boys were carrying away tobacco to sell to the soldiers."[23] During the course of his stroll, William Crook saw all there was to see in Petersburg—a desolate, nearly deserted ruin of a city, ravaged by looters.

President Lincoln and his party took the train back to City Point after his meeting with General Grant. Almost as soon as everyone arrived, they heard about the evacuation of Richmond for the first time—City Point was celebrating the event just as enthusiastically as everyone else throughout the North. About the only people in town who had not heard the news about Richmond were a long line of Confederate prisoners near the City Point dock. These prisoners

165

were boarding transports that would take them to prison camps in the North. At least one of them told the guards that every Yankee would be dead before they could get anywhere near Richmond. Nobody bothered to tell them the truth.

President Lincoln watched the prisoners as they waited their turn to board the ships, and was depressed by the sight. The men "were in a pitiable condition, ragged and thin; they looked half starved," William Crook wrote.[24] When the men took their rations out of their knapsacks to have lunch, everyone could see that their meal consisted of nothing but bread "which looked as if it had been mixed with tar." When they cut into it, "we could see how hard and heavy it was; it was more like cheese than bread." "'Poor fellows!' Mr. Lincoln said. 'It's a hard lot. Poor fellows.'" Crook could see that the president's face "was pitying and sorrowful. All the happiness had gone."

At City Point, the president had moved his quarters from the relative luxury of the *River Queen* to much more Spartan lodgings aboard Admiral Porter's flagship USS *Malvern*. Admiral Porter offered his own stateroom to Lincoln, but the president "positively declined" the suggestion.[25] Instead, he elected to sleep in a six-foot-long by four-and-a-half-foot-wide cabin. The cabin was usually occupied by the admiral's secretary.

While the president was asleep during his first night on board the *Malvern*, Admiral Porter ordered Lincoln's boots to be cleaned and his socks mended—the socks had holes in them. At breakfast, Lincoln announced to the admiral that a miracle had happened to him during the night. "When I went to bed I had two large holes in my socks," he explained, "and this morning there are no holes."[26] When the admiral inquired if the president had slept well, Lincoln replied that he had a good night's sleep, "but you can't put a long blade in a short scabbard. I was too long for the berth." He was also four inches too long for the cabin.

During the day, the admiral put all the ship's carpenters to work remodeling the president's cabin. By the end of the day, the cabin had been lengthened, widened, and completely refashioned. In the morning, Lincoln announced that a second miracle had taken place, "a greater miracle than ever happened last night; I shrank six inches in length and about a foot sideways."[27] The president was clearly enjoying himself. The time he was spending aboard the *Malvern* was helping to take his mind off the war.

But nothing could make him forget the war completely. The fires of Richmond were plainly visible from Admiral Porter's flagship. A rearguard of South Carolina troops had set fire to anything and everything that might be of use to the enemy—Federal troops would soon be occupying the city, everyone could see that. Tobacco warehouses were set alight, along with munitions works. A strong south wind helped to spread the flames, setting fire to the flour mills along the river. The wind destroyed just about everything the South Carolinians missed. Richmond, or at least a sizeable part of it, was burning to the ground.

All that evening, the evening after President Lincoln had visited Petersburg, "A lurid glare lit up the sky in the direction of Richmond," Commander John S. Barnes remembered.[28] "Heavy detonations followed each other in rapid succession, which Admiral Porter rightly interpreted as the blowing up of rebel ironclads." President Lincoln could see the fires and hear the explosions, as well. Commander Barnes noted that "Mr. Lincoln then made up his mind he would go to Richmond the next day."

While on board the *Malvern*, President Lincoln also discussed his views on the war, and what he hoped would happen after the war, with Admiral Porter. From the general tone of the conversation, the admiral recognized that Lincoln was determined to have the most generous and lenient terms for the Confederacy following the surrender. "Get them to plowing once," he said, in his own singular manner of speaking, "and gathering in their own little crops, eating pop-corn at their own firesides, and you can't get them to shoulder a musket again for half a century."[29] If the South was treated fairly and without malice, the president reasoned, another rebellion might be averted at some future point in time.

When he returned to City Point, the president read Secretary of War Stanton's telegram of earlier in the day. From the attitude of his reply, Lincoln probably had a good chuckle over Stanton's warning not to "expose the nation" and himself to possible assassination. "Thanks for your caution," he responded at five o'clock in the afternoon, "but I have already been to Petersburg, staid [sic] with Gen. Grant an hour & a half and returned here."[30]

Having said that, the president went on to make an admonition of his own. "It is certain now that Richmond is in our hands, and I think I will go there to-morrow. I will take care of myself."[31] In other words, if he was not afraid of going to Petersburg after the Confederates abandoned the city, then he was certainly not going to turn down the opportunity of going to the Confederate capital. He was determined to see Richmond and did not care if Secretary Stanton or anybody else objected.

THE PRESIDENT VISITS RICHMOND

The president was awake fairly early, and sent a telegram to Secretary Stanton to advise him of the latest news developments. General Weitzel had found a great deal of railroad stock that had not been destroyed by the retreating Confederates, Lincoln said, including twenty-eight locomotives. He also forwarded a telegram from General Grant that had been sent from Sutherland's Station. "General Sheridan picked up 1,200 prisoners to-day," the general telegraphed, and went on to advise that "the remnant of Lee's army" were scattered south of Richmond.[1] It was an encouraging message, further evidence that the war finally was winding down and would soon be ended.

Colonel Horace Porter noted that the army "caught but a few hours' sleep" during the night before, and were on the move again from Sutherland's Station at three o'clock in the morning on April 4.[2] General Grant did not want the Confederates to get any rest in their attempt to escape the pursuing Union army, which meant that Grant's own army would not be getting very much rest, either.

"The pursuit had become now become swift, unflagging, restless," as described by Colonel Porter.[3] Colonel Elisha Hunt Rhodes's Second Rhode Island Infantry was among the units pursuing General Lee. Colonel Rhodes wrote, "Still following the demoralized army. The road is filled with broken wagons and the things thrown away in the flight of the rebels."[4] President Lincoln was being kept informed of the fighting by General Grant and other Union officers, and was well aware of the state of Lee's army.

After contacting Secretary of War Stanton, President Lincoln began preparing for his trip to Richmond. When Secretary Stanton found out that the president intended to visit Richmond in spite of his warning, the exasperated Stanton reacted with anger and alarm. "That fool!" he shouted—as far as he was concerned, Lincoln should have known better than to risk his life unnecessarily.[5]

Commander John S. Barnes was not as vehement as Secretary Stanton when he heard the news of Lincoln's intent to see Richmond, but he did feel just as concerned for the president's safety. "I confess that I was much alarmed at the situation and the exposure of the President to assault or even assassination," he would later write.[6]

But the president was not going to Richmond just for the purpose of satisfying his own curiosity. Admiral Porter was of the opinion that Lincoln should visit the Confederate capital as soon as possible after the city surrendered. As William Crook put it, "In that way he could gather up the reins of government most readily and give an impression of confidence in the South that would be helpful in the reorganization of the government."[7] Once again, the president was looking beyond the end of the war and was thinking about the reunification of the country. If going to Richmond would help to accomplish this, and would "give an impression of confidence in the South," it was well worth the risk.

The president began his journey up the James River, along with his son Tad and his bodyguard William Crook, at about ten o'clock in the morning. The *Malvern* also made the trip, but Lincoln and his party were aboard the *River Queen*.

April 4 was Tad Lincoln's birthday, his twelfth. A trip to Richmond aboard a side-wheeler was the best birthday present a twelve-year-old could ever hope for, much better than birthday cake back at the White House. As soon as he came on board, Tad went belowdecks and began inspecting the ship and talking to the crew. His father remained on deck, where he and William Crook ate the contents of a large bowl of apples.

During the night and into the next morning, torpedo boats (which would be known as minesweepers in another era) cleared away the torpedoes, or sea mines, that had been blocking the channel. When Admiral Porter's flagship, USS *Malvern*, ran aground, the admiral decided that it would be best, and safest, for the president and his party if they continued on to Richmond in his own barge. The barge had a much shallower draft than the *Malvern*, and was rowed by twelve sailors, who would also accompany President Lincoln on shore. Commander Barnes was right behind the president's barge in a smaller boat.

In spite of all the precautions that had been taken to insure the president's safety, William Crook recalled that the trip was "exciting enough." There were still too many threats and hazards to suit him and his bodyguard's sense of security: "On either side dead horses, broken ordinance, wrecked boats floated near our boat, and we passed so close to torpedoes that we could have put out our hands and touched them."[8]

When Lincoln finally arrived on shore, the situation involving Lincoln's safety did not improve. Commander Barnes watched as the president "finally made a landing on the edge of town."[9] When the commander came ashore himself a few minutes after the president, he saw that Lincoln was being accompanied by "a few sailors, armed with carbines," and also that he was surrounded by "a dense mass of men, women, and children, mostly negroes." But in addition, Barnes noticed that the president's "tall form and high beaver hat towered above the crowd," which made him an excellent target for any snipers who happened to be in the vicinity.

William Crook was a lot more concerned about snipers and assassins than Commander Barnes—it was his job to protect the president. He was also very much aware that Lincoln was a very tall and inviting target. In an attempt to arrange some sort of defensive escort, Crook formed two lines of armed sailors, six in front of Lincoln and six behind him. Admiral Porter and Captain Penrose were to the president's right, while Crook and Tad were to his left. Crook had armed himself with a Colt revolver. "We looked more like prisoners than anything else as we walked up the streets of Richmond not thirty-six hours after the Confederates had evacuated."[10]

When the president first arrived, there were not very many people out on the streets except for a good many recently freed slaves—"Richmond was black with negroes," Crook remembered, and thought that they must have heard about Lincoln's entry into the city "through some sort of underground telegraph."[11] They were very glad to see President Lincoln, and went out of their way to show their enthusiasm. "By the time we were on shore hundreds of black hands were outstretched to the President." Lincoln shook hands with some of them, and thanked everyone for their wholehearted welcome.

As the president and his party made their way into Richmond, and as word of his arrival spread, more and more white residents of the city came out to see Lincoln. Crook said that the streets "were alive with spectators," and also noted, "Wherever it was possible for a human being to find a foothold there was some man or woman or boy straining his eyes after the President. Every window was crowded with heads."[12]

But it was an eerie and silent crowd—no one spoke or shouted or made a sound. To William Crook, there was something strange and oppressive about thousands of spectators looking on in complete silence as the president passed by. This was an unfriendly crowd. Unlike the freed slaves who had welcomed Lincoln when he first came ashore, these people were not glad to see the president. Lincoln was also aware of the hostility. According to William Crook, the president had the expression "of a brave man when he is ready for whatever may come."[13]

The president had not proceeded very far into the city when Crook noticed the blinds on the second story window of a house open slightly. A man dressed in gray came to the window and pointed something that looked like a gun directly at President Lincoln. Crook immediately dropped Tad's hand and stepped in front of the president—"I was sure he meant to shoot."[14]

Everyone in the president's following, including the president himself, was well aware of the danger. A mounted Union cavalryman was spotted at a nearby street corner; he was summoned and informed that "President Lincoln wishes for assistance."[15] The soldier galloped off to get help. A few minutes later "a small squadron of mounted men" rode up. The first thing the cavalry unit did was to clear the street. Afterward, they escorted the president and his party to General Weitzel's headquarters.

William Crook breathed a sigh of relief that Lincoln had not been shot. "It seems to me nothing short of miraculous that some attempt on his life was not made," he declared. "It is to the everlasting glory of the South that he was permitted to come and go in peace."[16]

When the president reached General Weitzel's headquarters, which he had established in Jefferson Davis's former residence, everyone realized that they were finally among friends. The house was made of stucco, and had a garden in the back. A black servant said that Mrs. Davis had ordered her staff to have the house in good condition for the Yankees when they arrived.

The Davis residence has been referred to as the Confederate White House, but Commander Barnes described it as "a modest and unpretentious building, brown in color, with small windows and doors."[17] The president entered the house via the front door and was escorted into Jefferson Davis's reception room. The room was "plainly but comfortably furnished." Commander Barnes noticed a print of the Confederate ironclad *Sumter* on one of the walls. Years later, the naval officer remembered that the picture of the warship "excited my covetousness."

While Commander Barnes was examining the room, President Lincoln sat down in President Davis's chair. Everyone in the room recognized the significance and the symbolism of the moment. Abraham

Lincoln was seated in the chair that had only two days before belonged to Confederate president Jefferson Davis—Commander Barnes commented that he was "seated in the chair almost warm from the pressure of the body of Jefferson Davis."[18] Some gathered by the door to look at the sight. Not much was said by anyone.

President Lincoln did not say very much, either. "There was no triumph in his gesture or attitude."[19] He leaned back in the chair, "like a tired man whose nerves had carried him beyond his strength," and asked for someone to bring him a drink of water. He seemed satisfied just to sit and relax for a few minutes and drink a glass of water before returning to the business of running the war.

President Lincoln congratulated General Weitzel on having captured Richmond, and a small celebration was held. One of the servants brought a tall, black bottle up from the cellar. Everyone who wanted a drink helped themselves as the bottle was passed around. The president was the only person in the room who decided that he did not want a drink.

General Weitzel asked President Lincoln what should be done with the "conquered people." The president replied that he did not want to issue any orders to the general regarding that particular subject, but he did give his wholehearted opinion. "If I were in your place I'd let 'em up easy," he said, "let 'em up easy."[20]

Following the celebration, a large carriage, which was described as an officer's ambulance, was driven up to the door. President Lincoln, Admiral Porter, General Weitzel, and some of his staff, along with Captain Penrose and Tad, climbed aboard—they were to be driven to several places that might be of interest in the Confederate capital. After everyone was on board, it was discovered that there was no room in the vehicle for Lincoln's bodyguard, William Crook. The president insisted that Crook accompany him on the tour of Richmond, which meant that a horse had to be produced at short notice. Crook took up a position alongside the ambulance, on the same side of the vehicle as the president. With Crook at Lincoln's side, the president and his party proceeded on their way.

As President Lincoln was driven through the city, he could see evidence of the war everywhere he looked. Hundreds of buildings and houses had been destroyed by fire. "The streets were crowded with furniture and every description of wares," a news reporter wrote, "dashed down to be trampled in the mud or burned up where it lay."[21] Among the landmarks they passed was the infamous Libby Prison, where hundreds of Union prisoners had been held in captivity. Crowds continued to turn out in large numbers to see Lincoln as he drove by, which made traveling slow and difficult. Some of the people actually cheered the president, especially in working-class districts. In the wealthier areas, the blinds remained closed and the residents stayed indoors, silent and forbidding.

The only stop made by the president and his entourage was at the former Confederate capitol, where the Confederate congress had convened. President Davis's cabinet room, which was in a very rundown and derelict condition, was the only room they visited. "The furniture was completely wrecked; the coverings of desks and chairs had been stripped off by relic-hunters, and the chairs were hacked to pieces," was William Crook's description of the cabinet chamber.[22] Official government documents were scattered all over the floor, along with now-worthless $1,000 Confederate bonds. Seeing Jefferson Davis's house might have been very inspiring and encouraging for Lincoln and his party, but the inside of the capitol was a depressing sight.

While he was in Richmond, President Lincoln met with former assistant justice, and Confederate assistant secretary of war, John A. Campbell, the only government official to remain in Richmond after the capital was evacuated. In fact, Campbell had informed John C. Breckinridge, the Confederate secretary of war, that he did not intend

175

to leave Richmond. His explanation was that "I should take an opportunity to see President Lincoln on the subject of peace."[23] The president was in full agreement with this point of view, and was more than willing to discuss peace with Campbell.

Judge Campbell, as he was frequently called, had talked peace terms with President Lincoln once before, at Hampton Roads, in February 1865. Confederate senator Robert M. T. Hunter of Virginia, Confederate vice-president Alexander H. Stephens, and Campbell met with Lincoln and Secretary of State Seward aboard the *River Queen* to discuss the possibility of reaching an agreement that would secure peace. The meeting, which went on for several hours, ended without results; the participants could not agree on terms that would be acceptable to both sides.

In his discussion with the president, Campbell's main concern was with the treatment of the former Confederate states by Lincoln and his government in the aftermath of the war, and he asked the president to treat them with "moderation, magnanimity, and kindness."[24] He also had anxieties over the civil liberties of the citizens of Richmond, and requested that no "requisitions" or restraints be made on the citizens "save as to police and preservation of order," and that there should be no interference regarding churches or religion.[25]

President Lincoln had no objection to these conditions. He had every intention of treating the South with magnanimity and generosity, and had no intention of interfering with civil liberties. As John A. Campbell succinctly stated, "He assented to this," and went on to say that General Weitzel also "cordially" assented.[26]

From President Lincoln's standpoint, the meeting was certainly encouraging. Campbell seemed to be in basic agreement with him regarding the future of the postwar South, although they had not gone into any details. The president invited Campbell to join him aboard the USS *Malvern* in the morning to continue the discussion. Campbell agreed, and suggested that the president also confer with some moderate political leaders at that time, if he could persuade them to come. Lincoln was only too willing to go along with the idea.

Following his meeting with John Campbell, the president was taken back to the wharf by ambulance. By this time, Admiral Porter's flagship, USS *Malvern*, had made her way to Richmond; President Lincoln was taken out to the flagship by tugboat, along with Admiral Porter, Tad, and William Crook. "It was with a decided sign of relief that we saw the president safe on board," Lincoln's bodyguard noted.[27]

The president spent the night aboard the *Malvern*, which would be starting back to City Point the next day. While on board the *Malvern*, President Lincoln received a visit from "a newspaperman, [and] an ardent rebel" named Duff Green.[28] The visit was not a pleasant one, but it did give Lincoln some idea of what lay ahead of him, as well as the rest of the Union, in dealing with the postwar South.

Duff Green came on board to see the president about a personal matter—he wanted a pass to visit a friend across the Confederate lines. As he approached the president, Lincoln held out his hand. Green refused to take it, announcing, "I did not come here to shake hands."[29] Lincoln chose to ignore the snub, and both men sat down. As soon as they both were seated, "Mr. Green began to abuse Mr. Lincoln for the part he had taken in the struggle between the North and the South." Admiral David Porter, who was present at the meeting, remembered that Green accused the president of cutting the throats "of thousands of my people," of traveling to Richmond "to gloat over the ruin and desolation you have caused," and of coming "to triumph over a poor, conquered town with only women and children in it."[30] According to William Crook, Green's last words were, "I do not know how God and your conscience will let you sleep at night after being guilty of the notorious crime of setting the niggers free."[31]

President Lincoln sat through this verbal barrage without showing any emotion and without saying a word. If he was angry about what Green had just said to him, he did not show it. After he finished his outburst, Green calmly told the president, "I would like, sir, to go to my friends." Lincoln turned to General Weitzel and said, just as calmly, "General, please give Mr. Green a pass to go to his friends."[32] Mr. Green was given his pass, went ashore, and was never seen again.

The incident probably bothered the president more than he let on. That night, he dropped in to see if Tad was all right and accidentally woke William Crook out of a sound sleep. When he realized that his bodyguard was awake, Lincoln stopped to talk for a few minutes. And the main topic on his mind was Duff Green's outburst. "The old man is pretty angry," he said, "but I think he will get over it."[33] After a while, he said goodnight and went back to his stateroom, probably still thinking about Green and what he had said that afternoon.

President Lincoln realized that Duff Green's point of view was not unique. There were millions of Duff Greens throughout the South, not only in Virginia but also in Mississippi, Georgia, Florida, Alabama, Missouri, and every other state throughout the former Confederacy, all of whom shared his inflammatory opinion. There was a pervasive resentment and hatred of Southerners toward the Federal troops who were occupying their cities, and revulsion toward President Lincoln for freeing the slaves. Winning the war was vital, but Lincoln could see that securing the peace would be something else again, and would be just as demanding.

John Wilkes Booth was among the Southerners who were despondent over the fall of Richmond. He had been depressed during the past few weeks over the Confederacy and its dismal future, as well as over its chances of winning the war. Whenever he spoke about the war, the subject made him either angry or dejected. He was every bit as incensed as Duff Green by the occupation of Richmond and by the freeing of the slaves, and he had no use at all for Abraham Lincoln. In Booth's opinion, Lincoln was a tyrant who was responsible for all of the South's troubles, and he thought something should be done to silence him permanently.

During the course of a conversation with a couple of friends, Booth announced that something astonishing would happen during the next two weeks. One of his friends was not impressed. "What are you going to do," he asked, "kill Jefferson Davis, take Richmond, or play Hamlet a hundred nights?"[34] But what John Wilkes Booth had in mind would turn out to be a lot more astonishing and shocking than any of these things.

Unifying the country and showing charity for the South were becoming increasingly central to President Lincoln. But his most pressing concern was putting an end to the war, as quickly as possible and with as little additional loss of life as possible. He recognized that General Grant was in close pursuit of General Lee and his army and also that the Confederates were downhearted and dispirited—senior officers, including General Grant, reported that morale among Lee's troops was low. But he also knew that they were still not willing to give up the fight. The fighting and the killing could still go on for several more weeks.

"April 4 was another active day," Colonel Horace Porter wrote, "the troops were made to realize that this campaign was to be won with legs."[35] They were competing in a "great walking-match" with General Lee's "demoralized army";[36] success now depended upon which army could out-walk the other. As Colonel Porter remarked, "success depended upon which army could make the best distance record."

General Grant was not nearly as casual about his pursuit of General Lee and his "demoralized army" as Colonel Porter. On the morning of

April 4, Grant was informed that Lee was moving farther west, still intending to make his way to Danville and join forces with General Johnston. To counter this movement, Grant immediately ordered General Philip Sheridan to move his forces into a position where he would be able to stop Lee from getting any rations or supplies. He also ordered General George Meade to join forces with the Army of the James, and to look for any opportunity to attack Lee and his army. General Grant's exact orders were that General Meade should make a "forced march," which was not exactly the same thing as Colonel Porter's "great walking-match."[37]

The end of the war was not very far off, both General Grant and President Lincoln could see that. Lee's army was still in the field, but the fighting spirit of his troops was low and he was having trouble keeping his men supplied with rations. Anything that could be done to bring the Confederates to the point of surrender—outfighting them, outmaneuvering them, or starving them into submission—would be done by Grant. The president was completely in favor of anything that Grant might do to shorten the war and bring it to an end.

APRIL 5, 1865, WEDNESDAY
RETURN TO CITY POINT

A telegram sent by President Lincoln to General Nathaniel P. Banks gives some idea of exactly how preoccupied he had become in recent weeks. General Banks had telegraphed the president that he was ready to leave for New Orleans and return to duty, as he had been instructed—"I am ready and desire any instructions you may have." The president wired back on the same day, admitting, "I have been so much occupied with other thoughts that I really have no directions to give you." His only orders for General Banks were to "go at once" to New Orleans and he would be in touch. Seeing the war to a successful conclusion, along with restoring the Union and securing the peace, had been too much on Lincoln's mind. He did not have any time to think about much else.[1]

Along with these items, another issue causing President Lincoln anxiety was the legal readmitting of the seceded states back into the Union. John A. Campbell came on board the USS *Malvern* to speak with the president, as Lincoln had invited him, especially to discuss the readmission of Virginia into the United States. Campbell tried to persuade several prominent Virginians to come along with him to visit the president, but only one man, a well-known Richmond attorney named Gustavus A. Myers, agreed to accompany him.

President Lincoln opened the meeting by handing out a document that listed three conditions for peace that he considered indispensable and non-negotiable. "He had prepared a paper which he commented on as he read each clause," Campbell said.[2] The first of Lincoln's terms

181

called for "The restoration of the national authority." The second condition stated that there should be "No receding by the Executive of the United States on the slavery question," and the final clause addressed the "cessation of hostilities," which would not take place short of an end of the war and "all forces hostile to the government" were disbanded. Lincoln's conditions also stated that "all propositions coming from those now in hostility to the government" would be "respectfully considered," but went on to say that "if the war be now further persisted in," the "additional cost" would be paid for by Confederate property that had been confiscated by the United States government.[3]

Both John Campbell and Gustavus Myers read their copy of the document. They had no objection to the clause that dealt with "the slavery question." According to a telegram sent by Lincoln's Assistant Secretary of War Charles A. Dana, "Slavery they admit to be defunct."[4] They also asked for "an amnesty and a military convention, to cover appearances." If amnesty could be offered, "the rebel army would dissolve and all the States return."

General Weitzel recalled that the president did not promise amnesty, "but told them he had the pardoning power, and would save any repentant sinner from hanging."[5] But arranging any sort of political agreement presented its share of difficulties. The main problem was that there were no Confederate authorities available to sign any documents or agreements relating to the restoring of national authority, the disbanding of hostile forces, or anything else. Jefferson Davis, along with the entire Confederate congress, had left Richmond and were nowhere to be found. The "Confederate government" existed in name only.

But President Lincoln had an idea of his own for bringing Virginia, as the first state to be admitted, back into the Union. According to Admiral Porter, Lincoln gave Campbell and Myers a written order that would allow the Virginia state legislature to convene in the Confederate capitol building "in the absence of all other governments."[6] Because the Confederate government had effectively been disbanded, the Virginia legislature would be acting in its place. Campbell stated that if members of the Virginia government were granted permission to meet in the Confederate capitol, they would proceed to vote Virginia back into the Union. President Lincoln gave Campbell his written permission, which General Weitzel promptly took ashore to deliver to the proper authorities. It looked as though the State of Virginia was well on its way toward withdrawing from the Confederacy and being reinstated into the United States of America.

But Admiral Porter had something to say that immediately changed the president's mind. The admiral reminded President Lincoln that Richmond was currently under military jurisdiction, which meant that no civil authority would be able to exercise any power without the permission of the general in command of the army—namely General Ulysses S. Grant. Admiral Porter went on to advise President Lincoln that "this order of yours should go through General Grant," who would be certain to "protest against this arrangement of Mr. Campbell's."[7]

By this time, General Weitzel had already gone ashore with the president's written order. As Admiral Porter remembered, Lincoln immediately called for the order to be returned to him as quickly as possible and asked the admiral to write an order that would rescind his original order. Admiral Porter wrote, "Return my permission to the Legislature of Virginia to meet, and don't allow it to meet at all."[8] Lincoln's order was returned, a possible embarrassment was avoided, and Campbell "never returned to try and reverse the decision."

John A. Campbell and the readmission of Virginia to the Union continued to occupy the president's mind. But Lincoln also decided that it was time to leave Richmond and return to City Point; his journey took precedence over everything else that day. Commander Barnes, aboard the USS *Bat*, left City Point first. The president left later in the day, aboard the USS *Malvern*, and took time to indulge in some sightseeing along the way. When the *Malvern* reached the Dutch

Gap Canal, "which was one of the engineering features of the day," President Lincoln wanted to go through it. Admiral Porter ordered a boat lowered, "and we passed through the canal to the James below."[9] The president enjoyed the diversion, and nobody aboard the *Malvern* objected to the delay it caused.

As soon as he returned to City Point, President Lincoln went to the telegraph office to read the dispatches that had come in while he was away. One of the telegrams informed him that Mary Lincoln would be returning from Washington with a group that included Lincoln's old friend Attorney General Joshua Speed, Senator Charles Sumner, French aristocrat the Marquis de Chambrun, and Elizabeth Keckley. One Lincoln biographer wrote that Mary Lincoln was "determined to show that she had recovered from her bout of paranoia."[10]

Another telegram, sent by Secretary of War Edwin M. Stanton, stated that Secretary of State William Seward had been seriously injured in a carriage accident at about four o'clock in that afternoon that day. "Mr. Seward was thrown from his carriage . . . his head and face much bruised and he is in my opinion dangerously injured."[11]

The horses pulling Secretary Seward's carriage had bolted and run off at full speed, with Seward inside the carriage. He tried to jump from the carriage when the horses slowed to make a turn but lost his balance and was thrown to the pavement. Bystanders carried the secretary to his nearby house, badly hurt and unconscious. Along with a broken arm, Secretary Seward's jaw had been fractured in two places, and his face was bruised and swollen almost beyond recognition.

"I think your presence here is needed," Secretary Stanton continued. "Please let me know when you might be expected."[12]

Earlier in the day, Secretary Seward had telegraphed the president on the subject of his returning to Washington. "We need your personal attention to several matters here which are important and urgent in conducting the Government but not at all critical or serious," he said.[13] "Are you coming up or shall I go down to you with the papers?" President Lincoln immediately replied, "I think there is no possibility of my remaining here more than two days longer. If that is too long come down."

Lincoln was hoping to stay at City Point until General Lee surrendered, which looked to be within the week. He enjoyed City Point, and felt completely refreshed by his visit. But the injury to Secretary Seward forced him to change his plans; there could be no possibility of Seward traveling to City Point, not in his condition. The president would have to go back to Washington sooner than he either wanted or expected.

At this point in time, while President Lincoln considered returning to Washington, General Robert E. Lee was at the village of Amelia Court House waiting for supplies and rations. General Grant received a dispatch from General Phil Sheridan informing him of the fact: "The whole of Lee's army is at or near Amelia Court House," and emphasized that "General Lee is at Amelia Court House in person."[14] General Sheridan also pointed out that the Confederates were out of rations, "or nearly so."

General Grant contacted General Sherman by written dispatch on April 5, although it would not reach him for three days. In his letter, Grant sent General Sheridan's estimate that Lee's "much demoralized" forces numbered about 20,000 troops, including cavalry.[15] Grant also advised Sherman, who was at Goldsboro, North Carolina, "All indications are not that Lee will attempt to reach Danville with the remnants of his force." He went on to advise "If you can possibly do so push on from where you are, and let us see if we cannot finish the job with Lee's and Johnston's armies," and to judge for himself whether it would be better for him to strike from Greensboro or nearer to Danville. He ended with, "Rebel armies are now the only strategic points to strike at."

General Grant decided to join General George Meade at his headquarters, which was about sixteen miles away. General Grant, Colonel Horace Porter, and three other officers, escorted by fourteen mounted soldiers and led by a scout named Campbell, started on their way when it was nearly dark. After riding for about two hours, enemy campfires could be seen off in the distance. The mounted escort also saw that fence rails had been taken down in several places, an indication that cavalry was on the move in that area. Everyone was well aware that no Federal cavalry units had been in that particular section of the country.

Colonel Porter began to grow suspicious of the scout Campbell. The colonel was well aware that "scouts are seldom trustworthy, and are often in the employ of both sides," and he did not know this particular scout very well.[16] Also, Campbell was acting in a suspicious manner. At one point, the scout dropped back and turned his horse into a patch of woods that General Grant and his escort had avoided.

From Colonel Porter's point of view, Campbell "seemed to be acting in a manner that indicated either confusion or treachery." Fearing that Campbell might be acting in some sort of conspiracy against General Grant, the colonel cocked his revolver and fell in behind the scout, watching to see if he gave any "suspicious signals" to some unseen contact.

As it turned out, the colonel's suspicions turned out to be completely groundless. Campbell was "only looking for a short cut through the woods," and had not been thinking of either treason or assassination. But Colonel Porter had not been overreacting. The threat of assassination was very much on everybody's mind, not just relating to President Lincoln but also concerning his general-in-chief and high-ranking government officials in Washington. Confederate agents and sympathizers were rumored to be everywhere. Colonel Porter did not want to take any chances with General Grant's safety.

General Grant did not even mention the incident, which was typical of him. In his *Personal Memoirs* all he said was "the night being dark our progress was slow through the woods in the absence of direct roads."[17] The possibility that his scout might be a Confederate assassin probably did not even occur to him. He did mention that he had some difficulty in convincing the soldiers on picket duty "of our identity" when he reached the Union lines, but did not go into any details.

Colonel Porter did give a few particulars of the general's arrival in camp, noting with amusement that the pickets "could hardly be made to understand that the general-in-chief was wandering about at that hour with so small an escort, and so near the enemy's lines."[18] When word of General Grant's arrival spread through the ranks, the reaction was spirited and a bit sardonic, as might be expected. "Why, there's the old man," one soldier said. "Boys, this means business." And, "Uncle Sam's joined the cavalry sure enough. You can bet there'll be lively times here in the morning."

After paying his respects to General Sheridan, and after "a good supper of beef, cold chicken, and coffee," General Grant rode over to General Meade's camp, which was not very far away.[19] He discovered that General Meade was not feeling well, still suffering the effects of a recent illness. General Meade had the idea of trying to outmaneuver General Lee, of moving by the right flank and overtaking him. But General Grant was afraid that Meade's strategy would only serve to give Lee "the coveted opportunity of escaping us."[20] He explained to Meade that "we did not want to follow the enemy; we wanted to get ahead of him." After listening to what Grant had to say, General Meade immediately changed his orders. "They were now given for an advance to Amelia Court House, at an hour early in the morning."

Back at City Point, President Lincoln was not aware of any of these details. His most immediate concern was the arrival of his wife, who was on her way from Washington with her entourage, along with thoughts of John A. Campbell and his proposal for bringing Virginia back into the Union. The best news of the day came in the form of his salary warrant in the amount of $1,981.67, his salary for the month of March, 1865.[21]

Jefferson Davis left Richmond on April 2, arriving in Danville the next afternoon. From Danville on April 5, he issued what he called a "proclamation" to rally his fellow Southerners to fight on in spite of the fall of Richmond and other recent reverses. In fact, President Davis said, losing the capital city was actually a blessing in disguise. General Lee and his army had been "greatly trammeled" by having to keep a "constant watch over the approaches to the capital."[22] But now that Richmond was in enemy hands, General Lee no longer had that responsibility.

"We have now entered upon a new phase of the struggle," President Davis announced. "Relieved from the necessity of guarding particular points, our army will be free to move from point to point, to strike the enemy in detail far from his base." He went on to state, "I will never consent to abandon to the enemy one foot of the soil of any of the States of the Confederacy," and promised that no peace would ever be made "with the infamous invaders" of Confederate territory. The proclamation ended with, "Let us, then, not despond, my countrymen, but rely on God, meet the foe with fresh defiance and with unconquered and unconquerable hearts."

This was exactly the attitude that President Lincoln did not want to hear, especially coming from Jefferson Davis. Lincoln wanted to end the war and stop the killing as quickly as possible. President Davis was doing his best to extend the war for as long as possible, to "meet the foe with fresh defiance," and never even consider the possibility of surrender. The war was clearly winding down. Lee's army was on the verge of crumbling, with hundreds of men deserting every day. Now that President Davis was no longer in Richmond, President Lincoln could only hope that Davis's call for defiance would go unheeded.

APRIL 6, 1865, THURSDAY
BRINGING THE FIGHTING TO AN END

The president received a telegram from Secretary of War Stanton, which gave him an update on the condition of Secretary of State Seward. The news was that Secretary Seward's injuries were not as severe as they had first appeared. "Mr. Seward although seriously injured is not in danger," Stanton reported, and went on to say that the surgeon general "saw no reason for alarm."[1] This came as very welcome news for the president. Not only did it mean that his secretary of state was not in any mortal danger, which everyone seemed to believe on April 5, but it also meant that he would now be able to stay on at City Point for a few more days. There would be no need for him to rush back to Washington and its stress and strain and partisan politics. Instead, he would be able to remain at army headquarters and read the dispatches from Grant and Sheridan as soon as they came in, which was much more satisfying.

John A. Campbell and his plan involving the Virginia legislature still had to be dealt with. Lincoln gave a great deal of thought to the situation, and telegraphed General Godfrey Weitzel in Richmond to give instructions regarding "the gentlemen who have acted as the Legislature of Virginia"—he did not want to say "the Virginia legislature," since this would imply that he was recognizing the Confederate governing body, and, by implication, the Confederacy itself.[2] Lincoln instructed General Weitzel that if these "gentlemen" wanted to assemble in Richmond "and take measures to withdraw Virginia troops" from General Lee's army, the general should "give them permission and protection" until such time that they might "attempt some action hostile to the United States." Anyone attempting any hostile action should be given "reasonable time to leave," and placed under arrest if they did not leave Richmond within the set time limits. The president ended his message by telling General Weitzel, "Allow Judge Campbell to see this but do not make it public."

President Lincoln also contacted General Grant regarding Judge Campbell and the "gentlemen" from the Virginia legislature, probably with Admiral Porter's advice regarding Richmond being under military jurisdiction in mind. The president first summed up what he had said to General Weitzel, namely that the legislature should be allowed to meet in Richmond for the purpose of withdrawing Virginia troops from the Confederate forces—he did not mention anything about the reinstating of Virginia to the Union—and then went on to give his thoughts on Judge Campbell's proposal.

The president had certainly mulled over his conversation with Judge Campbell and Gustavus Meyer aboard the *River Queen*, and he evidently had lost his enthusiasm for what had been discussed. "I do not think it very probable that anything will come of this," he advised General Grant, but thought it best to notify him of the meeting "so that if you should see signs, you may understand them."[3] He added that the measure regarding the withdrawal of Virginia troops from Lee's army was totally unnecessary—"it seems that you are pretty effectually withdrawing the Virginia troops from opposition to the government." This comment probably gave General Grant a small chuckle.

Mary Lincoln returned to City Point aboard the steamer *Monohasset* on April 6. She had not seen her husband since April 1 and was alarmed by his appearance. He seemed to be more tired and anxious than ever—anxious over how soon the war would end and anxious over the reunification of the country after it finally ended. But her worries concerning the president did not prevent her from taking a grand tour of Richmond. She had been in Washington when her husband and Tad had visited the Confederate capital and missed the cheering of the freed slaves, and had missed seeing Jefferson Davis's house.

Mary Lincoln wanted to see Richmond every bit as much as her husband, and decided to have her own tour of the city. Along with Senator Sumner, the Marquis de Chambrun, Robert Lincoln's girlfriend, and Elizabeth Keckley, Mrs. Lincoln saw everything worth seeing. As a biographer put it, "Mary Lincoln triumphantly toured the enemy capital."[4] The only person who enjoyed the sightseeing tour more than Mrs. Lincoln was Elizabeth Keckley, the former slave.

Mrs. Lincoln's perspective of the capital was not much different than her husband's had been. "Hundreds of Negroes" welcomed her party with "loud enthusiasm;" from the doorways, "terrified white people peeped out;" and she discovered that Jefferson Davis's residence was "a fine building with beautiful parlors," and also that the Confederate president "had carried away everything moveable in his hasty flight."[5] But Mrs. Lincoln also stopped at Libby Prison, which the president had decided not to visit during his tour of Richmond. The prison had once detained thousands of Federal inmates, but now housed about nine hundred Confederates. "Mrs. Lincoln was anxious to see them," the Marquis de Chambrun explained. "Almost all these unfortunates rose respectfully; some few, however, hissed or whistled." The marquis does not mention Mary Lincoln's reaction to this, or to anything else she experienced in Richmond, except that she had become angry and indignant when she learned of the mistreatment of Union prisoners. When she was informed that three thousand Union prisoners had been packed into the same space that now held nine hundred Confederates, he recalled that "our indignation overflowed."

About thirty five miles southwest of Richmond, General Ulysses S. Grant had his mind focused on a more immediate problem. General Robert E. Lee and his army had moved out from Amelia Court House during the night; Grant's forces were right behind the Confederates, doing their best to catch up with them. The army had been moving at a rate of thirty miles a day, sometimes more, past the discarded muskets and broken vehicles left behind by the retreating Confederates. General Lee was still moving westward, heading for the town of Farmville, a stop on the Southside Railroad. Lee was still trying for Danville and General Johnston's army in North Carolina. Grant was trying to stop him.

The two sides finally met at Sayler's Creek. According to General Grant's laconic account, "a heavy engagement took place in which infantry, artillery, and cavalry were all brought into action."[6] He went on to explain that his men had the advantage of occupying the high ground, and also that they were able to fire more rapidly—as the enemy retreated, they had to turn to face Grant's men every time they fired, which slowed their rate of fire.

Colonel Elisha Hunt Rhodes saw the battle from a completely different perspective. The first sign of the impending battle came during the afternoon, when Colonel Rhodes heard firing off to the right and front of his position. One of General Sheridan's senior officers said that Sayler's Creek was directly ahead of them, and that a Confederate wagon train was on the other side of it, guarded by a "Rebel corps" commanded by General Richard "Baldy" Ewell. The cavalry had stopped the advance of the wagon train. Colonel Rhodes's regiment, the Second Rhode Island Infantry, was ordered to attack.

When he reported back to his regiment, a captain asked Colonel Rhodes, "Colonel, are we to fight again?" When Rhodes said yes, the captain responded, "This will be the last battle if we win, and then you and I can go home."[7] Along with everyone else in the Second Rhode Island, Colonel Rhodes certainly hoped this would be the last battle.

Colonel Rhodes's unit moved down a hill, crossed the creek, and attacked the Confederate position. The Confederates retreated toward a patch of woods. When they came within fifty yards of the woods, a Confederate officer stepped out and shouted for the men to fire. "A long line of Rebels fired right into our faces and then charged through our line and getting between us and the river."[8] The Rhode Islanders regrouped and reformed, recrossed the river, and captured the Confederate wagon train. They also captured "about fifty Rebel officers," and kept after the retreating Confederates until after dark. The day's fighting cost the Second Rhode Island forty-four men killed and wounded. One of those killed was the captain that had asked if the regiment would be fighting that day.

The fighting at Sayler's Creek cost General Lee more than he could afford. "The enemy's loss was very heavy," General Grant said, in an understatement.[9] "Some six general officers fell into our hands in this engagement, and several thousand men were made prisoners." General Grant realized that the fighting could not go on much longer, not at the rate that General Lee was losing men.

One of the Confederate officers that had been captured was General Richard "Baldy" Ewell. In the course of the day, General Grant met a relative of General Ewell, a Dr. Smith, who told Grant about a conversation he had had with Ewell. According to Dr. Smith, General Ewell said that when General Grant's army crossed the James River in June 1864, "he knew their cause was lost."[10] Because of this, General Ewell was of the opinion that "the authorities" should have asked for an armistice at that time, "to make the best terms they could while they still had a right to claim concessions." But now it was too late—"the cause was lost and they had no right to claim anything."

General Ewell had gone on to say "that for every man that was killed after this in the war somebody"—somebody in the Confederate government, he meant—"was responsible and it would be very little better than murder."[11] General Ewell's mind was clearly on bringing the fighting to an end, but he was not sure if General Lee would be willing to surrender his army without being able to consult with President Davis beforehand. General Ewell hoped that he would.

APRIL 7, 1865, FRIDAY
"LET THE *THING* BE PRESSED"

President Lincoln first received word of Thursday's fighting at 11:15 that night. General Phil Sheridan telegraphed a brief report to General Grant; Grant forwarded it along to the president. The president forwarded it along to Secretary of War Stanton in the morning.

General Sheridan sounded confident and enthusiastic in his account of the day's fighting. He began by stating simply that "the enemy made a stand," but that he attacked with two divisions of the Sixth Corps "and routed them handsomely."[1] His listing of the Sixth Corps' activities sounded more impressive: "Up to the present time we have captured Generals [Richard] Ewell, [Joseph] Kershaw, [Seth M.] Barton, [Montgomery E.] Corse, [Dudley] DuBose, and Custis Lee, several thousand prisoners, 14 pieces of artillery with caissons and a large number of wagons." Sheridan ended with: "If the thing is pressed I think Lee will surrender."

Secretary Stanton immediately wired his congratulations to President Lincoln "on the glorious news of this morning."[2] He also let the president know that Secretary of State William Seward was recovering from his injuries, and that he was in good spirits. The communiqué concerning the results of yesterday's fighting was the main reason for Seward's high morale: "Your news stimulates him better than anything the apothecary could give."

General Sheridan's message had the same effect on Lincoln; it was the best news he could have hoped for. Later in the morning, he received even more encouraging news about Sayler's Creek. General

Grant forwarded three telegrams from generals who had taken part in the fighting. The first was from General Andrew A. Humphries, commander of the Second Corps. "Our last fight just before dark at Sailors Creek gave us two (2) guns 3 flags considerable number of prisoners 200 wagons 70 ambulances with mules & horses to about one half the wagons & ambulances," is the way General Humphries began his dispatch.[3] He went on to detail that more than two miles of road "is strewed with tents baggage cooking utensils" along with other equipment that had been discarded by the retreating Confederates, and explained that "it will take some time" to clear away all of the debris. Even though his men had given a very good account of themselves during the battle, General Humphries apologized for the fact "that I cannot follow rapidly during the night." He knew that the enemy was in full retreat and did not want to let up for any reason, even darkness.

General George Meade, commanding the Army of the Potomac, also sent a report that was read by President Lincoln. General Meade was known as the "goddamn goggle-eyed snapping turtle" because of his short temper and sour disposition, but even Meade managed to say something cheerful about the results of yesterday's action. "At daylight this morning I moved the 2d 5 & 6th Corps along the R R in the direction of Amelia C.H.," he started off, and went on to explain exactly how the many units of the three corps made their advance.[4] After this exciting beginning, Meade became—for him, at least—nothing short of enthusiastic. He referred to the corps commanders as "distinguished officers," and went on to pronounce, "it is evident todays works is going to be one of the most important of the recent brilliant operations." Saving the best for last, General Meade said exactly what President Lincoln and General Grant wanted to hear: "The pursuit will be continued so soon as the men have a little rest."

The third telegram that Lincoln read was from General Horatio Wright, commander of the veteran Sixth Corps, who gave a detailed account of his experiences at Sayler's Creek. "I proceeded across toward a nearly parallel road on which the Enemy was moving," he wrote, and "we swept down the road for a distance of about 2 miles."[5] There was also a second attack—"the Enemy had reformed his line on the opposite side where we attacked & drove him to a point a distance of a half mile further."

The major part of General Wright's lengthy account was a confusing combination of misspelled words and hard to follow phrases. But one particular sentence summed up the battle in a nutshell, plainly and concisely enough for anyone to follow: "The result has been a complete success."[6] The report went on to recount that "General Ewell & Curtis Lee & large numbers of other prisoners" were captured, but everything President Lincoln wanted to know was laid out in those seven words. All of the advancing and maneuvering against a heavily resisting enemy had ended in complete success.

President Lincoln probably did not understand every detail of the reports he read, most of which involved troop movements and strategy, and he may not even have read all of the telegrams in their entirety. But all of the telegrams boiled down to one conclusion: General Lee was on the run, General Grant was right behind him, and the end of the war was now only a matter of days away. The last sentence of General Sherman's dispatch made a particular impression: "If the thing is pressed I think Lee will surrender." At 11:00 a.,., Lincoln sent a telegram to General Grant that has become part of the Lincoln legend:

Head Quarters Armies of the United States,
City-Point, April 7. 11 AM. 1865

Lieut Gen. Grant.

Gen. Sheridan says "If the thing is pressed I think that Lee will surrender." Let the *thing* be pressed.

A. LINCOLN[7]

Robert E. Lee was the subject of a good many conversations and discussions during the first week of April, along with the surrender of his army. "It is desirable that Lee should be captured," Secretary of the Navy Gideon Welles wrote.[8] Secretary Welles did not have much use for General Lee, an opinion he had in common with many individuals throughout the North.

Welles was afraid that if General Lee managed to escape Grant, he would rally his "brigand force" and carry on a guerilla war in the interior. And Lee was "weak enough to try and continue hostilities," in Welles's opinion.[9] His "infidelity to the country which educated, and employed, and paid him shows gross ingratitude," Welles thought. "His true course would be to desert the country he has betrayed and never return."

Lincoln was in full agreement with Secretary Welles on this last point. President Lincoln would have had no objections at all if General Lee and every other high-ranking Confederate officer, along with President Jefferson Davis and the entire Confederate government, left the country permanently. If Lee and Davis were to take up permanent residence in Cuba or Canada or somewhere in Europe, they would no longer be in any position to cause more trouble.

But there were many throughout the North who thought that exile was too lenient a punishment for General Lee. They did not want Lee to be banished; they wanted to see him hanged. Lincoln did not approve of this point of view. The very last thing he wanted was to turn Jefferson Davis or Robert E. Lee into martyrs for the Lost Cause. He realized that he would have enough problems in trying to reunify the country without having Confederate martyrs to contend with.

The president expressed this point of view to several guests during a gathering aboard the *River Queen*, a get together that included Julia Grant, Mary Lincoln, longtime friend Elihu Washburne, the Marquis de Chambrun, and several other friends. Someone brought up the subject of the surrender of General Lee and his army, and also mentioned the possibility that Jefferson Davis and his cabinet might also be captured. President Lincoln was not happy about the second possibility. He pointed out that the "untimely capture" of President Davis would be the cause of "difficulty and embarrassment" for the government—Davis would become a bone of contention between those who favored clemency for the South, including himself, and those who saw Davis as a traitor and wanted vengeance.[10]

Another of the guests said of Davis, "Don't let him escape. He must be hanged." President Lincoln's response to this was, "Let us judge not, that we be not judged."[11] Libby Prison was also mentioned—the Confederate prison with all of its horrors should make any attempt at mercy or sympathy toward the South impossible. The president calmly repeated his Biblical quote, which he had also used in his second inaugural address. His goal for reunification was charity for all, including Jefferson Davis and Robert E. Lee.

Julia Grant was also asked for her opinion on the subject: "What shall be done with the Confederate President Jefferson David in the event of his capture?"[12] Mrs. Grant happened to catch the "friendly glance" of President Lincoln just as the question was being asked. After repeating the question slowly to herself, she very carefully replied, "I would trust him, I think, to the mercy of our always just and most gracious President." She later recalled that this answer "won me not a few compliments," and that those present said that it was "a most diplomatic answer." Mrs. Grant did not mention what the president himself had to say about her response.

Robert E. Lee was also on General Grant's mind, but for a completely different reason. The Confederate forces were still moving westward. General Phil Sheridan was right behind the retreating enemy and had made contact at the town of Farmville, a few miles to the west of Sayler's Creek. General Grant rode into Farmville later in the day, a few hours after the skirmish. General Sheridan sent a communiqué that seven trainloads of rations and provisions, supplies for Lee's army, had stopped at Appomattox, and that he was planning to capture them.

General Grant could see that Lee was running out of time and realized that it would be only a matter of a few days before his army would be completely isolated. If Phil Sheridan could capture the Confederate supply trains at Appomattox Station, Lee's army would be deprived from receiving any rations for some time, perhaps for several days. This, along with the conversation he had had with Dr. Smith the night before, gave General Grant the idea of asking Lee to surrender. He sat down and wrote:

HEADQUARTERS ARMIES OF THE UNITED STATES,
April 7, 1865—5 p. m.

General R. E. LEE,
Commanding C. S. Army:

GENERAL: The result of the last week must convince you of the hopelessness of further resistance on the part of the Army of Northern Virginia in this struggle. I feel that it is so, and regard it as my duty to shift from myself the responsibility of any further effusion of blood by asking of you the surrender of that portion of the C. S. Army known as the Army of Northern Virginia.

Very respectfully, your obedient servant,
U. S. GRANT,
Lieutenant-General, Commanding Armies of the United States.[13]

The letter was given to an officer, who rode from Farmville toward the north bank of the Appomattox River with a flag of truce.

General Grant spent the night in a small hotel in Farmville. He slept in the room that, he was told, had been occupied by General Lee the night before. Around midnight, he was awakened by a messenger with a reply from General Lee:

APRIL 7, 1865.

Lieutenant General U. S. GRANT,
Commanding Armies of the United States:

GENERAL: I have received your note of this date. Though not entertaining the opinion you express of the hopelessness of further resistance on the part of the Army of Northern Virginia, I recip-rocate your desire to avoid useless effusion of blood, and therefore, before considering your proposition, ask the terms you will offer on condition of its surrender.

R. E. LEE,
General.[14]

"That was not satisfactory," was General Grant's reaction to Lee's reply.[15] But he had not really expected General Lee to surrender on the basis of one letter. Still, he considered General Lee's reply "as deserving another letter," and decided to send him another surrender request in the morning, after he had a few more hours sleep.

President Lincoln did not know anything about Grant's letter to Lee, or about Lee's reply. The president would be making a return visit to Petersburg that day, and was more than preoccupied with the trip. Mary Lincoln had not seen Petersburg; she had been in Washington when the president made his first visit to the city, and she wanted to visit it before returning to Washington. The president decided to accompany her and her party. Mrs. Lincoln's group would include Tad, Senator

Charles Sumner, Elizabeth Keckley, and the Marquis de Chambrun. They would travel by train from City Point, and were on their way by noon.

Julia Grant had not been invited to join the Lincolns on their journey, and was offended by the exclusion. "I saw very little of the presidential party now," she wrote, "as Mrs. Lincoln had a good deal of company and seemed to have forgotten us."[16] "I felt this deeply and could not understand it," she said many years later. One possible explanation for Mrs. Grant's exclusion from the president's party was Mary Lincoln's embarrassment—she was still suffering from humiliation over her behavior regarding Mrs. Ord at the end of March. Even though the incident had taken place almost two weeks earlier, the president's wife was probably still too ashamed to face Julia Grant.

The train ride to Petersburg was ordinary and uneventful—entirely too ordinary and uneventful to suit the Marquis de Chambrun. Even though President Lincoln was the focal point of the journey—"we grouped ourselves around him"—the marquis pointed out that the president rode "in an ordinary day-car" along with a few unidentified officers and "several Negro waiters" from the *River Queen*.[17] This struck the marquis as not only unusual but also improper. In France, such a high-ranking government official would have his own private carriage, which would have been elegantly and lavishly decorated and would have been reserved for himself and members of his family. But President Lincoln rode in an ordinary, plebian "day-coach," which he deigned to share with officers and Negro waiters—the marquis referred to these passengers as "intruders." Instead of elegance, Lincoln apparently preferred plainness and simplicity, which the marquis found impossible to fathom.

This fondness for straightforwardness was one of the reasons behind President Lincoln's admiration for General Grant, who preferred to wear a private's simple blouse instead of a general's gold braid and was totally unconcerned with his own appearance. The president shared Grant's fondness for informality and lack of pretention.

President Lincoln had seen Petersburg before; it had not changed since his first visit. Marquis de Chambrun remarked that the city "looks less desolate than Richmond," and also that the president was "well received" by the local residents.[18] Lincoln received word that former US congressman Roger A. Pryor was in Petersburg. Roger Pryor had been a brigadier general in the Confederate army until he resigned his commission, and he was now living in the city. The president made an attempt to visit Pryor at his house; he had arranged for a parole when Pryor had been arrested for suspected espionage at the end of 1864. But Pryor's wife, Sarah, refused to allow Lincoln to see her husband— her reason was that General Lee was still in the field and, as such, her husband could not meet with the head of the opposing army. This was another indication for Lincoln that reunifying North and South was going to be a long and difficult undertaking.

Elizabeth Keckley had gone off on her own when she arrived at Petersburg. She had lived there when she was still a slave, and wanted to revisit some of the places she had known when she was young. But her brief stay only brought back "painful memories."[19] She had no desire to stay more than a few hours. "I was not sorry to turn my back again upon the city," she later wrote with a note of finality.

The president, Mrs. Lincoln, and the rest of their party returned to City Point by train later in the day. The Lincolns spent the evening aboard the *River Queen*, where they were visited by two congressmen, Elihu B. Washburne of Illinois and James G. Blaine of Maine. Both were on their way to see General Grant at Farmville, where they hoped to get their own perspectives on the war and how it was being fought. Congressman Washburne represented Grant's home district of Galena, Illinois, and was also an old friend of the general.

The get together with the Lincolns was friendly and affable; everybody enjoyed themselves and seemed to have a good time talking and telling stories. "Mr. Lincoln was in perfect health and excellent spirits," Congressman Washburne wrote.[20] He regaled his friends with tales of his visit to Richmond, "which had all the quaintness and originality for which he was distinguished," and kept up a constant stream of anecdotes. Before his guests left, Lincoln asked Congressman Washburne if he would take a letter to his son Robert, who was a member of General Grant's staff. The congressman personally collected the letter from the president on the following morning. "He was erect and buoyant, and it seemed to me I had never seen him look so great and grand." The time he was spending away from Washington, combined with the encouraging news from the war, was obviously having a beneficial effect on his health and morale.

It had not been a good day for Robert E. Lee. He was still doing his best to get to Danville and, if all went well, from Danville to General Joseph Johnston's army in North Carolina. But because the enemy was in possession of most of the railway lines in the vicinity, General Lee decided that it would be best to go to Danville by a longer, more indirect route. His plan was to meet a supply train filled with rations at Appomattox Station, give his men their first meal in five days, and keep moving westward.

Grant's army was still on the south side of the Appomattox River; the Army of Northern Virginia occupied the north side. The river in between was deep enough and wide enough to keep the Union army at bay, to stop it from making a crossing. This should allow General Lee's men enough time to catch their breath and put some distance between themselves and Grant's pursuing army. Two bridges connected the north bank and the south bank, but General Lee ordered both of them to be destroyed. Grant's engineers might build a pontoon bridge across the Appomattox, but the time spent in building a bridge would allow the Confederates to keep moving toward Danville without interference from the Union army.

During the afternoon of April 7, General Lee received word that enemy troops had crossed the Appomattox in force, and were now on the north side of the river. Only one of the two bridges across the river had been destroyed, which allowed an entire Federal division to cross over to the north bank. An attempt to recapture the bridge had been beaten back.

When he received the report, General Lee lost control of himself and indulged in a monumental temper tantrum. He was fully aware that the escape of his army was now in jeopardy because one of his officers had failed to carry out orders, and he could also see that this failure might turn out to be fatal. After regaining his composure, the general ordered artillery to be brought up in case the enemy mounted an attack.

Sometime after receiving this report, a messenger rode up with General Grant's letter asking him to surrender. General James Longstreet was sitting next to Lee when the letter was delivered. Lee read the note and handed it over to Longstreet without saying anything. The general read the letter and handed it back to Lee with a two-word response: "Not yet."[21]

A HOSPITAL VISIT AND A RECEPTION

The president had been at City Point since March 24, which was just over two weeks. He had hoped to stay in Virginia until General Lee surrendered his army, but even though General Grant was closing in on Lee and the end was now only a matter of days away, it was time for President Lincoln to return to Washington.

The visit had certainly helped to raise his spirits, although the telegrams from generals Grant and Sherman were probably just as responsible for his improved morale as the change in scenery. Since his arrival at City Point, Petersburg had been evacuated, Richmond had been captured, and both Grant and Sheridan had kept Lincoln informed that Lee's army was on the brink of surrender. It has been an exciting time for him. Four years of war were finally coming to an end. He had been in the war zone and had conferred with his general-in-chief while the fighting was building to a climax. But there was work to do at the White House that needed his attention and could not be left to another time. The president made plans to return to Washington later in the day.

Before he went back to Washington, though, President Lincoln wanted to pay a visit to the wounded soldiers at Depot Field Hospital, which was about a mile and a half southwest of City Point. The hospital was made up of several hundred tents, along with about one hundred wooden barracks, and treated thousands of patients within its wards. At about noon, the president, Senator Charles Sumner, Mary Lincoln, and the Marquis de Chambrun were driven to the sprawling hospital grounds, where they were met by the senior surgeon in charge. The surgeon escorted the presidential party to the nearest ward and the president began visiting the patients.

"We passed before all the wounded and amputated," the Marquis de Chambrun noted. "Almost all the wounded soldiers asked the President how the fight was progressing and inquired as to the political outlook, then smiled happily when told: 'Success all along the line.'"[1] Mary Lincoln did not stay with her husband throughout his visit to the hospital, but Chambrun and Senator Sumner remained nearby while the president was making his tour. Lincoln's greetings and consoling words were much appreciated by all the soldiers in the wards—and Lincoln visited many soldiers and shook a great many hands that afternoon. Senator Sumner seemed to be absolutely amazed that the president had taken the time to shake so many hands, although he seemed to be more moved than surprised by what President Lincoln had done.

The president's stay at Depot Field Hospital lasted until late afternoon. But the day's activities were not over yet. After leaving the hospital, President Lincoln and his party were driven to what the Marquis de Chambrun described as "headquarters." Headquarters was situated "on the far side of the town in a fine suburban mansion."[2] While Lincoln was busy conferring with "the generals commanding the garrison," Chambrun and the others visited the mansion and its abandoned gardens. The marquis was much impressed by the estate, and commented on how beautifully the grounds were laid out. But his escort brushed off the compliment, and dismissed the mansion's former owners with one hard comment: "These people were traitors." Residents of the South were not the only people who had hostile thoughts about the coming reunification.

The president was scheduled to depart City Point for Washington before the evening was over, but first he had to attend a reception aboard the *River Queen*. Enduring the rigors of a formal reception, and all the handshaking that went with it, was not something that the president anticipated with any pleasure. The afternoon at the hospital had already taken its toll; Lincoln was tired and needed a rest. Back on board the *River Queen*, he told his wife, "Mother, I have shaken so many hands today that my arms ache tonight. I almost wish that I could go to bed now."[3]

It was a nice party, at least according to most of those who were present. Julia Grant had not been invited; neither had Commander John S. Barnes. Commander Barnes was on board the *River Queen*, under orders from Admiral Porter, but he did not set eyes on Mary Lincoln. "Mrs. Lincoln was indisposed and I did not meet her," he said.[4] Nobody knew if the president's wife was not feeling well, or if she was still annoyed with Commander Barnes.

Elizabeth Keckley was there, and seemed to be enjoying the party and the entire scene. "As the twilight shadows deepened the lamps were lighted and the boat was brilliantly illuminated," she wrote. To her, the *River Queen* looked like "an enchanted floating palace."[5]

A military band played for the guests during the reception. The president asked the band play *La Marseillaise*, which was a selection he liked and had requested for his own enjoyment. After hearing it played once, Lincoln asked the musicians to perform it a second time. The encore was apparently for the benefit of the Marquis de Chambrun. The president turned toward Chambrun and said, with a touch of dry humor, "You have to come over to America to hear it"—at the time, Napoleon III had banned *La Marseillaise* as the French national anthem, calling it too revolutionary.[6]

Afterward, the president asked the marquis if he had ever heard "the rebel song *Dixie*." Chambrun confessed that he had not, and Lincoln asked "the surprised musicians" to play it. "That tune is now Federal property," President Lincoln explained, "and it good to show the rebels that, with us in power, they will be free to hear it again."

This was another instance of the president's intended policy toward "the rebels"—he did not even propose to ban *Dixie*, the Confederate national anthem.[7]

The reception began to wind down around ten o'clock. Officers came by to shake hands with the president and to say goodbye before going ashore. When someone asked Lincoln to make a speech, he replied that he was too tired just then. But, he told everyone present, he would be making a speech on Tuesday, after he returned to Washington.

Commander John S. Barnes remained on board the *River Queen*, expressly to look after President Lincoln. On Admiral Porter's instructions, Commander Barnes assigned two officers, along with a detachment of enlisted men, to guard "the president's person day and night."[8] As an added precaution, the crew of the *River Queen* had their identity papers and personnel records examined. "Mr. Lincoln's safety" was very much on Admiral Porter's mind, whether it was because he had heard rumors of an assassination attempt against the president, or if it was just a matter of concern because he considered the security of the president to be the Navy's responsibility. According to Commander Barnes, Admiral Porter "now became full of concern lest come mishap should occur during Mr. Lincoln's trip back to Washington, for which he or the Navy might be held responsible."

At about eleven o'clock, the *River Queen*'s lights and party decorations were taken down, and the boat began steaming down the James River toward Chesapeake Bay. She was accompanied by the USS *Bat*. Admiral Porter would like to have had the president's boat escorted by a few additional gunboats and other armed warships, but the *Queen* was too fast to allow for this possibility. The president wanted to return to Washington as quickly as the *River Queen*'s boilers would allow, which eliminated the possibility of being convoyed by slower and more heavily armed escorts. No other ship except the *Bat* could even hope to keep pace with the *River Queen*.

After the excitement of the day's activities, President Lincoln was in a quiet and thoughtful mood. "Mr. Lincoln stood a long while gazing at the hills," the Marquis de Chambrun observed.[9] The area had been a battleground throughout much of the war but the same ground, "so animated a few days before," was now "dark and silent." The president stayed out on deck "absorbed in thought" while the *River Queen* made its way downriver.

In the country west of Sayler's Creek, Colonel Elisha Hunt Rhodes was also in a thoughtful mood. His thoughts mainly concerned the ending of the war. "I have fifty men less than when I left Petersburg on the 2nd," he wrote.[10] "Some are dead, and some are wounded. God help them and bring us peace." Colonel Rhodes was also thinking about General Robert E. Lee, and about when he might surrender: "Still on, on, with cannon booming in our front, showing that Lee is not far away and perhaps may be at bay."

General Grant was also focusing on General Lee's army, which, in the general's estimation, was "rapidly crumbling."[11] Soldiers who had enlisted from that particular section of Virginia, he noted, "were continually dropping out of the ranks and going to their homes." General Grant came across a Confederate colonel who introduced himself as the proprietor of the hotel where Grant had spent the previous night. The colonel reported that he was the only man in his regiment who had not deserted. Since he was now all alone, he decided to drop out along with everybody else. Now he wanted to surrender and did not exactly know what to do. Grant advised him to stay where he was "and he would not be molested." Grant's reaction to the Confederate colonel's story was typically straightforward: "That was one regiment which had been eliminated from Lee's force by the crumbling process."

Colonel Horace Porter's account of this incident is a bit more sarcastic than General Grant's. Colonel Porter described the hotel proprietor as "a rather hungry-looking gentleman in gray, wearing the uniform of a colonel," who decided to "stop off" at home to look after his property after his regiment had crumbled to pieces.[12] "It is safe to say that his hotel had never before had so many guests in it," Colonel Porter remarked, "nor at such reduced rates." He went on to say that "His story was significant as indicating the disintegrating process which was going on in the ranks of the enemy." The colonel's regiment may have crumbled away, but at least he still had his hotel.

General Grant's intentions were to cross the Appomattox River to the north bank and then move westward with the units that were trying to make contact with Lee's rear guard. The troops were moving "with alacrity" and without any straggling. "They began to see the end of what they had been fighting four years for," Grant explained. "Nothing seemed to fatigue them."[13]

Before setting out from Farmville, General Grant sent another letter to General Lee regarding the Army of Northern Virginia's surrender:

APRIL 8, 1865.

General R. E. LEE,
Commanding C. S. Army:

GENERAL: Your note of last evening, in reply to mine of same date, asking the condition on which I will accept the surrender of the Army of Northern Virginia, is just received. In reply I would say that, peace being my great desire, there is but one condition I would insist upon, viz, that the men and officers surrender shall be disqualified for taking up arms again against the Government of the United States until properly exchanged. I will meet you, or will designate officers to meet any officers you may name for the same purpose, at any point agreeable to you, for the purpose of arranging definitely the terms upon which the surrender of the Army of Northern Virginia will be received.

Very respectfully, your obedient servant,
U. S. GRANT,
Commanding Armies of the United States.[14]

Bearing in mind what President Lincoln had said aboard the *River Queen* at the end of March, Grant offered General Lee the most generous terms possible—he wanted Lee to understand that he would accept just about any condition, and insisted upon only one definite term: that the men and officers would not take up arms again against the Federal government. Grant was also willing to meet Lee almost anywhere, "at any point agreeable to you," as long as General Lee agreed to surrender his army.

After giving his note to an orderly for delivery to General Lee, General Grant rode from Farmville to the north side of the Appomattox, where he joined the advancing columns of General George Gordon Meade. Grant was moving in "light marching order," taking no baggage or personal belongings with him. He and his staff wanted to be close to the front and did not waste any time in getting there. According to Colonel Porter, "we billeted ourselves at night in farm houses, or bivouacked on porches, and picked up meals at any camps that seemed to have something to spare in the way of rations."[15] When General Lee's reply arrived, Grant wanted to be in a position to respond to it and report to President Lincoln.

General Grant had been suffering from what Colonel Porter described as "a severe headache" all afternoon, which had been brought on by fatigue, anxiety, rushed meals or no meals at all, and lack of sleep. President Lincoln was not the only one who worried himself sick over the war. The general did his best to cure the headache by indulging in the colorful remedies of the day—soaking his feet in a mixture of hot water and mustard, and applying mustard plasters to his wrists and to the back of his neck. Nothing worked. He spent the night in a "double house." The general "threw himself on the sofa," while his staff slept on the floor.[16]

At around midnight, an officer brought "the expected letter" from General Lee. It was taken to General Grant's room, where the general was in too much pain to sleep. "Come in, I am awake," the general said, "I am suffering too much to get any sleep." He sat up on the sofa and, by the light of a candle that Colonel Porter had brought, read General Lee's reply:

APRIL 8, 1865.

Lieutenant-General GRANT,
Commanding Armies of the United States:

GENERAL: I received at a late hour your note of to-day. In mine of yesterday I did not intend to propose the surrender of the Army of Northern Virginia, but to ask the terms of your proposition. To be frank, I do not think the emergency has arisen to call for the surrender of this army; but as the restoration of peace should be the sole object of all, I desired to know whether your proposals would lead to that end. I cannot, therefore, meet you with a view to surrender the Army of Northern Virginia; but as far as your proposal may affect the C. S. forces under my command, and tend to the restoration of peace, I should be pleased to meet you at 10 a.m. to-morrow, on the old stage road to Richmond, between the picket-lines of the two armies.

Very respectfully, your obedient servant,
R. E. LEE,
General[17]

General Grant did not have the authority to negotiate anything connected with "the restoration of peace," which General Lee had mentioned twice in his letter. Only President Lincoln himself had the power to discuss peace terms. "It looks as if Lee still means to fight," Grant said, "I will reply in the morning."[18] After making "a few more comments," he stretched himself out on the sofa again. Colonel Porter expressed his hopes that the general might be able to get some sleep.

Abraham Lincoln's visit to City Point, as well as to Richmond and Petersburg, was more than just a vacation. "The expedition had been spoken of almost as if it were a pleasure trip," Lincoln's bodyguard, William Crook, wrote.[19] "Of course," Crook went on, "in one sense this was true." The trip did give the president some time away from the pressures and politics and politicians of Washington, which he confessed were killing him. Cynics would be quick to point out that the visit also got him away from his wife, which was another relief. But traveling to City Point accomplished a lot more than just giving the president some peace and quiet and relaxation.

As William Crook noted, Lincoln's City Point visit "was a matter or executive duty, and a very trying and saddening duty in many of its features." For one thing, going to army headquarters gave the president a first-hand look at the war. He had read all the dispatches and newspaper reports, but at Fort Stedman he saw for himself what artillery fire and the rifled musket could do, which seemed to add to his anxieties regarding the war and how soon it could be brought to an end. "This is the first time in the history of the war that the President has been personally present to encourage and animate the soldiers," an article in New York's the *Sun* reported.[20] The article went on to report that Lincoln's first-hand observation of the fighting, along with his consultation with his "military chiefs," combined to give ample evidence of "how anxiously he regarded . . . the great struggle."

William Crook, who accompanied the president during his time away from Washington, observed that his visits to Richmond and Petersburg also had an adverse effect on President Lincoln: "These things wore new furrows in his face" and also served to make Lincoln sadder, but at the same time made him more sympathetic toward the soldiers on both sides, including "the forlorn rebel prisoners."[21]

President Lincoln's stay at City Point also allowed him to see the war from a general's point of view. General Grant remembered that the president was with him "all the time" during his stay at army headquarters. "We visited the different camps," General Grant said many years after the war ended, and he also did his best to keep Lincoln both interested and informed.[22] The president certainly was kept informed as to what Grant and Meade and Sheridan were trying to accomplish. "He was very anxious about the war closing," General Grant said, and worried that a new campaign would begin if General Lee managed to join General Johnston's army in North Carolina. The more Grant saw of Lincoln, the more he was impressed by what he saw. After the war, Grant would say that Lincoln was "a great man."

"LEE HAS SURRENDERED"

The *River Queen* made a brief stop at Fortress Monroe, which was situated on the tip of the peninsula that separates the James River estuary from Chesapeake Bay. It was only a short stop-over, made for the purpose of picking up mail and dispatches as well as a Potomac River pilot. Commander John S. Barnes also departed the *River Queen* for the USS *Bat* at Fortress Monroe; the *Bat* was lying close by the *Queen* but was not at anchor. He shook hands and said goodbye to President Lincoln before leaving the ship. "Mr. Lincoln was kind enough to thank me for the good care taken of him," he recalled, and also took the time to crack a joke about what a comfortable life "navy men" led during wartime.[1] "Probably he never again thought of me," the commander said, "but the memory of his warm hand-clasp and kindly look remained with me and has never left me."

Both the *River Queen* and the *Bat* left Fortress Monroe during the afternoon and began steaming northward up Chesapeake Bay toward the Potomac River. President Lincoln was in a congenial, con-versational mood; his quiet and reflective frame of mind of the night before had passed. "That whole day the conversation turned on lit-erary subjects," the Marquis de Chambrun remembered.[2] "Mr. Lincoln read aloud to us for several hours." Most of the passages he read were from Shakespeare. He read from a beautiful quarto edition of Shake-speare's works, and recited several speeches from *Macbeth*, one of the president's favorite plays, including the "Duncan is in his grave" speech from act 3. "The lines after the murder of Duncan, when the new king [Macbeth] falls prey to moral torment, were dramatically dwelt on."

Duncan is in his grave;
After life's fitful fever he sleeps well;
Treason has done his worst: nor steel, nor poison,
Malice domestic, foreign levy, nothing,
Can touch him further.[3]

Lincoln read the speech twice, explaining that Shakespeare gave a picture of a murderer's mind, "when the dark deed achieved, its perpetrator already envies his victim's calm sleep."[4]

Macbeth's speech seemed to unnerve Lincoln's friend James Speed, one of the president's party, who proceeded to warn the president about growing rumors concerning threats of assassination. As the war wound down toward its finish, disgruntled Confederates were looking for a target for their frustrations. Lincoln was the most obvious target. But Lincoln was not interested in James Speed's warnings. He said that he would rather be dead than to live in constant fear. In that state of mind, it would have been more appropriate if he had read the passage from *Julius Caesar* where Caesar reacts to rumors of his own assassination, instead of the speech from *Macbeth*:

Cowards die many times before their deaths;
The valiant never taste of death but once:
Of all the wonders that I yet have heard,
It seems to me most strange that men should fear,
Seeing that death, a necessary end,
Will come when it will come.[5]

While President Lincoln was reading to his guests, the *River Queen* steamed north toward the Potomac River estuary. When the ship turned west and entered the Potomac, her escort, the USS *Bat*, almost immediately began falling behind. The *Bat*'s boilers had a habit of "foaming up," in Commander Barnes words, whenever there was a change from salt water to fresh, "so that we were hard put . . . to keep pace with the *Queen*."[6] The *River Queen* slowed down "once or twice" to allow the *Bat* to catch up. But in spite of all efforts, the *Bat* kept dropping back, "so that the *Queen* arrived at her dock at Washington some hours before us."

The president was not concerned with the fact that the *Bat* could not keep pace, which left the *River Queen* all alone in her journey up the Potomac. It had been a peaceful afternoon, with no communiques from anyone on shore and no news from the war. President Lincoln seemed to be calm and relaxed. When the *River Queen* passed Mount Vernon, Chambrun was moved to remark, "Mount Vernon, with its memories of Washington, and Springfield, with those of your own home—revolutionary and civil war—will be equally honored in America."[7] At that particular moment in time, Lincoln was not much interested in being honored and esteemed in the manner of George Washington, but his entire composure changed at the mention of his home in Springfield. "As though awakened from a trance," Chambrun would remember, "the President exclaimed: 'Springfield, how happy I shall be in four years hence to return there in peace and tranquility!'" He only wanted to finish his second term in the White House, put the country on the road to recovery and reconstruction after four years of civil war, and to go back to Springfield. Washington was welcome to his praise and adulation; all Lincoln required was to return home and start living a normal life again.

Chambrun also took note of two other conversations. The first was between the president and the marquis himself. Chambrun asked if the United States would become involved in the hostilities between France and Mexico, which had begun in 1862—"our Mexican expedition" is the way the Marquis phrased it—after the Confederate armies surrendered. The president's answer was straightforward and to the point. "We have had enough war," he said. "I know what the American people want and, thank God, I count for something in this country."[8] He concluded his short remark with, "Rest assured that during my second term there will be no more fighting."

The second exchange involved Mary Lincoln. As the *River Queen* steamed closer to Washington and the city's buildings and landmarks came into view, Mrs. Lincoln looked out at the town and said, "That city is full of enemies." The president was somewhat taken aback by his wife's remarks—she had not said very much up to that point—and answered sharply. "Enemies, never again must we repeat that word."[9] Mary Lincoln was not just referring to Lincoln's political adversaries. She had heard the assassination rumors along with everybody else and was frightened to think that some Confederate sympathizer might be waiting in one of the buildings she could see from the *River Queen*'s deck. The president brushed the remark aside.

The *River Queen* docked at Washington at around 6:00 p.m. By the time Commander Barnes had arrived in the capital aboard the USS *Bat*, the president had already been driven off into the city. Before he went ashore, President Lincoln said his goodbyes to Captain Penrose, shaking his hand and thanking him "for the manner in which he had performed his duty."[10] The president shared the carriage with his wife, his son Tad, and, by the bodyguard's own account, with William H. Crook.

As soon as the carriage left the wharf and began traveling through the streets, it became obvious that some sort of celebration was taking place. "The streets were alive with people, all very much excited," William Crook wrote. "There were bonfires everywhere."[11] Tad became so agitated by all the noise and activity that he could not sit still. Everyone in the vehicle had been aboard the *River Queen* all day. Nobody had heard any news, and they did not know what was happening. The driver stopped the carriage and asked a passerby about the cause of all the excitement. The man hesitated for a moment, and looked at the occupants in absolute astonishment. "Why, where have you been?" he asked in amazement, not recognizing President Lincoln. "Lee has surrendered."

General Grant had also been surprised by General Lee's surrender. After he had read Lee's most recent communiqué during the previous night, Grant was convinced that the Confederates meant to continue fighting. On the morning of April 9, he sent this reply:

Headquarters Armies of the U.S.
April 9, 1865

General R. E. Lee
Commanding C.S.A.

Your note of yesterday is received. As I have no authority to treat on the subject of peace, the meeting proposed for ten A.M. today could lead to no good. I will state, however, General, that I am equally anxious for peace with yourself, and the whole North entertains the same feeling. The terms upon which peace can be had are well understood. By the South laying down their arms they will hasten that most desirable event, save thousands of human lives, and hundreds of millions of property not yet destroyed. Seriously hoping that all our difficulties may be settled without the loss of another life. I subscribe myself, etc.

U. S. Grant,
Lieutenant General[12]

After sending his note to General Lee by courier, General Grant and several of his staff officers, including Colonel Horace Porter, rode off to meet with General Philip Sheridan. General Grant still had his migraine; it had been suggested to him that he ride on a covered ambulance instead of traveling by horseback, which might help to lessen the effects of his headache. But Grant elected to ride his big horse, Cincinnati, and rode off toward the village of Appomattox Court House. General Sheridan was up ahead, ready to throw his cavalry and infantry at the enemy. Grant wanted to join him at the front.

The general had not ridden very far when he and his party were overtaken by an officer from General Meade's staff. The officer handed General Grant a note from General Lee:

April 9, 1865

General: I received your note of this morning on the picket line, whither I had come to meet you and ascertain definitely what terms were embraced in your proposal of yesterday with reference to the surrender of this army. I now request an interview in accordance with the offer contained in your letter of yesterday for that purpose.

R. E. Lee, General[13]

"When the officer reached me I was still suffering from the sick headache," Grant would later write, "but the instant I saw the contents of the note I was cured."[14] He immediately wrote a reply:

Headquarters Army of the U.S.
April 9, 1865

General R. E. Lee
Commanding C.S.A.

Your note of this date is but this moment (11:30 A.M.) received, in consequence of my having passed from the Richmond and Lynchburg roads to the Farmville and Lynchburg road. I am writing this about four miles west of Walker's Church, and will push forward to the front for the purpose of meeting you. Notice sent to me on this road where you wish the interview to take place will meet me.

U. S. Grant
Lieutenant General[15]

General Grant met General Sheridan on the road approaching Appomattox Court House. After the usual salutes and greetings were exchanged, General Grant gestured toward the village and asked, "Is General Lee up there?" General Sheridan said yes; General Grant replied, "Very well. Let's go up."[16] They rode up to the substantial house of Wilmer McLean, where General Lee was waiting for them.

General Sheridan's men were in position to advance and did not know anything about any meeting between Lee and Grant. General Joshua Lawrence Chamberlain was about to order his troops to begin moving forward when a Confederate officer rode out from his lines with a white flag. The officer approached General Chamberlain and mentioned "a cessation of hostilities."[17] General Chamberlain sent him to the rear, explaining that he did not have the authority to negotiate surrender terms.

Shortly after this meeting, General Chamberlain received orders to cease firing and to halt, to stop his men from advancing any further. "There was not much firing to cease from," he remembered, "but to 'halt,' then and there?"[18] The men had been trained to keep moving forward, and had been advancing ever since they crossed the Rapidan River eleven months earlier—"forward to the end; forward to the new beginning; forward to the nation's second birth," General Chamberlain said.

But the word went out, "Halt! The rebels want to surrender," and the men halted where they were.[19] A general rode up and asked General Chamberlain why no one was moving up toward the enemy. "Only that Lee wants time to surrender," General Chamberlain answered with "stage solemnity." With that, the old general's entire demeanor changed. "Glory to God!" he shouted, and shook Chamberlain's hand "with an impetuosity that nearly unhorsed us both."

General Lee and General Grant signed the surrender terms later that afternoon. General Grant reported the surrender to the War Department in Washington at 4:30, after General Lee had ridden back to join his own army.

Honorable E. M. Stanton, Secretary of War, Washington

General Lee surrendered the Army of Northern Virginia this afternoon on terms proposed by myself. The accompanying additional correspondence will show the conditions fully.

U. S. Grant, Lieutenant-General[20]

It did not take very long for the news to spread and circulate. Staff officers began riding through the Union lines shouting "Lee surrendered!" General Chamberlain remembered that his men "rent the air with shouting and uproar" when they heard about the surrender.[21] Colonel Elisha Hunt Rhodes, who was with his unit outside Appomattox Court House, learned about Lee's surrender when he heard "loud cheering from the front."[22] A short time afterward, General George Gordon Meade "rode like mad down the road with his hat off, shouting, 'The war is over, and we are going home!'"

General Grant's wife, Julia, along with the wife of another officer and a half-dozen army and navy officers, were sitting "in the cabin of our boat" during the afternoon when a headquarters attaché entered the cabin.[23] As Mrs. Grant remembered the scene, the attaché was very agitated. He held a sheet of paper in his hand, and said, "Mrs. Grant, Madam, may I speak with you for a moment?" She followed the attaché into another stateroom and asked, "What news?"

"Glad news, but you must not tell on me," he said. "It would cost me my head if old Stanton knew I had brought the news to you."[24] He then proceeded to read everything that had been telegraphed to Washington regarding the surrender of General Lee to her husband, including the very generous terms of surrender.

"Now, Madam, forgive me if I have done wrong," he went on, "but I felt you must know as soon as anyone else, including the president. So I brought you the news."[25]

When Mrs. Grant returned to her guests, everyone did their best to coax the attaché's news out of her. She refused to say anything, but it did not really matter. About twenty minutes later, "a shout went up along the bluffs, and cries of 'The Union Forever, Hurrah, Boys! Hurrah!' then told them the glad tidings."[26]

After returning from City Point, the president's first stop in Washington was not the war office, but the house of Secretary of State William Seward. Secretary Seward was still in great pain from the injuries he had received from his accident, and was hardly able to speak. His daughter Fanny recalled that the president had already arrived when she came into her father's room. Frederick Seward, the secretary's son, was also present. "When I went into the room he was lying on the foot of father's bed, talking with him," she wrote.[27] It was a friendly visit— "kind, genial, and unaffected." The president was doing his best to lift the spirits of his secretary of state, who had also become his friend.

Lincoln told Seward all about his visit to Richmond, as well as his stopover at the Depot Field Hospital. There were seven thousand men in the wards, he explained, and he shook hands with every one of them. "He spoke of having worked as hard at it as sawing wood," Fanny said, "and seemed, in his goodness of heart, much satisfied at the labor."[28]

General Lee had surrendered his army, but the war was not quite over yet. General Joseph Johnston's army was still in the field in North Carolina, and other Confederate units were operating in other parts of the South. But Robert E. Lee and his Army of Northern Virginia *were* the Confederacy to many Southerners. As Winston S. Churchill somewhat romantically phrased it, General Lee and his army "carried the rebellion on its bayonets."[29] Now he had submitted to General Grant, and any hope of Confederate survival disappeared with his army. "With this surrender perishes the last hope of the rebels and their sympathizers, who have pinned their hopes upon Lee," an article in Washington's *Evening Star* stated.[30] "When Lee, the wisest and bravest of the confederate leaders, sees no ray of hope for the confederate cause, and voluntarily lays down his arms to prevent further and futile effusion of blood, the most credulous optimist among his followers must accept his judgement as decisive."

A British historian observed that Robert E. Lee never understood U. S. Grant, or Grant's basic strategy: "Lee never fathomed Grant."[31] He might have made the same observation regarding Lee and Abraham Lincoln. President Lincoln was just as determined as General Grant to see the war through to its final conclusion, until the Confederate armies had surrendered and all the seceded states had rejoined the Union. He also did everything possible to further the Union cause at the expense of the Confederacy. In September 1862, the president issued a proclamation that suspended habeas corpus. Under this proclamation, President Lincoln had 13,000 people jailed on the vague charge of "disloyalty." Most of these were Peace Democrats, who were extremely vocal in their support of the Confederacy and their opposition of the war—their point of view was that the war should be ended immediately, the separated Southern states should be granted their independence, and that the Confederate States should be allowed to keep their slaves.

The proclamation might not have been the most ethical course of action, but it kept thousands of Confederate sympathizers from giving the enemy whatever assistance they might be able to render, from moral support to information regarding troop movements. A Confederate supporter in a Federal prison was just as effectively taken out of the war as a Confederate soldier in a Union prisoner of war camp. Lincoln was prepared to bend the law, break the law, or create his own set of laws in order to put down the rebellion in the South.

General Lee did not understand what impact President Lincoln was having on the Union war effort, and had not even paid very much attention to Lincoln at all. Most of the South tended either to ignore Lincoln entirely or to ridicule him. The Southern press frequently referred to him as a gorilla or a baboon. (Many Northern newspapers were just as outspoken and insulting in their opinion of Lincoln.) But this tendency was a mistake. Lincoln's determination was as responsible for winning the war as Grant's. President Lincoln never lost faith in the Union's ability to win the war. That faith became infused in General Grant, and was as responsible for Appomattox as anything that Grant accomplished.

The terms that General Grant proposed to General Lee at Appomattox were simple and generous, in keeping with the terms that President Lincoln had outlined at City Point: all Confederate officers and men would be allowed to return home, and were not to be disturbed by any United States authorities; officers would be allowed to keep their side arms, horses, and personal property; the men in the ranks who claimed to own a horse or mule would be allowed to take the animal home. There would be no imprisonment for any of General Lee's men. This point of view was at least partially inspired by President Lincoln— Grant had shown consideration toward Confederate prisoners during his campaign against General Lee's army—and certainly followed Lincoln's tendency toward leniency for the South.

APRIL 10, 1865, MONDAY
RETURN TO THE WHITE HOUSE

When William Crook reported for work at the White House on Monday morning, he found that the president was already at his desk, sorting through the pile of unanswered mail. He looked up and said, "Good morning, Crook, how do you feel?"[1]

Crook responded that he was feeling "first rate," and asked the president how he was feeling that morning. "I am well, but rather tired," the president answered.[2] Crook noticed that President Lincoln did appear to be very tired; "his worn face made me understand, more clearly than I had done before, what a strain the experiences at Petersburg and Richmond had been." Now that all the excitement of the past few weeks was over, along with General Grant's campaign in Virginia, the stress Lincoln had been under was making itself even more obvious.

William Crook spent the entire day at the White House, close by the president. It turned out to be a particularly busy day. President Lincoln had been away from his office for over two weeks. "Seventeen days of absence," is the way Crook phrased it, which meant that seventeen days of correspondence had to be read and answered.[3] Also, the office was "thronged with visitors," as it usually was when Lincoln was present. Some people came to congratulate the president on General Lee's surrender, some came to offer advice on how to deal with Confederate leaders now that the war was almost over, and some came looking for jobs and appointments. "We settled back into the usual routine," Crook said. "It seemed odd to go on as if nothing had happened."

President Lincoln and William Crook must have been the only two people in the country, or at least in the North, who were having a normal, routine Monday. Throughout the North, the day had been proclaimed a legal holiday, as well as a day of thanksgiving. Newspapers spread the news of Lee's surrender. The *Detroit Free Press* announced, "Glory! Glory!! Glory!!! The Rebellion Ended! Lee's Whole Army Surrendered!"[4] The *New York Times* said, "Hang Out Your Banners, Union Victory! Peace! Surrender of General Lee and His Whole Army."[5] The *Albany Evening Journal* gave its headline a moral slant: "General Lee and His Army Have Surrendered! Slavery and Treason Buried in the Same Grave!"[6]

"The tidings were spread over the country over the night, and the nation seems delirious with joy," Gideon Welles remarked. "Guns are firing, bells ringing, flags flying, men laughing, children cheering."[7] Secretary Welles went on to speculate, "There may be some marauding and robbing and murder by desperadoes" in Texas "or at remote places beyond the Mississippi," but the surrender of General Lee, "the great Rebel captain," virtually assures the end of the war—"the termination of the Rebellion," in Secretary Welles's words.

Secretary Welles was wrong when he said that only unorganized resistance would be possible from remaining Confederate forces, or that any further fighting could only happen in Texas or west of the Mississippi. General Joseph Johnston's army was still active in North Carolina, and William Tecumseh Sherman was in position to move against it. In his memoirs, General Sherman wrote, "Promptly on Monday morning, April 10th, the army moved straight on Smithfield," where General Johnston's army was camped.[8] General Sherman had not yet heard the news of Appomattox and was advancing against Johnston, prepared to follow him "wherever he might go."

But as far as Washington, DC, was concerned, the war was over. The attitude of the general public in Washington was "forgive and forget," at least according to the Marquis de Chambrun.[9] "Columns of Confederate prisoners constantly traverse Washington," the Marquis reported. "Not a hostile shout greets their passage." Pedestrians seemed determined not to look at them, or pay any attention to them at all, "as though not wishing to hurt the feelings of these misled creatures."

Now that the war was over, "the words peace, pardon and clemency can be heard," a reaction that seemed to have taken the marquis completely by surprise. "It is impossible to imagine the rapidity with which the temper of the North has altered and to what extent it is spreading everywhere I go," he said.[10]

The marquis did not seem to be all that inclined toward clemency himself, at any rate not as far as slavery was concerned. He wrote that he would like to invite "our French Southern sympathizers" to travel to one of the Southern states, and to "become acquainted with the frightful details of the institution."[11] While he was visiting City Point, Chambrun had been shown "an instrument used to chain up the slaves on market days," which he described as "an iron manacle" that confined the wrist. "In seeing the irons worn by these unfortunates, and the corruption of the society which . . . profited by their labor," anyone who held a favorable opinion of the Confederacy "might alter their opinion of the regime."

During the afternoon, while the president was still sorting through his accumulated work, a crowd moved onto the White House grounds and began calling for Lincoln. Members of the band of the Quartermaster's regiment came along with the crowd, playing "excellent music." The president eventually came to the window and spoke to the "immense number of people."[12]

The president was in a pleasant mood. "I am very greatly rejoiced to find that an occasion has occurred so pleasurable that people cannot restrain themselves," he said, to everyone's amusement.[13] He went on to say that he was not planning to give a speech at that particular moment, because he had already prepared a speech for the following night, "and I shall have nothing to say if you dribble it out of me before." But so as not to disappoint everyone, President Lincoln requested the band to play "Dixie," calling it one of the best tunes he had ever heard. The Confederates had attempted to appropriate the song, he joked, but it had been captured fairly and was now a legal trophy. "I presented the question to the Attorney General," he explained, "and he gave it as his legal opinion that it is our lawful prize." The crowd burst into laughter and applause. The president disappeared from the window and went back to work.

A few hours later, another large group made their way to the White House to call for a speech. Just as he had done earlier, President Lincoln turned everyone away with a few good-natured remarks. He planned to give a speech on the following night, he said, but he was not ready to say anything just then. "Everything I say, you know, goes into print," he joked, and said that he did not want to make any mistakes or misstatements that would almost certainly find their way into the newspapers. With that, he said good evening and went back inside.[14]

But the president was not yet finished in his dealings with the public. At about six o'clock, a delegation of fifteen men presented themselves at the White House; President Lincoln met them in the corridor just inside the front door. After everyone was formally introduced, the man who made the introductions gave a short speech. "It was a very pretty speech," according to William Crook, "full of loyal sentiments and praise for the man who had safely guided the country through the great crisis."[15]

The president very politely listened to the speech. After the man finished, the delegation presented Lincoln with a portrait of himself. "When he saw his own rugged features facing him from an elaborate silver frame," Crook wrote, "a smile broadened his face."[16] The president then added a few words of his own, although they were probably not the remarks the delegation was expecting.

"Gentlemen, I thank you for this token of your esteem," he said. "You did your best. It wasn't your fault that the frame is so much more rare than the picture."[17] Every member of the group would have a story about President Lincoln when he went home, and another tale would be added to the Abraham Lincoln legend.

The fighting may have stopped, but the habit of war continued for the men in the field. "It seemed queer to sleep last night without fearing an attack," Colonel Elisha Hunt Rhodes wrote outside Appomattox Court House, "but the rebels are now all under guard."[18] Colonel Rhodes spoke with some of the Confederates, and discovered that they were as glad that the fighting had ended as the men of the Second Rhode Island regiment. "They all seemed surprised at our kind treatment of them, and I think General Grant's way of managing affairs will help us on the peace that must come." The men of both armies, Union and Confederate, were looking forward to the coming peace after four years of carnage.

General Joshua Lawrence Chamberlain was surprised by the number of Confederates who came over to the Union camp to visit— "to come over and see what we were really made of, and what we had left for trade."[19] They came to barter for food, for shoes, for tobacco, and sometimes just to talk, brothers-in-arms across the lines. "The inundation of visitors grew so that it looked like a county fair, including the cattle-show." So many Confederates came that senior officers finally had to forbid all visitors.

When General Grant tried to pass through the lines with several staff officers to meet with General Lee, he was stopped by Confederate pickets. They had been stopping Union troops for the past four years, and the habit was not easy to break. Colonel Horace Porter noted with a touch of sarcasm, "The practice which had so long been inculcated in Lee's army of keeping Grant out of its lines was not to be overturned in a day."[20] The general was "politely requested" by the pickets to wait until they contacted headquarters for instructions.

As soon as General Lee received word that General Grant was being detained at the picket line, he immediately rode out to receive his guest. They met on a knoll that overlooked the lines of both armies and saluted each other by raising their hats. The other officers also raised their hats before withdrawing, leaving Grant and Lee alone to confer with each other.

The topic of their conversation was the surrender of the remaining Confederate armies in the field. General Grant began the discussion by expressing his hope that the war would soon be over, not just in Virginia but throughout the country. General Lee responded by saying that he also hoped that all fighting would soon end and also trusted that everything possible would be done "to restore harmony and conciliate the people of the South."[21] The emancipation of the slaves should not be a hindrance to restoring relations between North and South, he went on to say. He did not know what the other Confederate forces would do, including Joseph Johnston's army, and he had no idea what course of action Jefferson Davis might pursue, but it was his considered opinion that all other Confederate armies should follow his lead, "as nothing could be gained by further resistance in the field."

Since General Lee was of the opinion that further resistance was useless, General Grant suggested that he should advise the remaining Confederate armies to surrender, "and thus exert his influence in favor of immediate peace."[22] General Lee responded that he would have to consult with Jefferson Davis before he could take any such action. When Grant suggested that he do just that, talk to President Davis about the subject, Lee responded that this would be stepping beyond his duties as a soldier. Besides, "the authorities" would almost certainly arrive at the same conclusion without his "interference." General Lee would not allow himself to become involved in any situation that might be taken as overstepping his authority as an officer, or with interfering with the authority of President Davis. General Grant later commented, "I knew there was no use to urge him to do anything against his ideas of what was right."[23] He let the matter drop.

A rumor began to circulate that General Grant asked General Lee to have a meeting with President Lincoln instead of Jefferson Davis. According to this story, General Lee refused to confer with Lincoln, explaining that he would have to confirm any such meeting with President Davis. But Colonel Horace Porter asked about this story when General Grant was on his death bed, and wrote that "his recollection was distinct that he had made no suggestion."[24] Grant did not suggest that General Lee have any sort of conference with Abraham Lincoln. Colonel Porter is of the opinion that when word first began to circulate that General Lee was asked to see the "president," it was generally assumed that the president in question was Abraham Lincoln, not Jefferson Davis. The rumor has persisted over the years, in spite of Colonel Porter's recollection.

The two generals continued to speak with one another for a little more than half an hour. At the end of the conversation, "The two commanders lifted their hats and bade each other good-bye."[25] Lee rode back to his camp, and Grant returned to his headquarters.

At the White House, President Lincoln continued to write and polish the speech he was preparing for the following evening.

APRIL 11, 1865, TUESDAY
A FAIR SPEECH

The president spent much of his day preparing for the speech he was to deliver that evening. Elizabeth Keckley came to the White House to help Mary Lincoln get ready for the event. On her way to Mrs. Lincoln's room, Lizzy decided to open the door to the president's office and take a look inside, just out of curiosity. What she saw was President Lincoln sitting at his desk, engrossed in his work, not even looking up, going over the text of his speech.

At around nine o'clock, the president met with General Benjamin F. Butler. According to General Butler's account, the two of them discussed the possibility of sending freed slaves to dig a canal across the Isthmus of Panama (General Butler referred to it as the "Isthmus of Darien"), as a well as an idea of establishing a black colony there. There are many who doubt General Butler's story. Washington's *Daily National Republican* mentions the meeting but gives no details, only noting, "Major General Butler had an interview with the President to-day."[1]

President Lincoln also issued a proclamation that closed more than thirty ports in Virginia, North Carolina, South Carolina, Florida, Alabama, Mississippi, Louisiana, and Texas "until they shall have again been opened by order of the President."[2] He also issued a second proclamation, which barred warships of any foreign country that had refused "privileges and immunities" to American warships. This proclamation ends by declaring, "the United States, whatever claim or pretense may have existed heretofore, are now, at least, entitled to claim and concede an entire and friendly equality of rights and hospitalities with all maritime nations."

The president's point was that the American fleet had expanded and had become more powerful during the war, and that the United States was now a bona fide naval power. The US Navy was now the equal of any other naval country, including Britain. Secretary of the Navy Gideon Welles agreed fully, stating, "we shall now assent our rights and, I hope, maintain them"—including against "the insolence of the petty officials of John Bull."[3]

President Lincoln's main activity for the day was his much-anticipated speech, which he delivered that evening. The Marquis de Chambrun received his invitation to attend the speech on Tuesday, when "a tall colored man" appeared at his door with a bouquet of flowers and a note, both of which were from Mary Lincoln.[4] The note informed the marquis that the president would be delivering a speech from a window in the White House, and asked if he would like to listen to his address with Mrs. Lincoln from an adjacent window. He accepted at once and spent most of the day as the guest of Mrs. Lincoln at the White House.

The city began celebrating long before the president spoke a word—the address was a true media event. Candles and lamps lit up all the public buildings in town—people commented that the Capitol dome could be seen for miles. The windows of the White House had rows of makeshift candle holders nailed in place for the occasion. Even Robert E. Lee's former home in Arlington, on the other side of the Potomac, was illuminated. The entire city was brilliantly lighted—this in an era long before electric lighting.

In spite of an "unpleasant drizzle" that continued all throughout the evening, thousands of people made their way along Pennsylvania Avenue toward the White House, which was the city's only paved street at the time.[5] The president's appearance "drew an immense throng to the White House, which not only filled up the grounds immediately in front of the mansion, but obstructed the sidewalks of the avenue from 15th to 17th streets."[6] As soon as the president came to one of the windows, the crowd erupted with cheers and applause. From another window, Mary Lincoln was also cheered and applauded.

Very shortly after he arrived at the window, without very much in the way of preliminaries, President Lincoln began reading from his text. "We meet this evening not in sorrow, but in gladness of heart," he began. "The evacuation of Petersburg and Richmond, and the surrender of the principal insurgent army, give hope of a righteous and speedy peace whose joyous expression can not be restrained."[7] The lighting was not very good, and the president was doing his best to read by the light of a candle, which he held in one hand, while he held the pages of his speech in the other hand. This very quickly proved to be a very awkward arrangement. He gestured to newspaper correspondent Noah Brooks, who was standing close by, to come to his assistance. Noah Brooks took the candle from Lincoln, which allowed the president to use both hands for his address. As he finished each page, he allowed it to fall to the floor. His son Tad picked up each page as it fell. Tad was having so much fun that he asked his father to let the pages fall faster.

The very beginning of the speech was positive and optimistic. After mentioning Petersburg and Appomattox, the president said that "a national thanksgiving" was being prepared, and followed by praising General Grant, "his skillful officers, and brave men," as well as by a tribute to "the gallant Navy." But following this uplifting start, President Lincoln shifted his focus to the more formal subject of reconstruction—a subject "fraught with great difficulty."

The rest of Lincoln's speech was all about the future and "the re-inauguration of the national authority," as he called reconstruction. His main focus was the recently established state government of Louisiana, which the president defended. Since 1862, Lincoln had been looking for a way to bring Louisiana back into the Union. The state had a good many pro-Unionists among its population; some Unionists insisted that they made up the majority. Now he was asking if the state government should be accepted as it existed, or should be rejected. "Can Louisiana be brought into proper practical relation with the Union *sooner* by *sustaining*," he asked, "or by *discarding* her new State Government?"

He admitted that the Louisiana government may not have been ideal, but pointed out that its new constitution abolished slavery, and that its legislature voted to ratify the Constitutional amendment abolishing slavery throughout the country. The president added that about twelve thousand voters in Louisiana gave "the benefit of public schools equally to black and white," and also authorized the state legislature "to confer the elective franchise upon the colored man." He also stated that "if we reject Louisiana, we also reject one vote in favor of the proposed amendment to the national Constitution"—namely the Thirteenth Amendment, which abolished slavery. (The Thirteenth amendment was ratified in December 1865.)

From a second story window in the White House, Elizabeth Keckley watched the president as he spoke. She was impressed by the sight of President Lincoln and Tad standing close together, and thought that the two of them presented "a striking tableau."[8] But the thought also occurred to her that the president made an excellent target as he stood there, illuminated "boldly in the darkness." It would have been a very simple matter to kill Lincoln as he stood in the window. "He could be shot from the crowd," she reflected, "and no one be able to tell who fired the shot."

Among the hundreds of people who stood watching the president were John Wilkes Booth and two friends. Booth had been angry and depressed ever since he had heard the news of Appomattox, and he had nothing but contempt for Abraham Lincoln. When he heard what

Alexander Gardner's well-known portrait of Abraham Lincoln, which was taken in February 1865. Nearly four years of war had taken its toll on the president; many people remarked on how tired and drawn he looked. *Image from the Library of Congress.*

Inauguration day, March 4, 1865. President Abraham Lincoln delivers his Second Inaugural Address from the steps of the Capitol. The brevity of the speech, which lasted only six or seven minutes, surprised the audience. John Wilkes Booth is one of the onlookers in the crowd behind and to the left of the president, just under the sculpture in the center of the photo. *Image from the Library of Congress.*

Abraham Lincoln's copy of his Second Inaugural Address, with changes in his own handwriting. This is the copy he read to the public on Inauguration Day. *Image from the Library of Congress.*

Vol. IX.—No. 429.]   NEW YORK, SATURDAY, MARCH 18, 1865.

Chief Justice Salmon P. Chase administers the oath of office after President Lincoln delivered his address. *Image from the Library of Congress.*

Secretary of State William H. Seward. Secretary Seward was seriously injured by one of John Wilkes Booth's co-conspirators, as was his son Francis. Both would survive, although Secretary Seward's face would bear the scars for the rest of his life. *Image from the Library of Congress.*

Although Secretary of War Edwin M. Stanton worried about President Lincoln's safety, and feared an assassination attempt, the president tended to dismiss Secretary Stanton's concerns. *Image from the Library of Congress.*

Gideon Welles served as President Lincoln's Secretary of the Navy, but he did not agree with the president's proposed policy of leniency toward the Confederacy after the war. *Image from the Library of Congress.*

Mary Lincoln accompanied her husband to City Point, Virginia, in March, but her behavior became a source of embarrassment for both President Lincoln and herself. *Image from the Library of Congress.*

Tad Lincoln with his father. Tad and the president spent a good deal of time together; his son's presence helped take President Lincoln's mind off the pressures of Washington. *Photo by Anthony Berger; image from the Library of Congress.*

The waterfront of City Point, Virginia. City Point was the supply center for General Grant's army and was also the meeting place between General Grant and President Lincoln. Mary Lincoln was not comfortable at City Point, but her husband enjoyed getting away from Washington and its pressures. *Image from the Library of Congress.*

General Grant, along with his wife, Julia, and his son Jesse, in front of the general's cabin at City Point. Julia Grant did her best to get along with Mary Lincoln, in spite of the latter's erratic behavior. *Image from Wikimedia Creative Commons.*

The side-wheeler *River Queen* took the Lincolns and their party from Washington to City Point. Aboard the *River Queen* along with General Grant, General Sherman, and Admiral Porter, President Lincoln drew up plans for the prosecution of the war and the rebuilding of the South. *Image from Wikipedia Creative Commons.*

A line of federal wagons makes its way through Petersburg after Confederate troops abandoned the city. With the evacuation of Petersburg, federal soldiers could see that the end of the war was in sight. *Photo John Reekie; image from the Library of Congress.*

Abraham and Mary Lincoln with their two sons, Robert and Tad. Robert Lincoln was an officer on General Grant's staff. *Lithograph by Currier and Ives; image from the Library of Congress.*

The ruins of Richmond, Virginia, in April 1865. The Confederate capital was a devastated ruin of a city, ravaged by looters. *Photo by Alexander Gardner; image from the Library of Congress.*

Escorted by armed sailors and accompanied by his son Tad, President Lincoln walks through the streets of Richmond on April 4. His bodyguard, William H. Crook, thought it was nothing short of a miracle that no attempt was made on the president's life. *Illustration by Thomas Nast; image from Wikimedia Creative Commons.*

Head Quarters Armies of the United States,

City Point, April). 11. Am 1865

Lieut Gen. Grant.

Gen. Sheridan says "If the thing is pressed I think that Lee will surrender." Let the thing be pressed.

A Lincoln

The original dispatch sent by Mr. Lincoln to me, Apl. 7th 1865,

U. S. Grant

"Gen. Sheridan says 'If the thing is pressed I think that Lee will surrender.' Let the <u>thing</u> be pressed." President Lincoln's famous communiqué of April 7 to General Grant. Under the president's message, General Grant wrote, "The original dispatch sent by Mr. Lincoln to me, April 7th 1865." *Image from the Library of Congress.*

On April 12, 1865, the Army of Northern Virginia formally surrendered at Appomattox, stacking their weapons and laying down their cartridge boxes. President Lincoln was not present at the ceremony, but he had been looking forward to the moment for the past eleven months. *Illustration by John R. Chapin; image from the Library of Congress.*

John Wilkes Booth regarded Abraham Lincoln as the cause of all of the South's problems. He imagined that he would be performing a heroic act for the Confederacy by assassinating the president. *Photo by Alexander Gardener; image from the Library of Congress.*

A sketch of the interior of Ford's Theatre by artist Alfred Waud, showing the box where President and Mrs. Lincoln sat during the performance of *Our American Cousin. Illustration by Alfred Waud; image from the Library of Congress.*

An artist's rendition of John Wilkes Booth firing his derringer at President Lincoln on the night of April 14. *Image from the Library of Congress.*

Andrew Johnson was a War Democrat from Tennessee who was named President Lincoln's running mate as a political expedient. He did not have either the personality or the political talent of Abraham Lincoln. *Image from the Library of Congress.*

Lincoln had to say in favor of giving the vote to "the colored man," Booth turned and said to one of his companions, "That means nigger citizenship," and promised that this would be the last speech that Lincoln would ever make: "Now, by God, I'll put him through."[9]

The president ended his speech by explaining, "What has been said of Louisiana will apply generally to other States"—he hoped to use Louisiana as a model for other seceded states as they rejoined the Union. He concluded with, "In the present *'situation'* as the phrase goes, it may be my duty to make some new announcement to the people of the South," without giving any details. "I am considering, and shall not fail to act, when satisfied that action will be proper."[10]

The audience cheered and applauded as the president read the main body of his speech, but not with the noise and enthusiasm they showed at the very beginning of the address. Most had been expecting a rousing victory speech. Instead, they were regaled with a long dissertation on the Louisiana legislature and reconstruction. Noah Brooks told the president that it was a fair speech, which was his way of saying that it said what the president wanted it to say but was not outstanding. The Marquis de Chambrun wrote, "It was a great event and a remarkable discourse."[11] William Crook also heard the address, and commented on its "two great principles."[12] The first was that "the mass of the Southern people shall be restored to their citizenship as soon as they desired it." The second principle: "punishment, *if punishment there be,* should fall upon those who had been to be chiefly instrumental in leading the south into rebellion." He did not even mention what the president had to say regarding giving the vote to former slaves.

The speech was printed in newspapers throughout the country, or at least throughout the North. Sometimes it was printed in its entirety, sometimes in an edited form. Nearly every report mentioned the illuminated buildings and the cheering crowds, but not every paper had a favorable opinion of what President Lincoln had to say. The *New-*

York Tribune complained that Lincoln's address "caused great disappointment and left a painful impression."[13] The Washington *Evening Star* noted that the speech had been "prepared with this deliberation, evidently in order that there should be no chance for misconception," which was a valid observation—the president worked very hard and spent a great deal of time in phrasing and polishing his address.[14]

After he finished delivering his speech and the crowd went home, President Lincoln tried his best to relax. Mary Lincoln and the Marquis de Chambrun walked through the White House to the president's room; Mrs. Lincoln opened the door without knocking. "There was Mr. Lincoln, stretched at full length, resting on a large sofa from his oratorical efforts."[15]

As soon as Mrs. Lincoln and Chambrun entered the room, President Lincoln "rose impulsively" and shook the marquis by the hand, "which he held in his own a long time as though better to show his pleasure and affection at seeing me again," the marquis recalled.[16] The two of them talked about the speech and the "extremely moderate ideas" that Lincoln had expressed. The president also spoke about the problems that lay ahead of him because of these ideas—Radical Republicans in Congress objected to any form of leniency that might be shown toward the Confederacy, and would oppose any measures for leniency that Lincoln might propose—but still declared "his firm resolution to stand firm for clemency against all opposition."

Chambrun and Mrs. Lincoln left the president after this conversation, and went downstairs to the parlor. A Miss Harris, described as the "daughter of one of the New York Senators," was waiting for them.[17] The three of them proceeded to have a very pleasant conversation, talking at length on a variety of subjects. "Mrs. Lincoln, full of the triumphs of the last few days, spoke with great confidence of the future and showed great satisfaction and pride in her husband's success."

APRIL 12, 1865, WEDNESDAY
ONLY A DREAM

O n the morning following the president's address on reconstruction, life at the White House went back to its normal routine. The usual stream of callers showed up—office seekers, well-wishers, casual visitors, people offering their congratulations for Appomattox. Washington may still have been celebrating, but it was an ordinary working Wednesday for President Lincoln and his staff. Among the items that Lincoln dealt with was a pardon for Private George Maynard of the Forty-Sixth New York Volunteers, who had been sentenced to death for desertion. The president's communiqué read simply, "Let the Prisoner be pardoned and returned to his Regiment."[1] Lincoln also asked Secretary of War Stanton to recommend Isaac G. Wilson of Illinois for an appointment to West Point.

President Lincoln also sent two telegrams to General Godfrey Weitzel in Richmond. His first telegraph concerned a reprimand that General Weitzel had received from Secretary Stanton. General Weitzel had not ordered prayers to be said for the president in churches throughout Richmond. Secretary Stanton telegraphed that he was extremely upset because General Weitzel had waived the requirement for clergymen to perform services without including "the usual prayer" for the president of the United States.[2] "If such has been your action it is strongly condemned by this Department," Stanton rebuked. If the clergy in Richmond could pray for "the rebel chief," Jefferson Davis, then they should be required to pray for President Lincoln as well.

President Lincoln had seen Secretary Stanton's dispatches, and sent his own response to General Weitzel on this small but niggling matter. "I do not remember hearing prayers spoken of while I was in Richmond," he said, "but I have no doubt you have acted in what appeared to you to be the spirit and temper manifested by me while there."[3] In other words, General Weitzel acted in the spirit of Lincoln's outlook of leniency toward the South, even if the general did not go along with Secretary Stanton's wishes. The president was of the opinion that Weitzel acted properly.

President Lincoln's second telegram to General Weitzel concerned John A. Campbell and "the gentlemen who have *acted* as the Legislature of Virginia."[4] The president was having second thoughts about allowing the Virginia legislature to meet. He had originally been of the opinion that having an assembly made up of prominent and influential Virginians would help to make Virginia's transition back into the Union smoother and more amiable. But Gideon Welles and Edwin M. Stanton did not agree with him. Secretary Welles objected to the convening of what he still considered to be a rebel governing body. "It was a recognition of them," he protested, and was afraid that if the "so-called legislature" met, they might "conspire against us" and make unreasonable demands.[5]

On April 7, John A. Campbell had sent General Weitzel a letter that made President Lincoln agree with Secretary Welles and change his mind about the Virginia Legislature. In his letter, Campbell stated, "The legislature of Virginia [will or should] be immediately convened."[6] (Brackets are in original.) He went on to state, "The spirit of the people is not broken and the resources of the country allow of a prolonged and embarrassing resistance," and made several other defiant comments that seemed to confirm Secretary Welles's misgivings that Campbell and the Virginia Legislature might very well "conspire against us" if they were permitted to meet.

President Lincoln was not happy with "Judge Campbell," as he called him, with the tone of Judge Campbell's letter, or with any of Campbell's pointed views regarding the Virginia legislature. On April 12, the same day he read the letter, the president telegraphed General Weitzel that he did not call "the insurgent Legislature of Virginia together, as the rightful Legislature of the State, to settle all differences with the United States."[7] He instructed General Weitzel, "Do not now allow them to assemble; but if any have come, allow them safe-return to their homes." Lincoln was determined to show Virginia and all the seceded states every possible consideration, but was not about to allow Judge Campbell or anyone else to show any form of insolence or disrespect toward the government of the United States.

On the same Wednesday morning, Robert E. Lee's Army of Northern Virginia formally surrendered to Union forces. Neither General Lee nor General Grant were present at the ceremony. General Joshua Lawrence Chamberlain accepted the Confederate flags and arms from General John B. Gordon, who represented General Lee.

General Chamberlain received orders to have his lines formed for the surrender ceremony at sunrise. His men watched as the Confederate forces, "on the opposite slopes," took down their tents for the last time and slowly formed their own ranks. After forming up, the gray lines slowly began moving forward—"The dusky swarms forge forward into gray columns of march," General Chamberlain later wrote.[8] The regimental battle flags were crowded so closely together, and the men of the regiments had been so thinned out by the fighting, that there seemed to be more flags than men, and "the whole column seemed crowned with red."

In the spirit of reconciliation shown by both General Grant and President Lincoln, General Chamberlain ordered his men to salute the surrendering Confederates, which he described as "a salute of arms."[9] Prompted by the bugler's call, the entire Union line gave "the soldier's salutation" of "carry arms," the marching salute. General Gordon was riding at the head of the Confederate column, depressed and with a downcast face. But as soon as he heard the snap of the muskets, he returned the salute by wheeling his horse toward the Union lines and touching the point of his sword to the toe of his boot. General Gordon also instructed his own men to salute the Union ranks as they passed by—"honor answering honor."

Each individual Confederate division then came forward to lay down its arms—the men fixed bayonets, stacked their muskets, removed their cartridge boxes and set them on the ground. The final part of the ceremony consisted of giving up their regimental battle flags. The flags were brought forward, "reluctantly, with agony of expression," rolled up, and set down next to the stacked muskets and cartridge boxes.[10] Some of the men rushed from the ranks to kneel over the standards and touch them for the last time.

The ceremony went on all day long; the divisions came forward, surrendered their weapons and flags, and withdrew. Federal wagons came to collect everything during the intervals between the coming and going of the Confederate units. Once in a while, the contents of the cartridge boxes were found to be unserviceable, and the ammunition would be emptied into the street.

Throughout the day, while the ceremony was taking place, General Chamberlain had the chance to speak with several Confederate generals. Most of them were completely taken by surprise concerning the generosity shown by both President Lincoln and General Grant. "You astonish us," one of them said, "by your honorable and generous conduct. I fear we should not have done the same by you had the case been reversed."[11] "I will go home," another Confederate officer said, "and tell Joe Johnston we can't fight such men as you. I will advise him to surrender."

But it was not all kind words and forgiveness and magnanimity.

General Chamberlain spoke with another Confederate officer concerning the good will that the men on both sides had shown toward each other, and remarked that brave men might become good friends in spite of the war. The Confederate officer did not agree at all. "You are mistaken, sir," he said. "You may forgive us, but we won't be forgiven. There is a rancor in our hearts . . . which you little dreamed of. We hate you, sir."[12]

General Chamberlain did his best to calm the officer, trying to make light conversation and mentioning that everyone would soon be going home. "Home!" the Confederate repeated with anger in his voice. "We haven't any. You have destroyed them. You have invaded Virginia, and ruined her. Her curse is on you."[13] Staff officers both in blue and gray who overheard the outburst thought it was comical and laughed at the display of bad temper. But the unhappy Confederate officer was not joking. Many thousands of Southerners were in full agreement with him.

President Lincoln was well aware that not everyone shared his, and General Grant's, feeling of generosity concerning the South. Many throughout the North felt the same anger and bitterness toward their former enemy, and cursed the former Confederate states. The next four years looked to be a long battle with the Radical Republicans for the president, but Lincoln was not worried. He would deal with his opponents, in Congress and elsewhere, when the time came, and he was confident that he would be able to carry out his program for reconciliation and reunification during the coming four years.

In North Carolina, General William Tecumseh Sherman was still in pursuit of General Joseph Johnston's army, and marched into Smithfield on Tuesday, April 11. Joe Johnston had already left Smithfield by the time General Sherman arrived. He was moving as quickly as he could toward Raleigh—he "retreated hastily," according to Sherman—and had burned several bridges during his retreat.[14] This left General

Sherman with the job of rebuilding the destroyed bridges, which took up most of the day.

That night, General Sherman received an urgent message from General Grant: General Lee had surrendered "his whole army" to him at Appomattox. He immediately announced the news to his troops in a special field order:

[Special Field Orders, No. 54]

HEADQUARTERS MILITARY DIVISION
OF THE MISSISSIPPI
IN THE FIELD, SMITHFIELD, NORTH CAROLINA, April
12, 1865.

The general commanding announces to the army that he has official notice from General Grant that General Lee surrendered to him his entire army, on the 9th inst., at Appomattox Court-House, Virginia.

Glory to God and our country, and all honor to our comrades in arms, toward whom we are marching!

A little more labor, a little more toil on our part, the great race is won, and our Government stands regenerated, after four long years of war.

W. T. SHERMAN, Major-General commanding.[15]

"Of course, this created a perfect *furor* of rejoicing," General Sherman wrote, in a massive understatement. Men cheered and shouted and threw their hats in the air, just as General Grant's men had done at Appomattox three days earlier. Now that General Lee had surrendered, the question on everyone's mind concerned General Johnston and what he would do. General Sherman wondered, "would he surrender at Raleigh? Or would he allow his army to disperse into guerilla bands, to 'die in the last ditch?'"[16]

"I know well that Johnston's army could not be caught," he said, "the men could escape us, disperse, and assemble again at some place agreed on, and thus the war might be prolonged indefinitely."[17] The general remembered what the president had said about the Confederate troops. Aboard the *River Queen* at City Point, President Lincoln had told Grant and Sherman that he wanted all surrendered troops "back at their homes, engaged in their civil pursuits." A guerilla war was the last thing General Sherman wanted.

That evening, part of his army had come in contact with the rear guard of Confederate troops under Wade Hampton as they moved toward Raleigh. General Sherman himself headed infantry units on a more southerly course, trying to prevent Joe Johnston from retreating southward and escaping to fight a guerilla war, the alternative both President Lincoln and himself hoped to avoid.

The many warnings that President Lincoln had received regarding assassination attempts began to affect his sleep. During the second week of April, Lincoln told his friend Ward Lamon, his wife, and one or two others who were present, the details of a recent dream. It was a frightening dream; the president had kept the details to himself for a few days, but he wanted to talk about it because it was disturbing him. Because it had put him in such a grave and solemn mood, Mrs. Lincoln wanted to hear about the dream as much as her husband wanted to talk about it.

Lincoln began by explaining that he had gone to bed fairly late on the night of the dream, which had been about ten days earlier, after waiting up for dispatches from the front. When he finally did go to bed, he had a disturbed sleep and began dreaming. In the dream that had distressed him so much, Lincoln heard "subdued sobs," as though a number of people were crying.[18] It seemed to him that he got out of bed and went downstairs, where he heard "the same pitiful sobbing," but he could not see anyone sobbing. "I went from room to room; no living person

249

was in sight." But he kept hearing the same "mournful sounds of distress" everywhere he went. He kept on looking, trying to find out exactly what was taking place and why anyone should be sobbing and behaving so strangely, and finally found himself in the East Room.

Inside the East Room, he saw a catafalque, along with a corpse "wrapped in funeral vestments" and with its face covered. Soldiers were stationed around the catafalque, acting as guards, and a crowd of people stood by, "weeping pitifully." Lincoln asked one of the soldiers, "Who is dead in the White House?"

"The President," the soldier replied, "he was killed by an assassin." This was followed by "a large burst of grief" from the crowd, which woke Lincoln from his dream. He was not able to sleep any more that night, and remained "strangely annoyed" by the dream ever since.

Mrs. Lincoln was also frightened by the dream. "This is horrid!" she said. "I wish you had not told it." She went on to say that she was glad that she did not believe in dreams, or else she would be living "in terror from this time forth."

"Well," the president answered, "it is only a dream, Mary. Let us say no more about it and try to forget it." But the dream had badly frightened President Lincoln. Ward Lamon noticed that Lincoln seemed to be "grave, gloomy, and at times visibly pale" because of his nightmare. He also remembered that the president quoted from *Hamlet*, "to sleep, perchance to dream, ay, *there's the rub!*" with an accent on the last three words.

The story of President Lincoln's White House nightmare has been told many times, and has been included in a number of Lincoln biographies. It is worth retelling because it gives some insight into Abraham Lincoln's frame of mind during this point in time. He had his hopes and plans for the future of the country now that the war was nearly over, as well as his own ideas concerning reconstruction. But at the same time he also feared, and was even resigned to the possibility, that he would not live long enough to carry them out.

"MELANCHOLY SEEMED TO BE DRIPPING FROM HIM"

P resident Lincoln was not in the best of spirits on this particular morning; he was in another one of his weary and sad moods. In an attempt to cheer himself up, he decided to go for a horseback ride through Washington. It was certainly a nice day for it; the weather was perfect. A ride might help, and it certainly could not hurt.

On his way through town, the president happened to come across Assistant Secretary of the Treasury Maunsell B. Field, who was riding in a carriage along Fourteenth Street. Secretary Field recalled that he heard a "clatter" coming up from behind, and saw the president approaching on horseback, followed by "the usual cavalry escort."[1] President Lincoln drew alongside the carriage and carried on a casual conversation with Assistant Secretary Field. "I noticed that he was in one of those moods when 'melancholy seemed to be dripping from him,' and his eye had that expression of profound weariness and sadness which I never saw in other human eyes." After talking for a while, Lincoln "put his spurs to his horse" and rode off with his escort.

In spite of his melancholy mood, President Lincoln did accomplish some routine paperwork. He wrote three passes for travelers with business in Alabama and Virginia, and also approved a recommendation for the post of collector of Internal Revenue for a district in California. The most important business undertaken by the president was a meeting with Secretary of War Stanton and General U. S. Grant involving the reduction of the Union army. Because the meeting involved General Grant, it also turned out to be the most exciting business of the day.

General Ulysses S. Grant was the man of the hour. The only man in the country, or at least in the North, more popular than General Grant was President Lincoln himself. When the public found out that the general and his wife were guests at the Willard, which was the most prestigious hotel in Washington, a crowd began to form outside the main entrance and eventually surrounded the entire building. In order for General Grant to leave the hotel to keep his appointment with the president, the manager had to send for the police. A police escort arrived shortly, and accompanied the general through the streets of Washington to the War Department. General Grant's entrance certainly livened up what otherwise would have been a mundane meeting with the president and Secretary Stanton, and may even have given Lincoln a lift out of his doldrums.

The subject of the meeting would also have been encouraging for President Lincoln; it involved preparations for the final winding down of the war. The president, his general-in-chief, and his secretary of war discussed the demobilization of the army along with the limiting of the purchase of arms and ammunition, which was costing the government millions of dollars every day. Now that General Lee had surrendered, it was agreed that there would be no more major battles or campaigns, which meant that there would no longer be any need for major military expenditures. This was exactly what President Lincoln wanted to hear.

Among the Lincoln papers is a document headed "Memorandum Respecting Reduction of the Regular Army."[2] The document details how the army was to be reduced, how existing regiments would be scaled down, and how discharged officers and enlisted men would be paid off, according to their rank at the time of discharge. Lincoln used the War of 1812 as a precedent. "At the close of the last British war—in 1815—the Regular Army was reduced and fixed at 14,000," he wrote.

Later in the same day, Secretary Stanton issued an order "to stop drafting and recruiting, to curtail purchases, to reduce the number of general and staff officers, and to remove all military restrictions."[3] Demobilization was finally under way. But the organizing of the postwar army, which would have a maximum number of 76,000 men, would not begin until July 28, 1866. The president and General Grant were in full agreement over downsizing the army and taking all necessary steps toward planning a peacetime military force.

Four days after Appomattox, the residents of Washington were still celebrating. "The city became disorderly with the men who were celebrating too hilariously," according to William Crook.[4] Mrs. Grant received visitors all day long, all of whom offered their congratulations to her husband and herself. Visitors also came to see President Lincoln at the White House throughout the day, shaking his hand, offering their congratulations, and sometimes just stopping to say hello. Everyone in town seemed to be intoxicated—sometimes literally, giving every bar in Washington capacity business—but also mentally and emotionally. The entire city seemed to be breathing a collective sigh of relief.

Julia Grant was excited by the holiday atmosphere; "all the bells rang out merry greetings, and the city was literally swathed in flags and bunting," she would later remember.[5] Even Secretary of War Edwin Stanton, who was normally anything but the most cheerful person in the world, "was in his happiest mood." He took Mrs. Grant aside to show her a few war trophies: "many stands of arms, flags, and, among other things, a stump of a large tree perforated on all sides by bullets, taken from the field at Shiloh."

Mary Lincoln was also in a cheerful mood. "We are rejoicing beyond expression over our great and glorious victories," is what she said to the *New York Herald's* James Gordon Bennett.[6] Her son Robert was home from the front and her husband would no longer have the strain and anxiety of the war to tax his health. Abraham Lincoln was probably about thirty pounds underweight, and appeared gaunt and unhealthy to everyone who saw him. Now that the war was nearly over, Mrs. Lincoln hoped that her husband's health and well-being would soon return.

After sundown, the city was illuminated once again. "Last night, Washington was ablaze with glory," according to the *Evening Star*. "The very heavens seemed to have come down."[7] The illumination was as much a social event as it was a celebration. "All the great men of the nation who were necessarily in Washington at that time were assembled that night," Julia Grant remembered.[8] "Such congratulations, such friendly, grateful grasps of the hand and speeches of gratitude."

General Grant and his wife had a minor disagreement over whether Mrs. Grant would be accompanied to the illumination by Secretary and Mrs. Stanton or by her husband. General Grant wanted his wife to go with the Stantons, while he escorted Mrs. Lincoln. But Julia Grant told her husband that she would not go at all unless he went with her. The general came up with another suggestion: he would ride out with Julia to the Stanton residence, leave her at the house, and then come back to escort Mrs. Lincoln to the illumination—the president elected not to go to the light show, leaving General Grant in charge. This arrangement suited Mrs. Grant; the Grants, Mrs. Lincoln, and the Stantons all watched the light show together.

The celebrations and excitement did not seem to amuse William Crook, the president's bodyguard. But the fact that the war was nearly over helped to calm him and put his mind at ease. "Those about the President lost somewhat of the feeling, usually present, that his life was not safe," he said somewhat awkwardly.[9] "It did not seem possible that, now that the war was over and the government . . . had been so magnanimous in its treatment of General Lee, after President Lincoln had offered himself a target for Southern bullets in the streets of Richmond and had come out unscathed, there could be danger." Crook had allowed himself to relax after the president left Richmond, "and had forgotten to be anxious since." With Lee's army having surrendered, the threat of assassination also ended, at least to William Crook's way of thinking.

FORD'S THEATRE

MORNING

President Lincoln had a full day ahead of him, as well as a full evening. He was out of bed by about seven o'clock, and was at breakfast by eight. Mary joined him for breakfast, along with their son Robert. Captain Robert Lincoln had come to Washington along with General Grant and was full of stories about what he had seen and done as a member of the general-in-chief's staff. One of his stories was about the surrender at Appomattox—he had been standing on the porch of Wilmer McLean's house when General Lee surrendered. He also brought a portrait of General Lee to show his father, setting it on the breakfast table. After looking at the picture for a while, the president pronounced that it was a good face—he made no insulting or disparaging remarks about General Lee.

Father and son also discussed Robert's postwar plans. President Lincoln said that he would like to see Robert go back to Harvard to finish law school. After graduating from Harvard, Lincoln joked, there might be enough evidence to tell if young Robert would make a good lawyer or not.

After breakfast, the president went to his office to deal with the business of the day. He met with lame-duck senator John P. Hale of New Hampshire, who had been appointed minister to Spain; spoke with an attorney from Detroit named William Alanson Howard; and received a visit from California congressman Cornelius Cole. President Lincoln also had an extended discussion with Speaker of the House Schuyler Colfax, although no one took any notes of this conversation. Speaker Colfax was interested in becoming a member of Lincoln's cabinet.

Among the messages President Lincoln sent were notes to Secretary of State William Seward and General Grant on the same subject: that day's cabinet meeting. He contacted Secretary Seward, "please assemble the Cabinet at 11 A.M. today," and requested that General Grant come at eleven o'clock instead of nine o'clock, as he had previously instructed.[1] The general was slightly upset by the president's note. He had been planning to leave for Burlington, New Jersey, with his wife to visit their children and was afraid that the two-hour postponement might prevent him from leaving Washington on time.

The cabinet meeting started on time. Frederick Seward, who was also assistant secretary of state, took his father's place at the meeting. William Seward was still too incapacitated by his injuries to attend. Everyone was anxious to meet General Grant. When the president shook the general's hand, the cabinet members broke into spontaneous applause. Grant was the hero of the hour, even to Secretary of War Stanton and Secretary of the Navy Welles, who could very well have been jaded by such an occasion.

President Lincoln sat at the head of the conference table, sitting sideways to make room for his long legs, and began the proceedings by asking the group if they had any news from General William Tecumseh Sherman in North Carolina. General Grant replied that he had not heard any recent news from General Sherman, which meant that General Joseph E. Johnston and his army were still at large. But he added that he was expecting word from North Carolina at any moment.

The president said he was sure they would be receiving news of

General Johnston's surrender very soon—he was certain of this, he said, because the night before he had had "the usual dream" that had always preceded good news. He had had the same dream several times before, he explained; it had come before nearly every successful battle and every great event that had taken place during the war: "Generally, the news had been favorable which succeeded the dream, and the dream itself was always the same."[2]

Secretary Welles asked about the nature of the president's dream. The president explained that it involved Welles's element, namely water. He went on to give details about his dream—that he seemed to be on board "some singular, indescribable vessel" that was moving very quickly toward an unknown destination on an indefinite shore.[3] The same dream had occurred to him before, he said, and it had always come before some "great and important event"—Antietam, Gettysburg, Stone River, and Vicksburg. General Grant interrupted to say that Stone River was no victory, and that "a few such fights would have ruined us." The president did not seem to be discouraged by General Grant's remarks, and repeated that everyone could expect some very good news soon. "I think it must be from Sherman," he said. "My thoughts are in that direction, as are most of yours." He was certainly right about that particular point—General Sherman and Joe Johnston were very much on everyone's mind.

The next topic of discussion was the restoration of Virginia and North Carolina to the Union. Secretary of War Stanton introduced a plan for reestablishing civilian rule to the Southern states. His idea would combine both Virginia and North Carolina into a single military department, which would be administered by the War Department. Secretary Welles objected that Virginia already had a legitimate state government under Governor Francis Pierpont, and reminded the president and the other members of the cabinet that "we had recognized and sustained him."[4] In North Carolina, on the other hand, "a legal government was now to be organized and the State reestablished in her proper relations with the Union." In other words, the two states should be dealt with individually, not lumped together.

President Lincoln remarked that the readmission of the Southern states "was a great question now before us,"[5] and added that he was glad Congress was not in session to interfere with the exertion and labor of reassembling the country after four years of war—"and there were none of the disturbing elements of that body to hinder and embarrass us," is the way Lincoln phrased it.[6]

Frederick Seward also had a few suggestions for the cabinet, speaking for his father. He explained that although it was extremely painful for the secretary of state to speak, he had managed to give young Frederick a number of ideas and recommendations before he left the house that morning. One item that Frederick's father wanted his son to mention was his idea that the War Department should occupy all forts throughout the Southern states, or destroy them if they were of no use to the army. Other items involving the readmission of seceded states to the Union included: turning all customs houses in Southern ports over to the US Treasury Department, which would also collect all revenues; taking possession of all Southern navy yards, including any Confederate naval vessels and warships; reestablishing post offices and postal districts throughout the South; and the reappointing of judges throughout the Southern states by the US attorney general.

All of these were good, sound ideas. The president realized that such measures would be necessary for the seceded states to be readmitted to the Union—the remnants of the Confederate army and navy needed to be dismantled, the courts and postal districts had to be restored, and a thousand other items would have to be addressed. But all of these things would have to be discussed and debated by the cabinet members, and President Lincoln knew all of the members well enough to realize that they would have their own thoughts and ideas for the items Secretary Seward had suggested. These ideas would be taken up at another meeting, where they would be given more study and consideration.

The topic of Confederate leaders, and what to do about them, was also brought up. President Lincoln's reaction to this question was the same as it had been previously. "I hope that there will be no persecution, no bloody work after the war is over," he said.[7] "No one need expect me to take any part in hanging or killing these men, even the worst of them." As he had also said before, he would not be disappointed if all the Confederate heads of government left the country. In fact, he would be more than happy if they departed and never came back. "Frighten them out of the country, open the gates, let down the bars, scare them off," shaking his hands "as if scaring sheep." He then came to his main point, telling the cabinet members, "enough lives have been sacrificed." There would never be any "harmony or union" unless old grievances and resentments could be forgotten.

Secretary of War Stanton had already discovered that the president meant what he said about opening the gates and letting them all go. Shortly after Appomattox, Stanton received a report that Jacob Thompson, a former US Congressman who had been the head of a secret Confederate delegation to Canada, was preparing to sail for England. Thompson had also organized raids across the Canadian border on towns in the United States, including a raid on St. Albans, Vermont, in October 1864, which resulted in the robbery of three banks, one St. Albans resident killed and another wounded, and the destruction of one building. "He had been organizing all sorts of trouble and getting up raids, of which the notorious attack on St. Albans, Vt., was a specimen," according to one source in the War Department.[8] Secretary Stanton did not share the president's sympathy for all Confederate leaders, and ordered Thompson to be captured and placed under arrest. But before his assistant secretary of war, Charles Dana, could leave the room, Stanton changed his mind. "No, wait," he said, "better go over and see the President."

Charles Dana went to the White House to see the president, and found him sitting in his office. "Halloo, Dana!" he said. "What is it? What's up?"[9] Dana told the president about Jacob Thompson's plans to leave the country for England, and also about Secretary Stanton wanting to have him arrested. He went on to say that Stanton decided to defer to the president's judgement before arresting Thompson. And the president's judgement was that Jacob Thompson should be allowed to leave the country. "When you have got an elephant by the hind leg and he's trying to run away, it's best to let him run." From President Lincoln's point of view, he would have one less problem to deal with Thompson on the other side of the Atlantic Ocean.

The remainder of the meeting was mainly concerned with restoring civilian rule to the former Confederate states. President Lincoln was adamant that the states would have to govern themselves, although the army might be needed to protect the new Unionist administration in some states. Voting rights for freed black slaves was also brought up, but was an issue that would require extensive discussion and deliberation, and so was deferred to a future meeting.

Before leaving the White House, Frederick Seward reminded Lincoln that a new British minister, Sir Frederick Bruce, had recently arrived in Washington and was awaiting his formal presentation to the president. The assistant secretary of state asked if the next day would be convenient for the appointment; President Lincoln replied that tomorrow at two o'clock would be fine. In the Blue Room? The president agreed to young Seward's suggestion. The British minister would be meeting President Lincoln the next day, Saturday, April 15, at two p.m. in the Blue Room.

AFTERNOON

At about 2:00 p.m., the meeting finally came to an end. Everyone stood up; some shook hands. All the cabinet members agreed that they should reconvene on the following Tuesday, April 18, to resume their discussion.

General Grant approached the president to shake his hand and exchange a few pleasantries, even though small talk was not really Grant's strong point. President Lincoln asked the general if he and Mrs. Grant would like to go to the theater that night—he and Mrs. Lincoln were going to Ford's Theatre to see the comedy *Our American Cousin*, and would love to have the Grants as their guests. But General Grant was not enthusiastic about the invitation. He did not want to go to the theater, and did not want to make any sort of public appearance—he was embarrassed by the outbursts of excitement and enthusiasm whenever he appeared in public. Also, Julia Grant had seen and heard enough of Mary Lincoln during their time together at City Point, and he knew that he wife did not want to go with the Lincolns, either.

Luckily, General Grant had a convenient excuse for declining the president's invitation. "The general said he would be very sorry to have to decline," Colonel Horace Porter recalled, "but that Mrs. Grant and he had made arrangements to go to Burlington, New Jersey, to see their children."[10] The Grants kept a house at 309 Wood Street, Burlington, and planned to leave Washington to visit their children in Burlington later that day. Going to Ford's Theatre would delay their departure for Burlington, the general explained, which would be a great frustration for Mrs. Grant. President Lincoln was disappointed by the general's refusal.

Julia Grant also received an invitation to go to Ford's Theatre that night. Her invitation had come by a messenger that may or may not have been sent by Mary Lincoln. As soon as she received the invitation, she immediately sent a note to her husband giving him two instructions: "that I did not want to go to the theater; that he must take me home."[11] Mrs. Grant was adamant about not going to the theater that night, and she wanted her husband to know it: "I not only wrote to him, but sent three of the staff officers who called to pay their respects to me to urge the General to go home that night."

Julia Grant not only did not like the tone of the invitation—she thought it "seemed like a command" instead of a request—but had also been taken aback by the look of the messenger. The man who brought the message was not dressed like someone who had been sent by the first lady but seemed a little too casual and even a bit sloppy in his dress—he wore "light-colored corduroy coat and trousers and with a rather shabby hat of the same color." The strange-looking messenger said, "Mrs. Lincoln sends me, madam, with her compliments, to say that she will call for you at exactly eight o'clock to go to the theater."

She replied, "with some feeling" in her voice, "You may return with my compliments to Mrs. Lincoln and say I regret that as General Grant and I intend leaving the city this afternoon, we will not therefore be here to accompany the president and Mrs. Lincoln to the theatre." The man hesitated for a moment before replying, "Madam, the papers announce that General Grant will be with the President tonight at the theater."

Mrs. Grant was not moved by this argument. "You may deliver my message to Mrs. Lincoln as I have given it to you," she said, probably with some impatience. "You may go." With that, the messenger turned and left.

Julia Grant was highly suspicious of the man in the corduroy suit and the shabby hat, and had the idea that he had not been sent by Mrs. Lincoln. "I have thought since that this man was one of the band of conspirators in that night's sad tragedy," she would write many years after the event.

General Grant was very glad to receive his wife's note. When he first declined the president's invitation, Lincoln replied that "people would be so delighted to see the general that he ought to stay and attend the play on that account."[12] The public's enthusiasm was one of the main reasons that Grant did not want to attend. Newspapers had, in fact, run announcements of General Grant's appearance at the theater. The *Evening Star* ran this item: "Lieut. General Grant, President and Mrs. Lincoln have secured the State Box at Ford's Theatre tonight to witness Miss Laura Keene's American Cousin."[13]

But Julia Grant's note very nicely deflated President Lincoln's objections. According to Colonel Horace Porter, "A note was now brought to [General Grant] from Mrs. Grant expressing increased anxiety to start for Burlington on the four o'clock train, and he told the President that he must decide definitely not to remain for the play."[14] When the president saw what Mrs. Grant had written, he realized that he would not be able to persuade General Grant to change his plans or to go against Julia Grant's wishes.

The Grants refusal to attend the theater left the Lincolns with the problem of who else they might be able to invite. The Stantons were asked to come, but Secretary Stanton declined on the grounds that the president ought to stay at home and did not want to encourage the Lincolns to go out that night—he was afraid that some fanatical Confederate might take a shot at Lincoln on his way to the theater. Also, Mrs. Stanton did not like Mary Lincoln any more than Julia Grant did. Governor Richard J. Oglesby of Illinois was also invited; he replied that he had a meeting that evening and could not get away. The governor of the Idaho Territory, William H. Wallace, also declined, as did Major Thomas T. Eckert, chief of the War Department's telegraph bureau— Secretary Stanton objected that Major Eckert was required for duty at the telegraph office. The Marquis de Chambrun was also invited but, according to his son Adelbert, excused himself on religious grounds— a devout Catholic, he did not want to attend a theatrical performance on Good Friday. Major Henry R. Rathbone, an acquaintance of the Lincolns, and his fiancée Clara Harris, the daughter of New York senator Ira Harris, were invited later in the afternoon, and accepted. The Lincolns would pick them up at Miss Harris's home on H Street. They had finally found another couple to make up their theater party.

When General Grant went back to the Willard after the cabinet meeting, his wife told him all about an incident that had happened at lunch. Mrs. Grant seemed very upset by what had happened. She and a friend, along with two of their children, had been sitting in a restaurant when four men came in and sat opposite them. Mrs. Grant thought one of the men was "the messenger of the morning."[15] Another was "a dark, pale man" who played with his soup spoon, "sometimes filling it and holding it half-lifted to his mouth, but never tasting it." The pale man seemed very intent on listening to everything that Mrs. Grant and her party were saying. Mrs. Grant was becoming frightened, and said to her friend, "I believe they are part of Mosby's guerillas and they have been listening to every word we have said."

General Grant did not seen to be fazed at all by his wife's story, or by the fact that these men stared at her and listened to her conversation. "Oh, I suppose he did so merely from curiosity," he said.[16] By this time, the general had become so used to being stared at and annoyed in public that he tended to shrug off such incidents. If Mrs. Grant had told her story to Secretary of War Stanton, who was always worrying about assassination plots and kidnapping attempts, his reaction would not have been nearly as nonchalant.

Later in the afternoon, at about 3:30, a similar incident occurred. The Grants, along with the wife of General Daniel S. Rucker, were riding in a carriage when "the same dark, pale man" rode past and stared at them. The rider galloped about twenty yards ahead of the carriage, then wheeled around and turned back. As he passed the carriage for the second time, "he thrust his face near the General's and glared in a disagreeable manner."[17] Grant was startled by this, and quickly drew back from the man. "This is the same man who sat down at the lunch-table near me," Mrs. Grant said. "I don't like his looks."[18]

The general did not like them either, but he said something casual about the incident to put his wife's mind at ease. In his memoirs, he does not even mention the incident. But in 1878, General Grant told reporter John Russell Young that he "learned afterward that the horseman was [John Wilkes] Booth."[19] The general did not say how he managed to acquire this information, or exactly how long afterward he had acquired it.

From his headquarters in Raleigh, North Carolina, General William Tecumseh Sherman read the Raleigh newspapers to keep informed of General Joseph E. Johnston's movements. He was preparing to cut off General Johnston's "only available line of retreat by Salisbury and Char-lotte," and expected that General Philip Sheridan would come down from Virginia to join him "with his superb cavalry corps."[20] General Sherman was getting ready for the possibility of another battle, and reasoned that he would be needing more cavalry when the time came. But because "the war was substantially over," to use his turn of phrase, General Sherman ordered his men not to wage war against the civilian population. "No further destruction of railroads, mills, cotton, and produce will be made without the specific orders of an army com-mander," General Sherman ordered, "and the inhabitants will be dealt with kindly, looking to an early reconciliation." This was from the general who had led his men on a march of destruction from Atlanta to the sea and ruined everything they passed. Sherman had paid attention to what President Lincoln had to say about reunification and reconcili-ation aboard the *River Queen* at City Point.

Shortly after issuing this order, General Sherman received a message from General Johnston. The message, dated April 13, dealt with the subject of surrender. "The results of the recent campaign in Virginia have changed the relative military condition of the belligerents," General Johnston's communiqué began.[21] "I am, therefore, induced to address you in this form the inquiry whether, to stop the further effusion of blood and devastation of property, you are willing to make a temporary suspension of active operations, and to communicate to Lieutenant-General Grant, commanding the armies of the United States, the request that he will take like action in regard to other armies, the object being to permit the civil authorities to enter into the needful arrangements to terminate the existing war."

General Sherman replied that he was "fully empowered" to arrange any suspension of hostilities between the two armies, and that he would "be willing to confer with you to that end."[22] He also stated that he would "undertake to abide by the same terms and conditions as were made by Generals Grant and Lee at Appomattox Court-House," and ended on a note that would have earned the full approval of President Lincoln: "I will add that I really desire to save the people of North Carolina the damage they would sustain by the march of this army through the central or western parts of the State."

Word of General Johnston's surrender communiqué, and of General Sherman's response to it, did not reach Washington that day. General Sherman sent his reply in the form of a letter, and had it delivered by messenger. When President Lincoln dropped in at the War Department's telegraph office, he asked Secretary Stanton if there had been any news from North Carolina. Stanton indicated that there had been no communication from General Sherman.

Early on Friday afternoon, a flag-raising ceremony was held at Fort Sumter, in Charleston harbor. Exactly four years earlier, on April 14, 1961, Major Robert Anderson had surrendered the fort to Confederate General P. G. T. Beauregard. On this Good Friday, Robert Anderson, now a general, raised the same flag over the recaptured fort in an elaborate ceremony. An estimated three thousand people were in attendance, including senators, congressmen, judges, and other dignitaries. The well-known orator Reverend Henry Ward Beecher delivered the somber keynote address, which ended, "in the name of God, we lift our banner and dedicate it to Peace, Union, and Liberty, now and forever more. Amen."[23]

The entire ceremony revolved around the raising of the flag, which was performed by General Anderson. The general made a short speech, which began, "After four long, long years of war, I restore to its proper place this flag which floated here during peace, before the first act of this cruel Rebellion."[24] Immediately afterward, three sailors attached the flag to the halyards, and General Anderson raised it to the top of the flagstaff—"with a firm and steady pull ran aloft the old flag," according to one onlooker.[25] "No sooner had it caught the breeze than there was one tumultuous shout. . . . Our flag was there, its crimson folds tattered, but not dishonored, regenerated and baptized anew in the fires of Liberty." When the flag reached the top of the staff, it was saluted by one hundred guns from Fort Sumter itself, along with the batteries of Fort Moultre and other forts that were "conspicuous in the inauguration of the rebellion." The audience cheered, applauded, cried, and sang "The Star-Spangled Banner."

The speeches and activities at Fort Sumter, including the flag raising, were meant to bring closure to the war, along with a tidy and conclusive end to it—four years to the day after the war began, it came to an end in the same place. "If Lincoln had lived," a historian commented many years later, "every textbook in American history would have shown the flag raising at Fort Sumter as the conclusion of the war. That's what it was meant to be."[26] The ceremony had been arranged to mark a final end to the war, an end to the fighting and the beginning of reconstruction and reunification. But events would not turn out to be as neat and conclusive as many people had hoped.

Vice-President Andrew Johnson had an appointment to meet with the president at the White House on Friday afternoon, but no exact time had been set. President Lincoln had asked Johnson to come sometime during the early afternoon, after the cabinet meeting had ended. But when the vice-president showed up for his appointment, a guard informed him that the cabinet meeting was still in session. Vice-President Johnson replied that he would stay within the White House grounds and keep himself available until the president was ready to see him.

Andrew Johnson had actually been waiting to see President Lincoln since Inauguration Day. He tried to arrange appointments several times but had never actually been able to talk to the president. But now the president had asked to see *him*. He waited for the cabinet meeting to end, and for Lincoln to call him into his office.

Abraham Lincoln neither liked nor disliked Andrew Johnson, although his embarrassing performance at the inauguration, called a "detestable discourse" by the Marquis de Chambrun,[27] did not help to enhance Lincoln's opinion of him. In common with most presidents before and since, President Lincoln tended to pay very little attention to his second-in-command and did not give him any jobs or assignments that might have made him a more useful member of the government. He also never asked Johnson to attend a cabinet meeting. In June 1864, when members of the Republican National Convention asked President Lincoln for advice on selecting a running mate—whether or not Johnson should replace Hannibal Hamlin, his current vice-president, on the ticket—Lincoln's reply was entirely noncommittal. "Wish not to interfere about V.P.," he said. "Can not interfere about platform. Convention must judge for itself."[28] Although Andrew Johnson might make a good candidate, Lincoln would not endorse him but also would not reject him.

After the Republican delegates went through their preliminaries, and had a roll-call vote to select their vice-presidential candidate, Andrew Johnson won by a large majority. The delegates were informed of the results of the roll-call vote by an official announcement. "Gentlemen of the convention—Andrew Johnson, having received a majority of all the votes, is declared duly nominated candidate of the National Union Party for the Vice-Presidency."[29] (The Republican Party was calling itself the National Union Party to accommodate War Democrats who supported Lincoln's war policy.) The Republican/National Union Party now had a coalition ticket: a Republican presidential candidate running in an alliance with a Democratic vice-presidential candidate. If all went according to plan, enough Republicans and War Democrats would vote for Lincoln/Johnson to outvote the Democratic candidate, George B. McClellan. "The selection for the Vice-Presidency strikes dismay into the ranks of the Copperheads," according to one account that disapproved of the Copperheads, or Peace Democrats, "who feel that it has strengthened the Union cause tremendously."[30]

President Lincoln hoped that a War Democrat would reinforce the Republican ticket and would improve his chances of being reelected. He had the feeling that the coming election was going to be close and that he was going to need all the help he could get. But he never sent Andrew Johnson a telegram to congratulate him on his nomination. As far as he was concerned, Johnson was on the ticket for the sole purpose of getting votes.

Their meeting on April 14 began after the cabinet meeting ended and after the president had lunch with Mary Lincoln. President Lincoln welcomed "Andy," shook his hand enthusiastically, and ushered him into the office. The two of them conferred for about twenty minutes. Not much is known about what took place during their conversation, but the main topic was probably reconstruction and the reunification of the country—the two most pressing concerns on the president's mind, now that General Lee had surrendered and General Johnston was about to. It is likely that the president advised Johnson of the proceedings of that morning's cabinet meeting.[31]

The conversation between President Lincoln and Vice-President Johnson was too short to be anything but superficial, but at least it gave the new vice-president some insight into what Lincoln had in mind for the future. When the president finished saying what he had to say, the two men shook hands again and the president ushered Johnson out of his office. Vice-President Johnson left the White House, and President Lincoln went back to work.

The president attended to several official chores. He accepted the resignation of a supreme court justice from the territory of Idaho and recommended his successor, he endorsed the release of a prisoner from Point Lookout prison in Maryland, and he endorsed several appointees in the state of Maryland, including postmaster, surveyor, and district attorney. The piece of business that probably meant most to him involved the issuing of passes to Richmond, which he ruled would no longer be necessary. "No pass is necessary now to authorize any one to go & return from Petersburg & Richmond. People go & return just as they did before the war."[32] It was a sign that life was finally beginning to return to normal.

The president also had an unscheduled conversation with Nancy Bushrod sometime during the afternoon. Nancy Bushrod and her husband, Tom, had been slaves on what is usually described as "the old Harwood plantation near Richmond."[33] When they heard about the Emancipation Proclamation, they left the plantation and came to Washington with their three children. Tom joined the army a short time afterward and always sent his pay back home to his wife. The money arrived regularly every month, until recently, when it had suddenly stopped. Nancy had twin boys and a baby girl to look after, and she now had no money to support them. Her children were crying from hunger, and she made up her mind to see President Lincoln about her predicament. On the afternoon of April 14, she came to the White House to ask the president if he could help her to get her husband's army pay.

At the White House, two sets of guards tried to keep Nancy from seeing the president, telling her that he was busy and that it was against orders to let her pass. But all the shouting between Nancy and the soldiers had its desired effect—"All of a sudden de do' open, an' Mistah Linkun stood lookin' at me." The president said to the soldiers, "There is time for all who need me. Let the good woman come in."

The president listened to what Nancy Bushrod had to say for about fifteen minutes. After sitting on the other side of the desk and hearing her story through, he said, "You are entitled to your soldier-husband's pay. Come this time tomorrow, and the papers will be signed and ready for you." Nancy thanked the president profusely; Lincoln simply bowed, and went back to a desk piled high with work. Nancy Bushrod lived to be more than eighty years of age, and never tired of telling the story of the day she met Abraham Lincoln.

The president and Mary Lincoln took a carriage ride out to the Navy Yard at about 5:00 p.m. The president wanted to be alone with his wife for a while and did not want anyone else to come along. He also just wanted to get out of the city, if even for only a couple of hours. At the Navy Yard, President Lincoln went aboard the monitor USS *Montauk*, which was still showing battle scars from her part in the attack on Charleston in 1863. The *Montauk*'s crew was glad to see him; the president took time to speak with several of them.

Lincoln was in a good mood and had been since morning. During the cabinet meeting, several members commented on how cheerful he seemed to be—almost unnaturally happy, considering his usually melancholy disposition. His happy mood continued into the afternoon, which came as a surprise to Mary. "Dear husband," she told him, "you almost startle me with your great cheerfulness."[34]

"And well I may feel so, Mary," he replied, and went on to explain, "I consider *this day* the war has come to a close."[35] After a moment, he said, "We must *both* be more cheerful in the future—between the war and the loss of our darling Willie, we have both been very miserable." He was certainly more than correct about that: the strain of the war, added to their personal problems, had combined to make them both very miserable indeed.

President Lincoln also talked about the future, especially about life after he left the White House in four years. He wanted to travel, to go to Europe, where he would be welcomed as a senior American statesman. He and Mary might even to go Jerusalem, which he had always wanted to see. They would also take a trip across the United States—visit some of the western states and ride out to California. After taking a long and much-needed rest, the Lincolns would go back to Springfield, where Lincoln would return to his law practice. The years ahead looked to be peaceful and prosperous, giving them both something to look forward to. "He longed, a little wistfully, for that time to come with its promise of peace," Mary mentioned to William Crook.[36]

The president and Mary returned to the White House for dinner and discovered that they had two visitors, both old friends of President Lincoln: General Isham Haynie and Governor Richard J. Oglesby, both from Illinois. Mary Lincoln allowed the three men to withdraw to Lincoln's office, where he proceeded to read passages from one of his favorite books, the comical *Nasby Letters*, written by David R. Locke under the pseudonym Petroleum Vesuvius Nasby. Reverend Nasby was an ardent Confederate supporter, who found life in the Confederate army dreary and decided to desert. Everyone enjoyed the Nasby jokes, especially the president himself, who kept on reading until it was time for dinner. Lincoln invited his friends to join him, but they both said they had previous engagements and would see him again soon.

Dinner was served earlier than usual that day, to allow the Lincolns to get to Ford's Theatre on time. Mary complained of a headache and said that she would rather not go out, but the president insisted, telling her that it would be good to get out and have a laugh. Also, he added, another night at home would not be either quiet or enjoyable—he would have callers all evening. Mary changed her mind and agreed to see the comedy with her husband.

After dinner, President Lincoln walked over to the War Department with William Crook to meet with Secretary of War Stanton. Crook mentions only that they went to the War Department "late on the afternoon of the 14th."[37] By that time the president's mood had changed dramatically, from happiness to depression. "I found that the President was more depressed than I had ever seen him and his step unusually slow," Crook observed. "I had heard of the transitions from almost wild spirits to abject melancholy which marked him . . . I wondered at him that day and felt uneasy."

On their short walk to the War Department, Lincoln said something that both upset and frightened Crook. "I believe there are men who want to take my life," he said, half to himself. "And I have no doubt they will do it."

William Crook was as alarmed by the president's straightforward tone of voice as by the statement itself. "Why do you think so, Mr. Lincoln?" was all he could say in response. "Other men have been assassinated," Lincoln said, unemotionally. The only response Crook could make was, "I hope you are mistaken, Mr. President."

The two of them walked a few paces in silence before President Lincoln spoke again. "I have perfect confidence in those who around me—in every one of you men," he said. "I know no one could do it and escape alive. But if it is to be done, it is impossible to prevent it."

They had arrived at the War Department by that time. President Lincoln went inside for his conference with Secretary Stanton, which was shorter than Crook expected. When he had come out of Stanton's office, Crook noticed that all the depression in the president's face had disappeared. He informed Crook in a normal tone of voice that he and Mrs. Lincoln were going to the theater that evening to see *Our American Cousin*. "It has been advertised that we will be there," he said, "and I cannot disappoint the people. Otherwise I would not go. I do not want to go."

Crook was surprised to hear this. He knew how much Lincoln loved the theater, and it seemed very unusual to hear him say that he did not want to go. When the two of them returned to the White House the president paused for a moment before going in. Crook said goodnight. "Good-bye, Crook," the president answered. This struck Crook as very strange—President Lincoln had always said "Good night, Crook" before. He walked home feeling "queer and sad."

President Lincoln found Speaker of the House Schuyler Colfax waiting for him when he entered the White House. Colfax wanted to know if the president had any intention of calling Congress back into session during the summer months, and seemed greatly relieved when Lincoln said that he had no such intention. This meant that Speaker Colfax would be free to take his planned trip to the west coast. Lincoln envied him the trip—he wished that he could go himself. Before he left, Speaker Colfax mentioned how nervous and anxious he had been when the president had gone to Richmond. Lincoln joked that he would also have been alarmed if anyone but himself had been president and had gone to Richmond. But since he had made the trip, he was not afraid about himself at all.

When Schuyler Colfax left, Congressman George Ashmun of Massachusetts was waiting to see the president on behalf of a friend who had a claim against the government. Lincoln was in no mood to hear about anybody's claims against the government and let the congressman know his feelings in an angry tone of voice. But when he saw that his angry response had offended Ashmun, he changed his manner

274

and said that he would make an appointment to see the congressman first thing in the morning. He took a card from his pocket and wrote, "April 14, 1865—Allow Mr. Ashmun & friend to come in at 9 A.M. to-morrow" and signed it.[38]

President Lincoln walked out onto the White House porch, where he joined Schuyler Colfax, Noah Brooks, and his wife. Brooks thought the president "was full of fun and anecdotes, feeling especially jubilant at the prospect before us."[39] He spoke about the country's future, mentioning that General Grant thought it possible to reduce the cost of maintaining the army by at least a half million dollars per day, which would reduce the national debt and help the economy to recover at a fairly rapid pace. While President Lincoln was talking, his carriage pulled up. At about the same time, former congressman Isaac N. Arnold arrived to have a word with the president. Arnold was an old friend and political ally, but Lincoln did not have time to talk at that precise moment. He excused himself, explained that he was on his way to the theater, and asked Arnold to come back in the morning.

EVENING

Before driving to Ford's Theatre, the Lincolns stopped at H Street to pick up Major Henry Rathbone and his fiancée, Clara Harris. On their way to the theater, Clara and Mrs. Lincoln had a pleasant conversation. The carriage had been escorted by two cavalrymen during the short trip. When the president and his party arrived at Ford's Theatre, the cavalrymen rode back to their barracks. Another escort would arrive in time to take the Lincolns and their guests back home after the play ended.

The performance had already started when the presidential party entered the theater at about 8:30. The conductor of the orchestra immediately stopped the show and struck up, "Hail to the Chief." The audience spontaneously rose to their feet and cheered, as the president walked slowly toward the state box, trailing behind Mary Lincoln and their two guests. He could not be seen very well by the audience; the corridor leading to the box was narrow and not very well lighted. When he reached the box, President Lincoln looked down and acknowledged the cheers and applause of the crowd by smiling and bowing to them.

The front of the box had been decorated with red, white, and blue bunting, along with the regimental flag of the Treasury Guard and a portrait of George Washington. After the Lincolns and their guests sat down, the audience could not see anyone in the state box—they were seated too far back to be seen from below. The president made it even more difficult by leaning back in an upholstered rocking chair, which the management of the theater had provided for his comfort. Most of the people in attendance had come to see the president, not the show; scalpers were charging $2.50 for tickets that normally sold for $0.75 to $1.00, and the house was nearly sold out. Many had hoped to see General Grant, as well. But everyone was very glad to see President Lincoln and more than happy to pay the inflated ticket prices just to get a glimpse of him.

Our American Cousin is a three-act British farce by Tom Taylor. The plot revolves around Asa Trenchard's visit to his relatives in England, where has gone to claim his inheritance. Asa Trenchard, the American cousin, is an awkward country bumpkin; his English relatives are aristocratic snobs and are generally not very bright. The play had first been performed in the United States in 1858 and was very well received—it had played for five consecutive months in New York.[40] Laura Keene, the well-known British actress, played the part of Florence Trenchard, the daughter of the patrician family. For this particular performance, new lines were added to bring the script up to date. One of the new exchanges occurred when a character complained about sitting too close to a drafty window: "If you please, ask the dairy maid to let me have a seat in the dairy. I am afraid of the draft here." Lord Dundreary responds, "Don't be alarmed. The draft has already been stopped by order of the President."[41]

Everyone seemed to be enjoying the play, including the Lincolns and their guests. Mary Lincoln frequently applauded the action down on stage, and the president laughed out loud whenever a line struck him as particularly funny. He would occasionally lean forward, which made him visible to the audience. Whenever this would happen, everyone would stop looking at the stage and turn toward the president's box. There was no doubt in anyone's mind that Abraham Lincoln was the star at Ford's Theatre that night.

Mary Lincoln was glad that her husband was having a good time, particularly after such a long and active day, and "seemed to take great pleasure in his enjoyment."[42] But the president's official duties did not end just because he happened to be at the theater. During an intermission, a message from the War Department was delivered to the president at his box. President Lincoln read the telegram and decided that his response could wait until morning. The sudden appearance of the messenger startled Clara Harris; she had not expected anyone to call on the president while he was at the theater.

The president saw Henry Rathbone take Clara's hand during the performance. Inspired by his guest's example, he decided to follow suit and took Mary's hand. She leaned close to her husband and whispered, "What will Miss Harris think of my hanging on to you so?" The president smiled and said, "She won't think anything about it."[43]

The performance carried on toward the play's inevitable happy ending. During the third act, when the comedy was nearly over, a loud noise came from the president's box. Afterward, people in the audience recalled that it was more of a "crack" than a "bang." Nobody thought that it was a gunshot. Immediately after the strange noise, which happened at about 10:13, a man with a knife in his hand jumped out of the box and landed on the stage. It was not a clean jump—the spur on his right boot caught on the Treasury Guard flag, which caused the man to land heavily on his left foot. He fell forward on his hands, got up, shouted something at the audience—some thought it was "Sic semper tyrannis," others thought it was "The South is avenged"—and limped off into the wings.[44]

The audience had no idea what had happened. Some of the spectators thought that something special had been added to the performance, an unusual bit of stage business to mark the president's appearance. Quite a few people recognized John Wilkes Booth as the man who jumped out of the Lincolns' box. Booth was very well known to the theater-going public, and had appeared at Ford's Theatre on any number of occasions. But when he landed on the stage, the performance came to a dead stop—none of the actors seemed to know what was happening either.

There was just as much confusion in the president's box. Mrs. Lincoln turned toward her husband when she heard the noise. Major Rathbone stood up and tried to stop the intruder. John Wilkes Booth dropped his derringer, drew a dagger, and stabbed the major in the arm, slashing it to the bone. Booth forced his way past Rathbone, shouted something about revenge for the South, and jumped over the edge of the box onto the stage. Major Rathbone shouted for someone to stop him. Mary Lincoln finally realized what had happened and began shrieking, "They have shot the President! They have shot the President!"[45]

The audience was also now aware of what had happened. Most people were on their feet. Some tried to leave the theater. Some wandered up onto the stage. From the stage, Laura Keene shouted for everyone to keep calm. But everyone was too excited to pay any attention. Some made their way out onto the street and began spreading the word that the president had been shot.

Charles A. Leale, a young army surgeon, managed to reach the president in spite of the chaos and found Lincoln slumped over in his rocking chair. He ordered some soldiers who were standing outside the box to lay President Lincoln on the floor, and began an examination to find the wound. The doctor was looking for a knife wound—he had heard someone say something about seeing a man with a knife and knew that Major Rathbone had been attacked with a knife. But after removing the president's shirt and undershirt, he could not find any sign of a knife wound. Dr. Leale looked at the president's head, and found the bullet wound that had been made by John Wilkes Booth's derringer.

The bullet—actually a .44 caliber lead ball—had entered the president's skull behind the left ear and had gone through the brain toward the right eye. "The ball entered through the occipital bone about one inch to the left of the median line," according to an autopsy report written by Dr. J. J. Woodward on April 15.[46] Dr. Leale examined the wound to determine if the lead ball had exited the skull, and found that it had not—it was still lodged in the brain.

The doctor cleared the blood clot that was forming around the bullet wound, which relieved pressure on the brain. Next, he opened the president's mouth and opened up his airway, so that he could breathe more easily. Another army surgeon, Dr. Charles Taft, was also admitted into the box. He assisted Dr. Leale by raising and lowering the president's arms while Dr. Leale administered artificial respiration. The two doctors soon had President Lincoln breathing again, but he did not regain consciousness. Both Dr. Leale and Dr. Taft agreed that the president's wound was mortal.[47]

While the doctors were doing their best to save President Lincoln, several other people had come into the president's box. Clara Harris was doing her best to comfort Mrs. Lincoln, Laura Keene had also entered the box, and a young obstetrician named Albert King had also managed to find his way to the president's side. It was evident that President Lincoln had to be moved out of this crowded setting. Dr. Leale ordered six soldiers to carry the president out of the box. They carried him down the stairs and out into the street. There was some discussion over where the president should be taken. Dr. Leale decided that moving him to the White House was out of the question. His concern was "that with the jostling in the street going back to the White House, they could have made the injuries far worse because the bullet was still in the brain, potentially bouncing around."[48] Instead, he was taken to the home of William Petersen, just across the street.

The president was carried up the steps, through the front door of the house, and into a small bedroom, where he was placed diagonally across a four-poster bed—he was too tall to fit lengthwise. Major Rathbone and Clara Harris went back to Ford's Theatre to bring Mrs. Lincoln over to Petersen's house. When she saw her husband, she screamed, asked someone to bring Tad, and shouted that she herself should have been shot instead of her husband. After a few minutes, she was gently led away to another room, where she cried uncontrollably.

News of the shooting had already begun to spread throughout Washington. The Marquis de Chambrun was getting ready to go to bed, at around 11 o'clock, when a "fellow lodger" knocked on his door and shouted, "The president had been assassinated."[49] The two of them rushed out into the street and made their way over to Ford's Theatre through the crowd that had already gathered. Just opposite the theater, "a cordon of troops" had been stationed in front of the Petersen house. "The soldiers were crying like children, but were also dangerously exasperated," Chambrun observed. "At the smallest move among the bystanders, they would have fired without hesitation."

Chambrun could see that there was absolutely no chance of getting anywhere near the Petersen house, so he decided to stand out in the street and wait for news. While he was waiting, the marquis recognized Clara Harris; he had spoken with Clara that afternoon at the White House. "The unhappy girl was spattered with blood but found words to tell me that the President was dead."[50] The blood was probably Major Rathbone's, not the president's, and Lincoln was not dead, Chambrun was informed—"slight pulsation could, it seemed, be detected, showing that the heart still beat."

General and Mrs. Grant first heard about the assassination in Philadelphia, where they had stopped on their way to Burlington, New Jersey. The general had not eaten anything since nine o'clock that morning; he and his wife were at a restaurant when the news came—a telegram from the War Department was handed to him while he waited for a dish of oysters:

War Department, Washington
April 14, 1865, midnight

Lieut. Gen. U. S. GRANT
On the night train to Burlington

"The President was assassinated at Ford's Theatre at 10 30 tonight & cannot live. The wound is a Pistol shot through the head. Secretary Seward & his son Frederick, were also assassinated at their residence & are in a dangerous condition. The Secretary of War desires that you return to Washington immediately. Please answer on receipt of this."

Thomas T. Eckert[51]

As soon as he read the dispatch, General Grant turned pale and his entire demeanor changed. He wife noted the change, and asked, "Is anything the matter?"[52]

"Yes, something *very* serious has happened," the general answered, and asked his wife not to cry out or show any emotion when she heard the news. "The President has been assassinated at the theater, and I must go back at once. I will take you to Burlington (an hour away), see the children, order a special train, and return as soon as it is ready."

The general did not say very much on the trip to Burlington. Julia Grant asked if he had any thoughts as to who might have shot the president and what might have been the motive. "Oh, I don't know," General Grant said. "But this fills me with the gloomiest apprehension. The President was inclined to be kind and magnanimous," he continued, "and his death at this time is an irreparable loss to the South, which now needs so much both his tenderness and magnanimity."

"This will make Andy Johnson President, will it not?" Mrs. Grant asked.

"Yes," General Grant answered, "and for some reason I dread the change."

When the Grants arrived at their house in Burlington, nobody went to bed; they had callers all through the night. "Crowds of people came thronging into our cottage to learn if the terrible news was true." Julia Grant remembered. General Grant left for Washington during the night, "while it was yet starlight."[53]

Secretary of State Seward and Vice-President Johnson had also been marked for assassination. Some believed that General Grant had been targeted, as well. Assistant secretary of war Charles Dana sent General Grant a warning about a possible assassination attempt, which arrived directly after the general received the War Department's telegram. "Permit me to suggest to you to keep a close watch on all persons who come near you in the cars or otherwise," Dana advised, "also that an engine be sent in front of the train to guard against anything being on the tracks."[54]

According to Colonel Horace Porter, Charles Dana's warning was well-founded. Colonel Porter gave an account of an incident involving General Grant that took place on the train to Burlington.

"Before the train reached Baltimore a man appeared on the front platform of the car, and tried to get in," he wrote, "but the conductor had locked the door so that the general would not be troubled by visitors."[55] On the following morning, a note written to General Grant arrived at the Grants' house in Burlington. Julia Grant opened and read it: "General Grant, thank God, as I do, that you still live. It was your life that fell to my lot, and I followed you on the cars. Your car door was locked, and thus you escaped me, thank God!"[56]

Vice-President Andrew Johnson was also to have been killed, but his intended murderer, George Atzerodt, did not carry out his assignment. Atzerodt had taken the room directly above Vice-President Johnson's at the Kirkwood House hotel, a short walk from Ford's Theatre. According to John Wilkes Booth's instructions, Atzerodt was supposed to have knocked on Johnson's door, entered his room, and stabbed him with a Bowie knife. But he could not go through with his assignment. Instead, he left the hotel and spent most of the night drinking in a local bar.

Lewis Powell very nearly carried out his assignment, which was the murder of Secretary of State William Seward. Powell arrived at Secretary Seward's house in Lafayette Square just after ten o'clock. He knocked on the door, walked past a servant, and walked up the stairs toward the secretary's bedroom. Frederick Seward met Powell at the top of the stairs. Powell told Frederick that he had some medicine for Secretary Seward, showed Frederick a small package he was carrying, and explained that he was under orders to deliver it to the secretary in person. Frederick assured Powell that he would make certain his father would receive the medicine. Powell appeared to turn around, as if to leave, but turned and drew a revolver from his coat. The revolver misfired; Powell struck Frederick Seward over the head with it, knocking him unconscious and fracturing his skull.

Secretary Seward was in bed, recovering from his carriage accident, and was being looked after by his daughter Fanny and an army nurse named George Foster Robinson. Private Robinson heard the scuffle, and opened the bedroom door to see about the noise. Powell punched Robinson—"struck at his breast," according to a newspaper account—ran past Fanny, and rushed toward Secretary Seward's bed with a large knife.

Seward was much too weak to evade his attacker. Powell jumped on the bed and began stabbing, cutting Seward's face, head, and neck. By this time, Robinson had recovered. He pulled Powell off the bed and onto the floor, which gave Secretary Seward the chance to roll off the bed and out of harm's way. Fanny had been screaming hysterically through all this, which awakened her brother Augustus Seward and sent him rushing off to his father's room. Young Augustus and Private Robinson wrestled with Powell, but somehow he managed to get away. He ran down the stairs and out to the street, shouting that he was mad, and rode off on his horse. When Secretary Seward rolled out of bed, he had dragged the sheets onto the floor; Robinson and Augustus found him wrapped in the sheets, "lying in a pool of blood."[57]

Gideon Welles came to see Secretary Seward shortly after Powell left the house. A messenger had informed him that both the president and Secretary Seward had been assassinated. Because the Seward residence "was on the east side of the square, mine being on the north," he decided to visit the secretary first—his house was just a short walk across Lafayette Square.[58]

As soon as Secretary Welles entered the house, the servants confirmed the fact that "an assassin or assassins had entered the house and assaulted the Secretary," and said that "Mr. Frederick was also badly injured." Frederick Seward's wife pointed the way to William Seward's room. "The Secretary was lying on his back, the upper part of his head covered by a cloth, which extended down over his eyes," Secretary Welles remembered. "His mouth was open and the lower jaw dropping down." His cheek had almost been cut off his face, and just flapped loose. A metal brace, which he had been wearing ever since his earlier accident, saved his jugular vein from being severed, and also saved his life.

Welles also looked in on Frederick Seward, who was lying in an adjoining room. "His eyes were open but he did not move them, nor a limb, nor did he speak," Welles wrote. The doctor in attendance said that he was "more dangerously injured than his father." Young Frederick's skull had been badly fractured; there was a good chance that he would not recover.

Secretary of War Edwin Stanton entered the Seward house directly after Secretary Welles. After visiting Secretary Seward and his son, they left the house together and decided to "attend the president immediately," riding by carriage over to the Petersen house. Quartermaster General Montgomery Meigs and District of Columbia chief justice David K. Cartter rode in the carriage along with them. Major Thomas T. Eckert of the War Department Telegraph Service rode behind the carriage, and two soldiers rode on either side.

The group and their escort made their way through the crowds that had taken over that part of Washington. "The streets were full of people," Secretary Welles would later write. "Not only on the sidewalk but the carriage way was to some extent occupied, all or nearly all hurrying towards 10th Street." When they reached Tenth Street and drove toward the Petersen house, "we found it pretty closely packed."

Gideon Welles, Secretary Stanton, and the others in the carriage entered the house and walked through to the president's room. "The giant sufferer lay extended across the bed, which was not long enough for him," Welles noted. "His large arms, which were occasionally exposed, were of a size which one would scarce have expected from his spare appearance." Lincoln still had the arms of a rail-splitter. "His slow, full respiration lifted the clothes with each breath that he took. His features were calm and striking."

Several people were already in the room when Secretary Welles arrived; he estimated that at least six of them were doctors. Senator Sumner was also there, along with Speaker Colfax and all of the cabinet members except for William Seward. "The room was small and over-crowded," was Secretary Welles's understatement. He asked one of the doctors about the president's "true condition," fearing that he already knew it. Lincoln had already deteriorated during the time that Welles had been in the Petersen house—"his right eye began to swell and that part of his face became discolored." The doctor confirmed Welles's worst suspicions. "He replied the President was dead to all intents, although he might live three hours, perhaps longer."

A NEW WORLD

O ut in the streets of Washington, nobody had any real idea of what was happening. The only source of information that night was rumor, but there were so many rumors that they only served to add to the collective confusion and anxiety. And the fact that so many of them contradicted one another did not help the situation. Some of the stories in circulation claimed that the president had only suffered a slight wound, but that Andrew Johnson was dead. One account insisted that the entire cabinet, including William Seward, had been assassinated. Another said that General Grant had been killed aboard a train on his way to New Jersey.

Several of the rumors being circulated involved Confederate leaders: the Confederate government had been behind the president's shooting, which was the signal for a general uprising; guerilla warfare would soon break out, with armed Confederate extremists seizing bridges and other strategic points around the city. But none of these rumors gave any indication of who these mysterious conspirators might be, when they were planning their insurrection, or even how many of them were under suspicion. There were certainly enough soldiers on the street to make anyone believe that something sinister was about to take place—mounted cavalry and foot soldiers could be seen all over the city. During the early hours of Saturday morning, the best thing anyone could hope for was that the coming day would bring better news, or at least more reliable information.

At the Petersen house, the assembled family members, cabinet members, friends, and colleagues were fully aware that President Lincoln had absolutely no chance of surviving, or even of living through the night, and they waited for him to die. By about one o'clock, the doctors had already pronounced him brain dead—"he would have some movements, some twitching, things like that," a doctor would state more than 150 years after the event, "and it's a foregone conclusion that he was brain-dead by about 1:00 a.m."[1] Robert Lincoln had also joined the group, but there was nothing he could do except look at his father and wait, along with all the others.

The president's pillow had become saturated with blood. During the early morning hours, his head was raised and a new pillow was placed under his head. His breathing was uneven, sometimes shallow and sometimes with a heavy rasping noise. Mary Lincoln came into the room every now and again, distraught and on the verge of hysteria, shouting at her husband to wake up and unnerving everyone present. At one point, when the president's breathing became particularly loud, Mary let out a penetrating scream and fell to the floor. Secretary Stanton, who was never the soul of tact and discretion under the best of circumstances, lost his temper and shouted, "Take that woman out and do not let her in again."[2]

Everyone's nerves were being taxed to the limit; they had been listening to President Lincoln's groans and had been watching him expire before their eyes for the past few hours. At about six o'clock, Gideon Welles decided that he had to get away from that house, if only for a few minutes, and took a short walk: "It was a dark and gloomy morning, and rain set in before I returned to the house," which was about fifteen minutes later.[3] He passed several groups of people along the way, "all anxious and solicitous," and all asking about the president. When he replied that Lincoln could not survive, the reaction was always overwhelming grief.

After returning to the house, Secretary Welles settled into what he called the "back parlor," where Secretary Stanton and several others were discussing the assassination. He went back to the president's room a short while before seven o'clock. It was evident that President Lincoln "was rapidly drawing near the closing moments."[4] Robert Lincoln stood near the head of the bed. On two occasions, according to Secretary Welles, "he gave way to overpowering grief and sobbed aloud," leaning on Senator Sumner's shoulder. But, as Welles pointed out, the end was not far off: "The respiration of the President became suspended at intervals, and at last entirely ceased at twenty-two minutes past seven." Secretary Stanton famously pronounced, "Now he belongs to the ages."[5]

A Presbyterian minister, Dr. Phineas Gurley, knelt on the floor and said a prayer. Mary Lincoln was escorted out of William Petersen's house and back to the White House, screaming when she saw Ford's Theatre across the street. After the doctors, friends, and relatives left the room, a cabinet meeting was held in the same room. According to a newspaper account, "Immediately after the President's death a cabinet meeting was called by Secretary Stanton, and held in the room in which the corpse lay. Secretaries Stanton, Welles and Usher [John P. Usher, Secretary of the Interior], Postmaster General Dennison, and Attorney General Speed present."[6] The account concludes with, "The results of the Conference are yet unknown."

The meeting's main activity was to contact Andrew Johnson by letter, to inform him officially of the president's death and also to let him know that "the government devolved upon him."[7] The letter was straightforward and to the point:

WASHINGTON CITY, April 15, 1865.

SIR: ABRAHAM LINCOLN, President of the United States, was shot by an assassin last evening at Ford's Theatre, in this city, and died at the hour of twenty-two minutes after seven o'clock. About the same time at which the President was shot, an assassin entered the sick chamber of Hon. W. H. SEWARD, Secretary of State, and stabbed him in several places in the throat, neck and face, severely, if not mortally, wounding him. Other members of the Secretary's family were dangerously wounded by the assassin while making his escape.

By the death of President LINCOLN, the office of President has devolved, under the Constitution, upon you. The emergency of the government demands that you should immediately qualify, according to the requirements of the Constitution, and enter upon the duties of President of the United States. If you will please make known your pleasure, such arrangements as you deem proper will be made.

Your obedient servants,
HUGH MCCULLOCH,
Secretary of the Treasury.

EDWIN M. STANTON,
Secretary of War.

GIDEON WELLES,
Secretary of the Navy.

WILLIAM DENNISON.
Postmaster-General.

J. P. USHER,
Secretary of the Interior.

JAMES SPEED,
Attorney-General.[8]

Secretary Welles went to his house for breakfast, where he discovered that his wife had gone to the White House—Mary Lincoln had sent for her. Mrs. Welles would stay at the White House throughout the day, in spite of the fact that she had been unwell during the entire past week. The secretary himself—"wearied, shocked, exhausted, but not inclined to sleep"—rode over to the White House after breakfast through "a cheerless cold rain."[9] Several hundred recently freed slaves stood about in front of the White House, loudly weeping and showing their grief over the loss of President Lincoln. The crowd did not disperse throughout the entire day, even though the rain would not let up.

"At the White House, all was silent and sad," Secretary Welles noted. Mrs. Lincoln, accompanied by Mrs. Welles, met him in the library, where they were soon joined by Attorney General Speed. They also met young Tad Lincoln, who asked, "Oh, Mr. Welles, who killed my father?" Nobody knew what to say. "Neither Speed nor myself could restrain our tears, nor give the poor boy any satisfactory answer."[10]

Andrew Johnson was sworn in as president a few hours later, at about ten o'clock. By Johnson's request, the short ceremony was held in his room at the Kirkwood Hotel; it was administered by Chief Justice Salmon Chase. Before leaving to perform the ceremony, the chief justice checked the US Constitution to make certain he was proceeding correctly—no president had ever been assassinated before, and he wanted to check to be sure that Johnson's swearing in was correct according to the Constitution. After satisfying himself that the succession procedure was accurate and that he could go ahead, he left for the Kirkwood to perform the ceremony.

About ten people had assembled in Andrew Johnson's room to witness the procedure, including Hugh McCulloch, secretary of the treasury; Attorney General Speed; and several senators. Johnson put his left hand on the Bible, raised his right hand, and repeated the oath as Chief Justice Chase recited it: "I do solemnly swear that I will faithfully execute the office of President of the United States, and will, to the best of my ability, preserve, protect and defend the Constitution of the United States." When the ceremony had ended, Chief Justice Chase duly informed Andrew Johnson that he was now president of the United States. President Johnson responded by making a short speech, which began, "Gentlemen, I must be permitted to say that I have been almost overwhelmed by the announcement of the sad event which has so recently occurred."[11]

"I hardly thought that the authority could be passed so easily from one who was great and popular into the hands of a man who has yet neither power nor prestige," the Marquis de Chambrun wrote. "But such is the law!"[12]

"Washington, as well as the whole country, was plunged in an agony of grief, and the excitement knew no bounds," Colonel Horace Porter wrote.[13] General Grant made the same observation: "The joy that I had witnessed among the people in the street and in public places in Washington . . . had been turned into grief; the city was in reality a city of mourning."[14] Along with the rest of the country, the city not only mourned, it also seethed with anger. The headline of the *New York Times* ran: "AWFUL EVENT—President Lincoln Shot by an Assassin—The Deed Done at Ford's Theatre Last Night—The Act of a Desperate Rebel."[15]

In just about every town throughout the North, flags flew at half-staff and were frequently draped in black crepe. All official government buildings were also hung with black—city halls, town halls, court houses, libraries. Dry good shops ran out of their supply of black cloth within the space of an hour or so. Banks and businesses closed for the day. Newspapers announced that they would not print an edition on the following day. "The Washington tragedy absorbed all thought and all conversation," a news reporter observed. "In the stores, on the street corners, in the railroad cars, men, women and children of all classes could talk of nothing else. All agreed that the crime that had been committed was the greatest of modern times."[16]

The day following the president's death, April 16, was Easter Sunday. Clergymen throughout the North memorialized President Lincoln in their sermons. Some pointed out the Lincoln, like Jesus, was killed on Good Friday. Also like Jesus, Lincoln was a martyr—Jesus died for the sins of mankind, while Lincoln died for the sins of his country, especially slavery. Other sermons compared Lincoln with Moses. They both led their people to the Promised Land, but had not been allowed to go there themselves: "I have let you see it with your eyes, but you shall not go there."[17] The *Chicago Tribune* also thought that Lincoln was a martyr to slavery: "On the sacred anniversary on the day made holy by the crucifixion of Him . . . we mourn another martyrdom . . . another martyr to the demon—Slavery."[18]

There was a widespread feeling that John Wilkes Booth had acted with the approval of Jefferson Davis, a suspicion that turned out to be completely unfounded. Throughout the North, there were many who called for some measure of revenge against Confederate leaders, as well as for defensive measures to prevent any further assassinations or possible insurrections or uprisings. These feelings were not just held by the public at large.

General Ulysses S. Grant was also on edge, and he issued an order to keep a heightened lookout and tighten all security—he still had Charles Dana's warning on his mind to keep a close watch on all suspicious persons. As soon as he returned to Washington from Burlington, General Grant ordered General Edward Ord to arrest the mayor of Richmond, as well as all members of the city council. He also wanted General Ord to round up and arrest any Confederate officers who had not taken the oath of allegiance to the United States. General Ord objected that such measures might serve to incite an open rebellion. General Lee was in Richmond; arresting General Lee in the former Confederate capital might cause residents to riot in the streets, or even to take up arms. Grant saw the rationale behind General Ord's objections and canceled his order. But he still advised Ord to increase his vigilance against anyone in Richmond who even looked suspicious, who might turn out to be an assassin or a saboteur.

General Grant also ordered General Philip Sheridan to prepare to make an advance against General Joseph E. Johnston. General Johnston and his army were still at large in North Carolina, and General Sherman did not have enough cavalry to suit General Grant. Phil Sheridan had an outstanding cavalry corps, one of the best in the Union army. Grant ordered him to move south, and to keep himself in readiness to go after Joe Johnston if necessary. All of this took place less than a week after Appomattox, where General Grant offered Lee the most generous and lenient terms possible. His change of heart gives a good indication of how the country at large felt about the South following the assassination.

William Crook did not hear anything at all about the assassination until Saturday morning, April 15. He had gone to bed early on Friday night, and had slept right through all the hysteria of the night before. His reaction to the president's death was completely different from anyone else's: "My first thought was, If I had been on duty at the theatre, I would be dead now."[19] If he had been stationed outside the president's box at Ford's Theatre, William Crook reasoned that he would have confronted John Wilkes Booth and would have been killed by Booth instead of President Lincoln. But he had not been assigned to protect the president that night. That job had been given to John F. Parker, a policeman on Washington's metropolitan force, who was to have guarded President Lincoln from four o'clock in the afternoon until midnight.

John F. Parker had been at his station when the president arrived at Ford's Theatre, and had sat in a chair outside the president's box. But at around nine o'clock he left the theater and went to a nearby bar to have a drink. When John Wilkes Booth came to the theater, Parker was still at the bar.

William Crook's next thought was to wonder if John F. Parker was dead. "Had Parker been at his post at the back of the box—Booth still being determined to make the attempt that night—he would have been stabbed, probably killed."[20] Crook reasoned that the struggle between Parker and Booth "would have given the alarm," and that Major Rathbone and President Lincoln himself could have disarmed Booth, "who was not a man of great physical strength." Crook was angered and frustrated by Parker's dereliction of duty. "It makes me feel rather bitter," he said, "when I remember what the President had said, just a few hours before, that he knew he could trust all his guards."

Parker was never brought up on charges for his misconduct on the night of April 14. During the early morning hours of April 15, he walked into his precinct station with a prostitute named Lizzie Williams in tow. The desk sergeant dismissed her, simply because there was no evidence of any criminal activities against her. The sergeant did not ask Parker any questions, either about Ford's Theatre or the assassination. When his shift ended, Parker went home. He remained a member of the Washington police force for three more years, when his lackadaisical attitude toward his job finally caught up with him—he was found asleep on his shift, when he should have been walking his beat, and was dishonorably dismissed from the police force.

Commander John S. Barnes, who had worried about the president's safety while he was in Richmond, was awakened by an orderly early on Saturday morning. The orderly said that the flagship, the USS *Minnesota*, had hoisted her colors at half-mast, and also that Admiral Porter had signaled for Commander Barnes to come on board at once. It was a very early hour in the day to receive such an order; the commander was afraid that something must have happened to Admiral Porter. He dressed as quickly as he could and was rowed over to the *Minnesota*.

Commander Barnes was met at the gangway by Commodore Rockendorf, who escorted Barnes to his cabin. Once they were out of sight of the ship's crew, the commodore handed Commander Barnes a telegram from Gideon Welles, secretary of the navy: "President Lincoln was assassinated last night in Ford's Theater, and is dead."[21]

Barnes read and reread the dispatch, while Commodore Rock-endorf tactfully walked away in silence. "It seemed as though the fact could not impress itself upon my mind. For some moments I could not utter a word."[22] When the impact of Secretary Welles's telegram finally took effect, "I am not ashamed to say I sat down and gave way to a bitter grief that was heartfelt and sincere."

Elisha Hunt Rhodes learned of the assassination in camp at Burkes-ville, Virginia. A corporal informed him that "President Lincoln was dead, murdered."[23] Colonel Rhodes told the corporal not to repeat the story to anyone in camp, but a short while later a messenger rode up with a circular from General Meade that gave the news in more detail. The dispatch was read to the officers and men of the regiment by the adjutant. "The sad news was received in grief and silence, for we feel that we have lost a personal friend," Colonel Rhodes remembered. "The soldiers feel that the leaders of the Rebellion are responsible, and I fear that if Lee's Army had not surrendered that they would have fared hard at our hands."

Joshua Lawrence Chamberlain did not hear the news until Sunday afternoon. He had made his headquarters in a grand prewar manor house—"an old mansion of the ancient regime," he called it—and was listening to a German band from his former brigade playing cheerful tunes. While the general was enjoying his peaceful day, a cavalryman rode up with a message. There was nothing unusual about receiving a military telegram, even on a Sunday afternoon, but there was something about the messenger's look and manner that caught Chamberlain's attention.

The rider dismounted and handed the telegram to General Chamberlain's chief of staff, saying, "I think the general would wish to treat this as personal."[24] The officer walked over to General Chamberlain and handed him the "flimsy," a telegram written on yellow tissue paper.

Washington, April 15, 1865

The President died this morning. Wilkes Booth the assassin. Secretary Seward dangerously wounded. The rest of the Cabinet, General Grant, and other high officers of the Government included in the plot of destruction.

General Chamberlain's first thought was of the effect this news would have on the men; he was afraid that they would rise up against the local residents and destroy their town. "It might take but little to rouse them to a frenzy of blind revenge," he reflected. "They, for every reason, must be held in hand." He ordered a double guard to be placed on the entire camp immediately. "Tell the regimental commanders to get all their men in, and allow no one to leave." Next, he called a meeting with his officers to tell them the "appalling news," as well as to issue an order that word of the assassination was to be kept secret from the soldiers. The news must be "prudently broken" to the men; "what if now this blackest crime should fire their hearts to reckless and implacable vengeance?"

The general was so shaken by the telegram that it affected his demeanor. The lady of the prewar mansion—"there were never any men at home in those days"—came out to ask the general what was wrong. "It is bad news for the South," he answered.

"Is it Lee or Davis?" she asked, with some anxiety in her voice. "I must tell you, madam, with a warning," he replied. "I have put your house under a strict guard. It is Lincoln." When he spoke, the woman's face brightened with relief. General Chamberlain was sorry to see her change of expression. "The South has lost its best friend, madam," was the only thing he could say to her.

After meeting with his officers, the general and two other officers rode off to see General George Gordon Meade. "We found him sad—very sad," as well as filled with foreboding. At that point in time, nobody knew who was behind the assassination—possibly Jefferson Davis and other members of the Confederate government had planned it. "The plan is to destroy the Government by assassination," General Meade said. "They probably have means to get possession of the capital before anybody can stop them. There is nothing for it but to push the army to Washington, and make Grant military dictator until we can restore constitutional government." If General Meade was thinking along these lines, this gives some idea of how the army as a whole was thinking.

Secretary of State William Seward learned of President Lincoln's death on the morning after Ford's Theatre, according to his daughter Fanny. The *New York Tribune* reported that "he bore up well under the depressing announcement with remarkable fortitude."[25] A few days later, Secretary Seward asked to have his bed moved closer to the window. When he saw the flags at the War Department flying at half-staff, he said to an attendant that he now fully realized that the president was dead. "If he had been alive he would have been the first to call on me; but he has not been here, nor has he sent to know how I am, and there's the flag at half mast." The truth had finally registered in his mind.[26]

Jefferson Davis received the news of President Lincoln's assassination on April 18, when he arrived in Charlotte, North Carolina. John C. Breckinridge, Davis's Secretary of War, had learned of the assassination in a telegram from General Sherman; Breckinridge passed the information along to President Davis. The messenger who delivered the dispatch also read its contents to some nearby Confederate troops. The soldiers cheered the news, "not appreciating the evil it portended," but President Davis immediately realized the full implication of Lincoln's death.[27]

"For an enemy so relentless in the war for our subjugation, we could not be expected to mourn," President Davis would write, "yet in view of the political consequences, it could not be regarded otherwise than a great misfortune to the South." He was not about to call Abraham Lincoln a friend of the South, but he could see that Lincoln was not an enemy, either, and was probably the closest thing to a friend that the South could have hoped for.

"He had power over the Northern people, and was without personal malignity toward the people of the South," Davis continued, "his successor was without power in the North and the embodiment of malignity toward the Southern people, perhaps the more so because he had betrayed and deserted them in their hour of need." When Tennessee had seceded from the Union, Andrew Johnson did not go with his state; he retained his seat in the US Senate. In 1862, President Lincoln appointed Johnson military governor of the state. To the North, Andrew Johnson was considered a courageous Southern Unionist who refused to commit treason and desert his country, but to Jefferson Davis and most of the South he was a traitor who turned his back on his native state.

General Robert E. Lee declared that President Lincoln's assassination was nothing less than a disgrace and a horrible crime. The war was over. General Lee wanted nothing more than for the former Confederate states to come back into the Union in peace and honor. Lincoln's death at the hands of a fanatical Confederate sympathizer could only impede an honorable peace, and would also stand in the way of a true reconciliation between North and South. The general realized that Lincoln's death was not an auspicious event, either to the South or to the restoration of peace.

Not everyone in the South agreed with General Lee. As far as many Southerners were concerned, Abraham Lincoln was a monster and a tyrant and should have been killed a lot sooner. A woman from North Carolina referred to the president as "Lincoln the oppressor" and wondered why Booth had not shot him before. But she also wondered exactly what Andrew Johnson would be like, and wrote, "Lincoln the rail splitter was bad enough, Johnson, the renegade tailor, is worse."[28]

Newspapers throughout the South varied in their carrying of the news of the assassination, as well as in their points of view regarding the incident itself. A North Carolina paper lamented the news of Lincoln's death, and also feared that it might be the cause for additional hostility from the North. "Abraham Lincoln was the best friend the South had in all the North," the paper's editor wrote. "We pray God that his untimely and cruel death may not add to the miseries of our afflicted state. North Carolina had no agency in the awful deed."[29]

Not every editor was as diplomatic, or even pretended to have any regrets over Lincoln's death. Some even ridiculed other Southern newspapers that lamented the assassination. At least one Texas newspaper came right out and said it was glad that President Lincoln was dead. "It is certainly a matter of congratulation that Lincoln is dead," the paper's editor wrote, "because the world is now happily rid of the monster that disgraced the form of humanity."[30]

Some editors did not give any opinion at all regarding what had happened at Ford's Theatre. A South Carolina newspaper treated the story as a foreign news event, and reported the overseas reaction to the assassination: "The news of the assassination of President Lincoln and attempted assassination of Secretary Seward had reached England, producing there, and throughout Europe, a most profound sensation of horror, and calling forth expressions everywhere of earnest sympathy and respect."[31]

And not every editor managed to get his facts straight. A newspaper in Alabama ran this as its headline: "GLORIOUS NEWS— Lincoln and Seward Assassinated!—LEE DEFEATS GRANT—Andy Johnson Inaugurated President."[32] The short piece went on to state that Lincoln and Seward were both dead. "Lincoln was shot through the head in the theatre; Seward was slain while in bed," and added, "This is said to be true beyond a doubt." The article added, "A gentleman just from Selma says it is believed in Selma that Lee and Johnston had effected a junction and whipped Grant soundly."

Nearly every account in every newspaper, North and South, had one item in common—now that President Lincoln was gone, editors and reporters wondered what would happen next. Andrew Johnson was a completely unknown entity. Many in the North regarded him with suspicion; Southerners tended to look at him with foreboding. Nobody, North or South, knew exactly what to expect. The assassination had created an entirely new world. Nobody could say whether this new world would be better or worse, but everyone had their anxieties.

John Wilkes Booth wrote a letter explaining exactly why he felt compelled to kill the president: he had not done anything to support the Confederacy for four years, and now he had to something great and decisive to make up for his inactivity. In a letter to his mother dated 1864, he explained, "For, four years I have lived (I may say) A slave in the north (A favored slave its [sic] true, but no less hateful to me on that account.)" After saying this, he went on to make his point, "Not daring to express my thoughts or sentiments, even in my own home Constantly hearing every principle, dear to my heart, denounced as treasonable, And knowing the vile and savage acts committed on my countrymen their wives & helpless children, that I have cursed my willful idleness, And begun to deem myself a coward and to despise my own existence."[33]

An entry in Booth's diary, dated "April 13th/14 Friday the Ides," he attempted another explanation: "Until to day [sic] nothing was ever thought of sacrificing to our country's wrongs. For six months we had worked to capture. But our cause being almost lost, something decisive & great must be done."[34] He also gave his own account of what happened at Ford's Theatre on the night of April 14: "I struck boldly and not as the papers say. I walked with a firm step through a thousand of his friends, was stopped, but pushed on. A Col- was at his side. I shouted Sic semper *before* I fired. In jumping broke my leg. I passed all his pickets, rode sixty miles that night, with the bones of my leg tearing the flesh at every jump. I can never repent it, though we hated to kill: Our country owed all her troubles to him, and God simply made me the instrument of his punishment. The country is not what it *was*. This forced union is not what I *have* loved. I care not what *becomes* of me. I have no desire to out-live my country."

According to his own version, he is the hero of the story. "After being hunted like a dog through swamps, woods, and last night being chased by gun boats till I was forced to return wet cold and starving, with every mans hand against me, I am here in despair," Booth wrote. "And why; For doing what Brutus was honored for, what made Tell a Hero." Comparing himself to Brutus, who assassinated Julius Caesar, and the Swiss folk hero William Tell, he wrote, "My action was purer than either of theirs."[35]

John Wilkes Booth was trailed and cornered in a barn near Bowling Green, Virginia. The barn was set alight; Booth was fatally shot by one of the pursuing troops. After being dragged from the barn, he asked the soldiers to tell his mother that he died for his country. David Herold, Lewis Powell, George Atzerodt, and Mary Surratt, who owned the boarding house where the conspirators sometimes met, were tried and convicted of conspiracy to murder the president, the vice-president, and the general-in-chief of the army. They were found guilty and sentenced to death. On July 7, 1865, all four were hanged at Washington's Old Arsenal Penitentiary.

"THE LOSS THIS COUNTRY HAS SUFFERED"

F ollowing his brother's death in 1963, Senator Robert F. Kennedy said, "An assassin never changed the course of history."[1] Even when he made this statement, Senator Kennedy knew that it was not true; he was saying it only in an attempt to soften the blow of President Kennedy's murder. Assassins have changed the course of history many times throughout the centuries, from Brutus and Julius Caesar in 44 BCE to Gavrilo Princip, the killer of Archduke Franz Ferdinand, in 1914. And John Wilkes Booth changed it as well.

With the powers of insight and observation of someone born in another country, the Marquis de Chambrun realized that a "great Change" would take place now that Andrew Johnson was in the White House.[2] Abraham Lincoln had the determination, the political shrewdness, and the personality, along with the necessary unscrupulousness, to implement whatever measures would be needed to reunify the country. He was determined to make Reconstruction succeed according to his own moderate terms, and was willing to make any alliances and break any rules to accomplish his goals.

But Chambrun had absolutely no faith in Andrew Johnson's political judgment and had the feeling that he would not be able to implement President Lincoln's policy of leniency toward the South. Now that Lincoln was dead, Chambrun feared that Reconstruction would be a failure, or at least would not be the conciliatory program that Lincoln wanted to pursue, and might end up doing more harm than good. Only Lincoln had the drive and the ability to push through Lincoln's ideas for a lenient and tolerant reunification. "I firmly believe that it is impossible to compute as yet the loss that this country has suffered," Chambrun would write. "Without any doubt, Mr. Lincoln was embarked on a course which was perilous even for himself, but he alone could have followed it. Without him, there is no way out. Only the common road, where nothing can oppose the radical program."[3]

The most immediate and noticeable change brought about by President Lincoln's assassination was in the attitude of the North toward the South. "Vengeance on the rebel leaders is the universal cry heard from one end of the country to another," the marquis noted. "Lincoln's recommendations are forgotten. . . . Today, all idea of pardon is obliterated."[4]

In the days immediately after being sworn in as president, Andrew Johnson seemed intent on a program of retribution toward the South—the polar opposite of what President Lincoln had in mind. As far as President Johnson was concerned, Southerners were nothing but traitors and did not deserve either clemency or leniency, only revenge. General Grant summed up President Johnson's point of view with this simple sentence, which he heard Johnson repeat many times: "Treason is a crime and must be made odious."[5] The Marquis de Chambrun frequently also heard the president say the same thing. "He is always saying, 'I'll show them; I'll teach them that treason is a crime . . . and must be punished.'"[6] Chambrun thought President Johnson had become obsessed with punishing traitors, and wondered what effect this preoccupation would have on the country. "To punish traitors may be the order of the day, but afterwards what?"

Not everyone was as reflective as the marquis. Many thousands throughout the North agreed with Andrew Johnson's policy of punishment for the former Confederate states, and wanted nothing but vengeance for the South. The radical wing of the Republican Party looked forward to a Carthaginian peace—the Radicals intended to make punitive measures against the South official policy and also wanted to execute or imprison every Confederate leader that could be brought to justice, including Jefferson Davis. Andrew Johnson's remarks that treason was a crime that must be punished was just what they wanted to hear. "Johnson is *right*," a well-known radical senator wrote in a letter to his wife. "He now thinks just as we do and desires to carry out radical measures and punish treason and traitors."[7]

But shortly after taking office, President Johnson changed his entire outlook concerning Reconstruction. He made it very clear to the country, as well as to the Congress, that he intended to carry out most of Abraham Lincoln's plans for a soft peace. President Johnson's Amnesty Proclamation of May 1865 promised a full pardon to all Southerners who swore an oath of allegiance to the United States. The proclamation also restored all property, except slaves, that had been confiscated by the Federal government. Excluded from the proclamation were high-ranking Confederate officials, including anyone "who held the pretended offices of Governors of States in insurrection against the United States," any and all "military and naval officers in the rebel service who were educated by the government in the Military Academy at West Point, or the United States Naval Academy," and anyone with taxable property worth more than twenty thousand dollars. A total of fourteen "classes of persons" were excluded from the proclamation.[8]

At the end of May, President Johnson also issued Proclamation 135—"Reorganizing a Constitutional Government in North Carolina." Under this proclamation, the president appointed a provisional governor who would head a convention to form a new government and also write a new constitution. But only men who had been registered to vote in 1861 would be eligible to elect delegates to the convention.[9]

These proclamations made residents of the former Confederate states not only happy and satisfied but also relieved—after hearing what President Johnson had been saying about punishing traitors, they did not know what to expect. Democrats and most Republicans were also glad to hear about the president's proclamations. But the Radical Republicans were taken completely by surprise, and were more than just slightly annoyed by the president's change of heart. The Radicals did not like the new policy, and they also did not like the new president's failure to grant recently freed slaves the right to vote. A good many Radicals had been secretly relieved—and some not so secretly—when President Lincoln had been shot; they did not want anything to do with his plans for clemency and reconciliation. But now it looked as though they were going to have to deal with Lincoln's "charity for all" program just the same, and they were not happy about it.

Andrew Johnson's views on Reconstruction might have changed, but there were many throughout the North who were in full agreement with the Radical Republicans. These angry and unforgiving people did not want charity for the South either; they wanted revenge. General William Tecumseh Sherman found out about this feeling toward the South the hard way in mid-April, about a month before President Johnson's Amnesty Proclamations were issued, when he drew up surrender terms with General Joseph E. Johnston. General Sherman received word from the Confederate general on April 16, the day following President Lincoln's death. "On the 16th I received a reply from General Johnston, agreeing to meet me the next day at a point midway between our own advance at Durham and his rear at Hillsboro," he wrote in his memoirs.[10]

General Sherman had ordered one locomotive and a railway carriage to take him to Durham at eight o'clock on the morning of April 17. Just as he was boarding the train, the camp's telegraph operator stopped him—a very important dispatch was just coming in, and General Sherman ought to see it before leaving. The telegraph was from Secretary of War Stanton, informing him of President Lincoln's assassination. General Sherman ordered the operator not to reveal the contents of the dispatch to anyone until he returned from his meeting with General Johnston.

At Durham, General Sherman and a detachment of cavalry rode off to meet General Johnston and his attendants. After all the handshakes and preliminaries had been seen to, the two generals rode to a nearby farm house. This was the first time the two men had met. Their staff officers waited outside in the garden while the two generals went inside the house to talk.

The first thing General Sherman did was to show General Johnston the assassination dispatch. He carefully watched Johnston's reaction. "The perspiration came out in large drops on his forehead, and he did not attempt to conceal his distress," General Sherman recalled. "He denounced the act as a disgrace to the age, and hoped I did not charge it to the Confederate Government."[11] General Sherman put Johnston's mind at ease by saying that he did not think General Lee or any Confederate officers had anything to do with it—"but I would not say as much for Jeff. Davis . . ." He also explained that his men had not yet been informed of the assassination and feared what might happen when they found out. His particular fear was "that a foolish woman or man in Raleigh might say something or do something that would madden our men," which would result in the army burning Raleigh to the ground. As it turned out, General Sherman's fears were unfounded. When word of the assassination was read to the men, "there was not a single act of retaliation" by any of his soldiers.

General Sherman did not discuss surrender terms with General Johnston until the following day, April 18. In his surrender document, Sherman offered Johnston terms that were more than generous and lenient, issued in the spirit of both President Lincoln and General Grant. But in addition to issues pertaining to the surrendering of Johnston's army, the document also addressed political matters. Lincoln had expressly prohibited General Sherman from even mentioning politics or matters pertaining to the government, and Sherman did not have the authority to discuss these items. In his generosity, General Sherman had overstepped and exceeded his authority. His intentions were well meant, but his actions would bring the full fury of a vengeful North down on him.

"Sherman thought, no doubt, in adding to the terms that I had made with General Lee, that he was but carrying out the wishes of the President of the United States," General Grant would later write.[12] The general did not hear from Sherman until April 21, when he received a dispatch dated April 18: "I enclose herewith a copy of an agreement made this day between General Joseph E. Johnston and myself, which, if approved by the President of the United States, will produce peace from the Potomac to the Rio Grande."[13] As soon as he read the message, Grant realized that General Sherman had gone far beyond his authority, and he could see that the surrender terms Sherman had given General Johnston would be the cause of a great many problems.

According to the agreement drawn up by Sherman and Johnston, the Confederate armies would disband and move to their various state capitals, where they would deposit their weapons in their state arsenals. Every officer and man would then agree "to cease from acts of war and abide by the action of both State and Federal authority." The surrendered troops would be under the jurisdiction of both Federal and Confederate state governments, which actually gave the state governments as much authority as the federal government in Washington, DC.

Another clause in the agreement called for "the recognition by the Executive of the United States of the several State governments on their officers and legislatures taking the oaths prescribed by the Constitution of the United States." General Sherman had given himself the authority to require the President of the United States to recognize the governments of the Confederate states, as well as the power to require officers and legislatures to take oaths prescribed by the US Constitution. There was more to the agreement than this, but these were the two principal items that bothered General Grant.[14]

Grant sent the agreement along to Secretary of War Stanton, along with the recommendation that President Johnson and his cabinet take action pertaining to the document as soon as possible. The president and his entire cabinet abided by General Grant's suggestion. They met that day and rejected the agreement immediately—General Sherman knew that he was going beyond his authority, and he had made it a point that all terms should be conditional and would not take effect unless approved by Washington. Washington emphatically did not approve. General Grant was ordered go to North Carolina to visit General Sherman and take control of his army.

But President Johnson did more than just order Grant to go and see General Sherman. "Instead of recognizing that Sherman had made an honest mistake in exceeding his authority," Colonel Horace Porter commented, "the President and the Secretary of War characterized his conduct as akin to treason, and the Secretary denounced him in unmeasured terms."[15] General Grant left for North Carolina on April 22. He did not notify General Sherman of his visit, for two reasons. The first consideration was security—no one wanted to alert a possible assassin that the general was traveling by train to North Carolina. Also, General Grant did not want to embarrass his old friend with news that he was coming down from Washington to chastise him.

Grant arrived at Raleigh, North Carolina, during the early morning hours of April 23. He discussed the surrender agreement with General Sherman in detail, and informed Sherman in no uncertain terms that the agreement had been rejected by the president and his cabinet. Under the circumstances, Sherman had no other option than to make another appointment to meet with General Johnston to renegotiate the terms of the surrender. But when General Sherman went to talk to Johnston, Grant was not present. He made a point of remaining discreetly in the background—back in Raleigh, according to Horace Porter—"lest he might be seen to share in the honor of receiving the surrender, the credit for which he wished to belong wholly to Sherman."[16]

As soon as the rewriting of the surrender document had been accomplished—essentially under the same terms that General Grant had offered General Lee at Appomattox—Grant returned to Washington and General Sherman put the incident behind him.

But the incident was far from over. Newspapers throughout the country printed Secretary Stanton's negative remarks about the surrender document, which infuriated Sherman and turned the entire North against him. In his comments, Stanton listed reasons why he considered General Sherman's surrender terms to be not only insubordinate but also treasonable. The last of these was probably the most damning: "It formed no bases of true and lasting peace, but relieved rebels from the pressure of our victories and left them in condition to renew their effort to overthrow the United States Government, and subdue the loyal States, whenever their strength was recruited, and any opportunity should offer."[17] In Secretary Stanton's opinion, General Sherman's surrender agreement not only wasted the army's victories in the field but also put the rebellious states in a position to start another war against the US government.

When the North read what Secretary Stanton had to say, the general reaction was resentment and outrage toward General Sherman. President Lincoln had been dead for just over a week, and anger toward the South had not dissipated at all during this time. If anything, it had increased. The public was indignant toward General Sherman because of his lenient attitude toward the rebels. "Some people went so far as to denounce him as a traitor," General Grant wrote.[18] The North was in no mood to show any forgiveness toward the South, and had no use for anyone who showed any mercy toward the rebels. This included General William Tecumseh Sherman, in spite of his war record.

Most of the army felt the same way about the South as the civilian population. On April 19, the War Department issued an order that all army units should stop where they were as a gesture of respect for President Lincoln's funeral, which was taking place in Washington that day. General Joshua Lawrence Chamberlain had the idea of holding a memorial service for the president in camp, to have their own funeral. Headquarters tents were draped in black for the day, along with all regimental flags, and the senior chaplain was asked to give a memorial sermon eulogizing the president.

When the time came for the memorial service, the men formed a hollow square, flags were brought to the head of their regiments, arms were stacked and, after a stirring hymn played by a regimental band, the pastor began to speak. He reminded the soldiers of President Lincoln's love for them all, and also spoke about the assassination. "And you will endure this sacrilege?" he shouted. "Can heavenly charity tolerate such crime under the flag of this delivered nation?"[19]

General Chamberlain could see the men reacting to the pastor's sermon; their faces tensed up and turned red. He quietly asked the chaplain to tone down his rhetoric, but his warning was ignored. "Better to die glorious than to live infamous," the pastor continued. "Better to be buried beneath a nation's tears than walk the earth guilty of a nation's blood. Better, thousandfold, forever better, Lincoln dead than Davis living." General Chamberlain may have been upset by these remarks, but the chaplain was only saying out loud what most of the North was thinking. Even General Grant's wife, Julia, possibly with the assassination attempt of her husband in mind, did not agree with a policy of clemency toward the South. "Too much precious blood has been shed, too much treasure wasted, for the great sin of rebellion to be too lightly condoned by the government so lately threatened," she would write.[20]

One of the most obvious targets for the North, and especially for the Radicals, was Robert E. Lee, the Confederacy's most famous general. President Johnson wanted to have General Lee put on trial for treason, but General Grant threatened to resign his command if the president arrested Lee, which would violate the surrender terms he had signed at Appomattox. In June 1865, General Lee wrote a letter to Andrew Johnson regarding the restoration of "all rights and privileges" he had lost when Virginia seceded from the Union and Lee went out of the Union with his state.

Richmond, Virginia, June 13, 1865

His Excellency Andrew Johnson,
President of the United States

Sir: Being excluded from the provisions of amnesty & pardon contained in the proclamation of the 29th ult; I hereby apply for the benefits, & full restoration of all rights & privileges extended to those included in its terms. I graduated at the Mil. Academy at West Point in June 1829. Resigned from the U.S. Army April '61. Was a General in the Confederate Army, & included in the surrender of the Army of N. Va. 9 April '65. I have the honor to be, very respectfully,

Your obedient servant,
R. E. Lee[21]

Although he freely admitted that he had resigned his commission in the US Army and had been a general in the Confederate army, General Lee did not see that his behavior was any different from that of another famous rebel: George Washington. "At one time, he [Washington] fought against the French under Braddock, in the service of the King of Great Britain," he wrote to P. G. T. Beauregard, "at another, he fought

312

with the French at Yorktown, under the orders of the Continental Congress of America, against him. He has not been branded by the world with reproach for this; but his course has been applauded."[22] But the Radicals in Congress were not satisfied with such an explanation and were of the considered opinion that Robert E. Lee was a traitor and should be treated like one. The son of the US ambassador to Great Britain, Henry Adams, thought that General Lee should have been hanged.

Andrew Johnson opposed the Radical Republicans and their program for Reconstruction, but he did not have the diplomacy or the political ability to do anything about it. He was a veteran politician, beginning his career as an alderman and working his way up to the Tennessee legislature and then to governor of Tennessee, serving two terms, and then to the US Senate. But throughout his political career, he made few friends and even fewer allies. Gideon Welles complained that Andrew Johnson had no confidants and did not want any. During his two terms as governor, he rarely made any effort to work with the legislature.

As a politician, Johnson was solitary at best and difficult at worst. For one thing, he was convinced of his own self-righteousness—according to his point of view, he was always right and anyone who disagreed with him was wrong. The office of president, especially in the days immediately following the Civil War, required tact and diplomacy and the ability at least to try to cooperate with the opposing Radicals. Abraham Lincoln had all of these qualities, along with the ability to make deals and reach compromises. Andrew Johnson lacked every one of these attributes. Instead of being flexible and willing to negotiate, Johnson was stubborn, intolerant, and obstinate. These traits would not serve him well during the next four years.

During Andrew Johnson's four-year term in the White House, four Reconstruction Acts were passed by Congress. President Johnson vetoed all four of these acts; Congress overturned every one of the president's vetoes. Three of the reversals came on the same day that the president issued his veto. The president's unwillingness to compromise was playing into the hands of the Radicals. When the first Reconstruction Act had been introduced, he had been advised to exercise a pocket veto to override the act, which would have at least temporarily defused any confrontation with the Radicals. But President Johnson decided to ignore his advisors and defy Congress, which allowed both the House and the Senate to override his veto and to give him a decisive political defeat.

President Johnson had vetoed the First Reconstruction Act with a message that condemned the measure as "absolute despotism."[23] Under the provisions of the act, the South would be divided into five military districts, much like the division of Germany after the Second World War. Each district was to be placed under the control of a Union general, who was given the authority, and the troops, to enforce Federal laws. The act also instructed the ten former Confederate states to draw up new constitutions that would guarantee universal male suffrage, and also stipulated that after a state adopted a new constitution and elected a new governor and legislature, the new government would not be recognized until it ratified the Fourteenth Amendment. (The first section of the Fourteenth Amendment grants citizenship to freed slaves; the second section specifies that all persons residing within a state, including freed slaves, would be counted toward representation in Congress, but that a state that denies any of its citizens the right to vote would have its representation in Congress decreased in proportion; the third section denies the right to hold office to any former Confederate officials; the fourth section prohibits questioning the validity of the United States public debt. The fifth section gives Congress the authority to enforce the previous four sections of the amendment.)

Andrew Johnson might have responded to the First Reconstruction Act with a moderate response to Congress, listing the reasons for his disagreement with the act's provisions in a reasonable and cogent manner. But he did not have the personality or the political finesse to respond in such a way, which Abraham Lincoln would have done. Instead, he stated that the act was unconstitutional and unnecessary, and went on to say that it reduced the position of the ten affected states to "the most abject and degrading slavery," and that it would also "force the right of suffrage out of the hands of the white people and into the hands of the negroes."[24] Congress was not impressed by Johnson's scolding. Both houses voted to override his veto on the same day: the Senate vote was 38 to 10; the House voted 135 to 48.

General Grant called President Johnson's veto statement "one of the most ridiculous messages that ever emanated from any president."[25] By this time, any hope of Abraham Lincoln's policy for leniency and benevolence toward the South was long dead. The Radicals had completely overturned Lincoln's—and Johnson's—Reconstruction program and replaced it with their own, much harsher, version. Under the Radical's program, the South was treated like an occupied and conquered territory. Lincoln's notion of malice toward none and charity for all died with him.

On the same day that President Johnson's veto of the First Reconstruction Act was overridden, which was March 2, 1867, Congress also acted to override another of the president's vetoes. In February, both houses had passed the Tenure of Office Act, which prohibited the president from removing any official that had been appointed by the Senate unless the Senate approved the president's dismissal. President Johnson considered the act an infringement on the power of the chief executive, and vetoed it. On March 2, Congress voted to overrule the president's veto.

The Tenure of Office Act would turn out to be Andrew Johnson's undoing. It would give the Radicals the legislative excuse they needed to impeach the unpopular president. In August, 1867, President Johnson dismissed Secretary of War Edwin M. Stanton from the cabinet and replaced him with Ulysses S. Grant. Six months later, the House of Representatives voted to impeach Andrew Johnson on eleven charges, including violation of the Tenure of Office Act. The trial began in the Senate in March and lasted until May; Johnson was acquitted by one vote.

In July of 1868, Horatio Seymour received the Democratic Party's nomination when Andrew Johnson received less than one-third of the votes necessary for the nomination. But replacing Johnson as their candidate did not help the Democrats in November. They lost the election, and the White House, to Republican candidate Ulysses S. Grant.

"It was unfortunate that Johnson was not a wiser, abler, nobler man," lamented one of Andrew Johnson's biographers.[26] In other words, it was unfortunate that Johnson was not Abraham Lincoln, or at least was not more like the public's image of Abraham Lincoln. It was even more unfortunate that President Johnson did not have his predecessor's talents for persuasion, political manipulation, and deal making, which were the traits he needed in dealing with the Radicals. Wisdom and nobility may be commendable virtues, but Johnson would have been much better off if he possessed the much more practical assets of tact and diplomacy.

Abraham Lincoln and Andrew Johnson did not have very much in common, much to Johnson's detriment. "The new president was different from the dead President, whom we missed every day," noted William Crook, who served as bodyguard to both presidents. "He was short, while Mr. Lincoln was remarkably tall; he was burly, while Mr. Lincoln was gaunt."[27] But even more important than height and appearance was President Johnson's dissimilarity in personality with Abraham Lincoln. "He was a man who found it impossible to conciliate or temporize," Crook went on to comment regarding Johnson. "Andrew Johnson's opinions and policies did not change. . . . It was inevitable, when other men were going in opposite ways, that there should be a collision."[28]

But Abraham Lincoln never had to deal with the problems that Andrew Johnson had to face: citizenship for the freed slaves, voting rights for blacks, and all the other difficulties that were part of Reconstruction. About a year before his own assassination, President John F. Kennedy gave his opinion concerning President Lincoln and his place among the other US presidents. Being the head of state during wartime "made it easier for a President to achieve greatness," President Kennedy said.[29] And the fact that Lincoln had been killed while the war was still winding down, only five days after Appomattox, helped to enhance his reputation—he died at the height of his popularity. "But would Lincoln have been judged so great a President if he had lived long enough to face the almost insoluble problem of Reconstruction?"

APPENDIX

LETTER FROM PRESIDENT LINCOLN TO GENERAL GRANT ON HIS PROMOTION, AND GRANT'S REPLY

[see Introduction, note 4]

Executive MANSION, WASHINGTON, April 30, 1864.

Lieut.-Gen. Grant:

Not expecting to see you before the Spring campaign opens, I wish to express in this war, my entire satisfaction with what you have done up to this time, so far as I understand it. The particulars of your plans I neither know, nor seek to know. You are vigilant and self-reliant; and pleased with this, I wish not to obtrude any restraints or constraints upon you. While I am very anxious that any great disaster, or capture of our men in great numbers, shall be avoided, I know that these points are less likely to escape your attention than they would be mine. If there be anything wanting which is within my power to give, do not fail to let me know it.

And now, with a brave army and a just cause, may God sustain you.

Yours, very truly.
A. LINCOLN.

HEADQUARTERS ARMIES OF THE UNITED STATES,
CULPEPPER COURT-HOUSE, May 1, 1864.

THE PRESIDENT: Your very kind letter of yesterday is just received. The confidence you express for the future and satisfaction for the past in my military administration, is acknowledged with pride. It shall be my earnest endeavor that you and the country shall not be disappointed. From my first entrance into the volunteer service of the country to the present day, I have never had cause of complaint, have never expressed or implied a complaint against the Administration or the Secretary of War, for throwing any embarrassment in the way of my vigorously prosecuting what appeared to be my duty.

Indeed, since the promotion which placed me in command of all the armies, and in view of the great responsibility and importance of success, I have been astonished at the readiness which everything asked for has been yielded, without even an explanation being asked. Should my success be less than I desire and expect, the least I can say is, the fault is not with you.

Very truly, your obedient servant,
U. S. GRANT, Lieut.-Gen.

LINCOLN'S SECOND INAUGURAL ADDRESS

[see March 4, 1865, note 9]

[Fellow Countrymen:] At this second appearing to take the oath of the presidential office, there is less occasion for an extended address than there was at the first. Then a statement, somewhat in detail, of a course to be pursued, seemed fitting and proper. Now, at the expiration of four years, during which public declarations have been constantly called forth on every point and phase of the great contest which still absorbs the attention, and engrosses the enerergies [*sic*] of the nation, little that is new could be presented. The progress of our arms, upon which all else chiefly depends, is as well known to the public as to myself; and it is, I trust, reasonably satisfactory and encouraging to all. With high hope for the future, no prediction in regard to it is ventured.

On the occasion corresponding to this four years ago, all thoughts were anxiously directed to an impending civil-war. All dreaded it—all sought to avert it. While the inaugural address was being delivered from this place, devoted altogether to *saving* the Union without war, insurgent agents were in the city seeking to *destroy* it without war—seeking to dissol[v]e the Union, and divide effects, by negotiation. Both parties deprecated war; but one of them would *make* war rather than let the nation survive; and the other would *accept* war rather than let it perish. And the war came.

One eighth of the whole population were colored slaves, not distributed generally over the Union, but localized in the Southern part of it. These slaves constituted a peculiar and powerful interest. All knew that this interest was, somehow, the cause of the war. To strengthen, perpetuate, and extend this interest was the object for which the insurgents would rend the Union, even by war; while the government claimed no right to do more than to restrict the territorial enlargement of it.

Neither party expected for the war, the magnitude, or the duration, which it has already attained. Neither anticipated that the *cause* of the conflict might cease with, or even before, the conflict itself should cease. Each looked for an easier triumph, and a result less fundamental and astounding.

Both read the same Bible, and pray to the same God; and each invokes His aid against the other. It may seem strange that any men should dare to ask a just God's assistance in wringing their bread from the sweat of other men's faces; but let us judge not that we be not judged. The prayers of both could not be answered; that of neither has been answered fully. The Almighty has His own purposes. "Woe unto the world because of offences! for it must needs be that offences come; but woe to that man by whom the offence cometh!" If we shall suppose that American Slavery is one of those offences which, in the providence of God, must needs come, but which, having continued through His appointed time, He now wills to remove, and that He gives to both North and South, this terrible war, as the woe due to those by whom the offence came, shall we discern therein any departure from those divine attributes which the believers in a Living God always ascribe to Him? Fondly do we hope—fervently do we pray—that this mighty scourge of war may speedily pass away. Yet, if God wills that it continue, until all the wealth piled by the bond-man's two hundred and fifty years of unrequited toil shall be sunk, and until every drop of blood drawn with the lash, shall be paid by another drawn with the sword, as was said three thousand years ago, so still it must be said "the judgments of the Lord, are true and righteous altogether."

With malice toward none; with charity for all; with firmness in the right, as God gives us to see the right, let us strive on to finish the work we are in; to bind up the nation's wounds; to care for him who shall have borne the battle, and for his widow, and his orphan— to do all which may achieve and cherish a just, and a lasting peace, among ourselves, and with all nations.

LINCOLN'S CONDITIONS FOR PEACE

[see April 5, 1865, note 3]

1. The restoration of the national authority throughout all the States.

2. No receding by the Executive of the United States on the slavery question, from the position assumed thereon, in the late Annual Message to Congress, and in preceding documents.

3. No cessation of hostilities short of an end of the war, and the disbanding of all force hostile to the government.

That all propositions coming from those now in hostility to the government; and not inconsistent with the foregoing, will be respectfully considered, and passed upon in a spirit of sincere liberality.

I now add that it seems useless for me to be more specific with those who will not say they are ready for the indispensable terms, even on conditions to be named by themselves. If there be any who are ready for those indispensable terms, on any conditions whatever, let them say so, and state their conditions, so that such conditions can be distinctly known, and considered.

It is further added that, the remission of confiscations being within the executive power, if the war be now further persisted in, by those opposing the government, the making of confiscated property at the least to bear the additional cost, will be insisted on; but that confiscations (except in cases of third party intervening interests) will be remitted to the people of any State which shall now promptly, and in good faith, withdraw its troops and other support, from further resistance to the government.

What is now said as to remission of confiscations has no reference to supposed property in slaves.

JEFFERSON DAVIS'S PROCLAMATION TO RALLY THE SOUTH TO KEEP FIGHTING

[see April 5, 1865, note 22]

The General-in-Chief found it necessary to make such movements of his troops as to uncover the capital. It would be unwise to conceal the moral and material injury to our cause resulting from its occupation by the enemy. It is equally unwise and unworthy of us to allow our energies to falter and our efforts to become relaxed under reverses, however calamitous they may be. For many months the largest and finest army of the Confederacy, under a leader whose presence inspires equal confidence in the troops and the people, has been greatly trammeled by the necessity of keeping constant watch over the approaches to the capital, and has thus been forced to forego more than one opportunity for promising enterprise. It is for us, my countrymen, to show by our bearing under reverses, how wretched has been the self-deception of those who have believed us less able to endure misfortune with fortitude than to encounter danger with courage.

We have now entered upon a new phase of the struggle. Relieved from the necessity of guarding particular points, our army will be free to move from point to point, to strike the enemy in detail far from his base. Let us but will it, and we are free.

Animated by that confidence in your spirit and fortitude which never yet failed me, I announce to you, fellow-countrymen, that it is my purpose to maintain your cause with my whole heart and soul; that I will never consent to abandon to the enemy one foot of the soil of any of the States of the Confederacy; that Virginia—noble State, whose ancient renown has been eclipsed by her still more glorious recent history; whose bosom has been bared to receive the main shock of this war; whose sons and daughters have exhibited heroism so sublime as to render her illustrious in all time to come—that Virginia, with the help of the people and by the blessing of Providence, shall be held and defended, and no peace ever be made with the infamous invaders of her territory.

If, by the stress of numbers, we should be compelled to a temporary withdrawal from her limits or those of any other border State, we will return until the baffled and exhausted enemy shall abandon in despair his endless and impossible task of making slaves of a people resolved to be free.

Let us, then, not despond, my countrymen, but, relying on God, meet the foe with fresh defiance and with unconquered and unconquerable hearts.

Jefferson Davis

LINCOLN'S REMARKS AFTER APPOMATTOX, PART 1

[see April 10, 1865, note 13]

FELLOW CITIZENS: I am very greatly rejoiced to find that an occasion has occurred so pleasurable that the people cannot restrain themselves. I suppose that arrangements are being made for some sort of a formal demonstration, this, or perhaps, to-morrow night. If there should be such a demonstration, I, of course, will be called upon to respond, and I shall have nothing to say if you dribble it all out of me before. I see you have a band of music with you. I propose closing up this interview by the band performing a particular tune which I will name. Before this is done, however, I wish to mention one or two little circumstances connected with it. I have always thought "Dixie" one of the best tunes I have ever heard. Our adversaries over the way attempted to appropriate it, but I insisted yesterday that we fairly captured it. I presented the question to the Attorney General, and he gave it as his legal opinion that it is our lawful prize. I now request the band to favor me with its performance.

LINCOLN'S REMARKS AFTER APPOMATTOX, PART 2

[see April 10, 1865, note 14]

MY FRIENDS: I am informed that you have assembled here this afternoon under the impression that I had made an appointment to speak at this time. This is a mistake. I have made no such appointment. More or less persons have been gathering here at different times during the day, and in the exuberance of their feeling, and for all of which they are greatly justified, calling upon me to say something; and I have, from time to time, been sending out what I supposed was proper to disperse them for the present.

I said to a larger audience this morning what I desire now to repeat. It is this: That I supposed in consequence of the glorious news we have been receiving lately, there is to be some general demonstration, either on this or to-morrow evening, when I will be expected, I presume, to say something. Just here I will remark that I would much prefer having this demonstration take place to-morrow evening, as I would then be much better prepared to say what I have to say than I am now or can be this evening.

I therefore say to you that I shall be quite willing, and I hope ready, to say something then; whereas just now I am not ready to say anything that one in my position ought to say. Everything I say, you know, goes into print. If I make a mistake it doesn't merely affect me nor you but the country. I, therefore, ought at least try not to make mistakes.

If, then, a general demonstration be made to-morrow evening, and it is agreeable, I will endeavor to say something, and not make a mistake, without at least trying carefully to avoid it. Thanking you for the compliment of this call, I bid you good evening.

LINCOLN'S OFFICIAL ADDRESS AFTER APPOMATTOX

[see April 11, 1865, note 10]

We meet this evening, not in sorrow, but in gladness of heart. The evacuation of Petersburg and Richmond, and the surrender of the principal insurgent army, give hope of a righteous and speedy peace whose joyous expression can not be restrained. In the midst of this, however, He from whom all blessings flow, must not be forgotten. A call for a national thanksgiving is being prepared, and will be duly promulgated. Nor must those whose harder part gives us the cause of rejoicing, be overlooked. Their honors must not be parcelled out with others. I myself was near the front, and had the high pleasure of transmitting much of the good news to you; but no part of the honor, for plan or execution, is mine. To Gen. Grant, his skilful officers, and brave men, all belongs. The gallant Navy stood ready, but was not in reach to take active part.

By these recent successes the re-inauguration of the national authority—reconstruction—which has had a large share of thought from the first, is pressed much more closely upon our attention. It is fraught with great difficulty. Unlike a case of a war between independent nations, there is no authorized organ for us to treat with. No one man has authority to give up the rebellion for any other man. We simply must begin with, and mould from, disorganized and discordant elements. Nor is it a small additional embarrassment that we, the loyal people, differ among ourselves as to the mode, manner, and means of reconstruction.

As a general rule, I abstain from reading the reports of attacks upon myself, wishing not to be provoked by that to which I can not properly offer an answer. In spite of this precaution, however, it comes to my knowledge that I am much censured for some supposed agency in setting up, and seeking to sustain, the new State government of Louisiana. In this I have done just so much as, and no more than, the public knows. In the Annual Message of Dec. 1863 and accompanying Proclamation, I presented *a* plan of re-construction (as the phrase goes) which, I promised, if adopted by any State, should be acceptable to, and sustained by, the Executive government of the nation. I distinctly stated that this was not the only plan which might possibly be acceptable; and I also distinctly protested that the Executive claimed no right to say when, or whether members should be admitted to seats in Congress from such States. This plan was, in advance, submitted to the then Cabinet, and distinctly approved by every member of it. One of them suggested that I should then, and in that connection, apply the Emancipation Proclamation to the theretofore excepted parts of Virginia and Louisiana; that I should drop the suggestion about apprenticeship for freed-people, and that I should omit the protest against my own power, in regard to the admission of members to Congress; but even he approved every part and parcel of the plan which has since been employed or touched by the action of Louisiana. The new constitution of Louisiana, declaring emancipation for the whole State, practically applies the Proclamation to the part previously excepted. It does not adopt apprenticeship for freed-people; and it is silent, as it could not well be otherwise, about the admission of members to Congress. So that, as it applies to Louisiana, every member of the Cabinet fully approved the plan. The message went to Congress, and I received many commendations of the plan, written and verbal; and not a single objection to it, from any professed emancipationist, came to my knowledge, until after the news reached Washington that the people of Louisiana had begun to move in accordance with it. From about July 1862, I had corresponded with different persons, supposed to be interested, seeking a reconstruction of a State government for Louisiana. When the message of 1863, with the plan before mentioned, reached New-Orleans, Gen. Banks wrote me that he was confident the people, with his military co-operation, would reconstruct, substantially on that plan. I wrote him, and some of them to try it; they tried it, and the result is known. Such only has been my agency in getting up the Louisiana government. As to sustaining it, my promise is out, as before stated. But, as bad promises are better broken than kept, I shall treat this as a bad promise, and break it, whenever I shall be convinced that keeping it is adverse to the public interest. But I have not yet been so convinced.

I have been shown a letter on this subject, supposed to be an able one, in which the writer expresses regret that my mind has not seemed to be definitely fixed on the question whether the seceding States, so called, are in the Union or out of it. It would perhaps, add astonishment to his regret, were he to learn that since I have found professed Union men endeavoring to make that question, I have *purposely* forborne any public expression upon it. As appears to me that question has not been, nor yet is, a practically material one, and that any discussion of it, while it thus remains practically immaterial, could have no effect other than the mischievous one of dividing our friends. As yet, whatever it may hereafter become, that question is bad, as the basis of a controversy, and good for nothing at all—a merely pernicious abstraction.

We all agree that the seceded States, so called, are out of their proper relation with the Union; and that the sole object of the government, civil and military, in regard to those States is to again get them into that proper practical relation. I believe it is not only possible, but in fact, easier to do this, without deciding, or even considering, whether these States have ever been out of the Union, than with it. Finding themselves safely at home, it would be utterly immaterial whether they had ever been abroad. Let us all join in doing the acts necessary to restoring the proper practical relations between these States and the Union; and each forever after, innocently indulge his own opinion whether, in doing the acts, he brought the States from without, into the Union, or only gave them proper assistance, they never having been out of it.

The amount of constituency, so to speak, on which the new Louisiana government rests, would be more satisfactory to all, if it contained fifty, thirty, or even twenty thousand, instead of only about twelve thousand, as it does. It is also unsatisfactory to some that the elective franchise is not given to the colored man. I would myself prefer that it were now conferred on the very intelligent, and on those who serve our cause as soldiers. Still the question is not whether the Louisiana government, as it stands, is quite all that is desirable. The question is, "Will it be wiser to take it as it is, and help to improve it; or to reject, and disperse it?" "Can Louisiana be brought into proper practical relation with the Union *sooner* by *sustaining*, or by *discarding* her new State government?"

Some twelve thousand voters in the heretofore slave-state of Louisiana have sworn allegiance to the Union, assumed to be the rightful political power of the State, held elections, organized a State government, adopted a free-state constitution, giving the benefit of public schools equally to black and white, and empowering the Legislature to confer the elective franchise upon the colored man. Their Legislature has already voted to ratify the constitutional amendment recently passed by Congress, abolishing slavery throughout the nation. These twelve thousand persons are thus fully committed to the Union, and to perpetual freedom in the state—committed to the very things, and nearly all the things the nation wants—and they ask the nations recognition and it's assistance to make good their committal. Now, if we reject, and spurn them, we do our utmost to disorganize and disperse them. We in effect say to the white men "You are worthless, or worse—we will neither help you, nor be helped by you." To the blacks we say "This cup of liberty which these, your old masters, hold to your lips, we will dash from you, and leave you to the chances of gathering the spilled and scattered contents in some vague and undefined when, where, and how." If this course, discouraging and paralyzing both white and black, has any tendency to bring Louisiana into proper practical relations with the Union, I have, so far, been unable to perceive it. If, on the contrary, we recognize, and sustain the new government of Louisiana the converse of all this is made true. We encourage the hearts, and nerve the arms of the twelve thousand to adhere to their work, and argue for it, and proselyte for it, and fight for it, and feed it, and grow it, and ripen it to a complete success. The colored man too, in seeing all united for him, is inspired with vigilance, and energy, and daring, to the same end. Grant that he desires the elective franchise, will he not attain it sooner by saving the already advanced steps toward it, than by running backward over them? Concede that the new government of Louisiana is only to what it should be as the egg is to the fowl, we shall sooner have the fowl by hatching the egg than by smashing it? Again, if we reject Louisiana, we also reject one vote in favor of the proposed amendment to the national Constitution. To meet this proposition, it has been argued that no more than three fourths of those States which have not attempted secession are necessary to validly ratify the amendment. I do not commit myself against this, further than to say that such a ratification would be questionable, and sure to be persistently questioned; while a ratification by three-fourths of all the States would be unquestioned and unquestionable.

I repeat the question, "Can Louisiana be brought into proper practical relation with the Union *sooner* by *sustaining* or by *discarding* her new State Government?"

What has been said of Louisiana will apply generally to other States. And yet so great peculiarities pertain to each state, and such important and sudden changes occur in the same state; and withal, so new and unprecedented is the whole case, that no exclusive, and inflexible plan can be safely prescribed as to details and colatterals [*sic*]. Such exclusive, and inflexible plan, would surely become a new entanglement. Important principles may, and must, be inflexible.

In the present "*situation*" as the phrase goes, it may be my duty to make some new announcement to the people of the South. I am considering, and shall not fail to act, when satisfied that action will be proper.

ANDREW JOHNSON'S INAUGURAL SPEECH

[see April 15, 1865, note 11]

Gentlemen, I must be permitted, to say that I have been almost overwhelmed by the announcement of the sad event which has so recently occurred. I feel incompetent to perform duties so important and responsible as those which have been so unexpectedly thrown upon me. As to an indication of any policy which may be presented by me in the administration of the government. I have to say that that must be left for development as the Administration progresses. The message or declaration must be made by the acts as they transpire. The only assurance that I can now give of the future is by reference to the past. The course which I have taken in the past in connection with this rebellion, must be regarded as a guarantee of the future. My past public life, which has been long and laborious, has been founded as I, in good conscience believe, upon a great principle of right, which lies at the basis of all things. The best energies of my life have been spent in endeavoring to establish and perpetuate the principles of free government, and I believe that the government, in passing through its present trials, will settle down upon principles consonant with popular rights, more permanent and enduring than heretofore. I must be permitted to say, if I understand the feelings of my own heart, I have long labored to ameliorate and alleviate the condition of the great mass of the American people. Toil and an honest advocacy of the great principles of free government have been my lot. The duties have been mine—the consequences are God's. This has been the foundation of my political creed. I feel that in the end the government will triumph, and that these great principles will be permanently established. In conclusion, gentlemen, let me say that I want your encouragement and countenance. I shall ask and rely upon you and others in carrying the government through its present perils. I feel in making this request that it will be heartily responded to by you and all other patriots and lovers of the rights and interests of a free people.

ANDREW JOHNSON'S AMNESTY PROCLAMATION

[see Epilogue, note 8]

Whereas, The President of the United States, on the 8th day of December, A.D. eighteen hundred and sixty-three, and on the 26th day of March, A.D. eighteen hundred and sixty-four, did, with the object to suppress the existing rebellion, to induce all persons to return to their loyalty, and to restore the authority of the United States, issue proclamations offering amnesty and pardon to certain persons, who had directly or by implication participated in the said rebellion; and

Whereas, Many persons, who had so engaged in said rebellion, have, since the issuance of said proclamations, failed or neglected to take the benefits offered thereby; and

Whereas, Many persons, who have been justly deprived of all claim to amnesty or pardon thereunder, by reason of their participation, directly or by implication, in said rebellion, and continued hostility to the Government of the United States since the date of said proclamations, now desire to apply for and obtain amnesty and pardon;

To the end, therefore, that the authority of the Government of the United States may be restored, and that peace, order and freedom may be established, I, ANDREW JOHNSON, President of the United States, do proclaim and declare that I hereby grant to all persons who have directly or indirectly participated in the existing rebellion, except as hereinafter excepted, amnesty and pardon, with restoration of all rights of property, except as to slaves, and except in cases where legal proceedings under the laws of the United States providing for the confiscation of property of persons engaged in rebellion have been instituted; but on the condition, nevertheless, that every such person shall take and subscribe the following oath or affirmation, and thenceforward keep and maintain said oath inviolate, and which oath shall be registered for permanent preservation, and shall be of the tenor and effect following, to wit:

"I, _____, do solemnly swear or affirm, in presence of Almighty God, that I will henceforth faithfully support and defend the Constitution of the United States and the Union of the States thereunder. And that I will, in like manner, abide by and faithfully support all laws and proclamations which have been made during the existing rebellion with reference to the emancipation of slaves, so help me God."

The following classes of persons are excepted from the benefits of this proclamation:

First—All who are or shall have been pretended civil or diplomatic officers, or otherwise domestic or foreign agents of the pretended Confederate Government.

Second—All who left judicial stations under the United States to aid the rebellion.

Third—All who shall have been military or naval officers of said pretended Confederate Government above the rank of Colonel in the army or Lieutenant in the navy.

Fourth—All who left seats in the Congress of the United States to aid the rebellion.

Fifth—All who resigned or tendered resignations of their commissions in the army or navy of the United States, to evade duty in resisting the rebellion.

Sixth—All who have engaged in any way in treating otherwise than lawfully as prisoners of war persons found in the United States service, as officers, soldiers, seamen, or in other capacities.

Seventh—All persons who have been or are absentees from the United States for the purpose of aiding the rebellion.

Eighth—All military and naval officers in the rebel service who were educated by the government in the Military Academy at West Point, or the United States Naval Academy.

Ninth—All persons who held the pretended offices of Governors of States in insurrection against the United States.

Tenth—All persons who left their homes within the jurisdiction and protection of the United States and passed beyond the Federal military lines into the so-called Confederate States, for the purpose of aiding the rebellion.

Eleventh—All parties who have been engaged in the destruction of the commerce of the United States upon the high seas, and all persons who have made raids into the United States from Canada, or been engaged in destroying the commerce of the United States upon the lakes and rivers that separate the British Provinces from the United States.

Twelfth—All persons who at the time when they seek to obtain the benefits hereof by taking the oath herein prescribed, are in military naval, or civil confinement, or custody, or under bonds of the civil, military or naval authorities or agents of the United States, as prisoners of war, or persons detained for offences of any kind either before or after conviction.

Thirteenth—All persons who have voluntarily participated in said rebellion, and the estimated value of whoso taxable property is over twenty thousand dollars.

Fourteenth—All persons who have taken the oath of amnesty as prescribed in the President's Proclamation of December 8, A.D., 1863, or an oath of allegiance to the Government of the United States since the dates of said proclamation, and who have not thenceforward kept and maintained the same inviolate—provided that special application may be made to the President for pardon by any person belonging to the excepted classes, and such clemency will be liberally extended as may be consistent with the facts of the case and the peace and dignity of the United States.

The Secretary of State will establish rules and regulations for administering and recording the said amnesty oath so as to insure its benefit to the people and guard the government against fraud.

In testimony whereof I have hereunto set my hand and caused the seal of the United States to be affixed. Done at the City of Washington the Twenty-ninth day of May, in the year of Our Lord, one thousand eight hundred and sixty-five, and of the Independence of the United States the eighty-ninth.

By the President: ANDREW JOHNSON. WM. H. SEWARD, Secretary of State.

NOTES

Introduction

1. Carl Sandburg, *Abraham Lincoln: The Prairie Years and the War Years*, one vol. ed. (New York: Harcourt, Brace & World, 1954), p. 679.

2. Quotes from the second inaugural address are from Abraham Lincoln, *The Collected Works of Abraham Lincoln*, ed. Roy P. Basler, vol. 8 (New Brunswick, NJ: Rutgers University Press, 1953), pp. 332–33.

3. Elisha Hunt Rhodes, *All for the Union: The Civil War Diary and Letters of Elisha Hunt Rhodes* (New York: Vintage Books, 1991), p. 219.

4. "Gen. Grant and the President," *New York Times*, September 23, 1864, p. 4. Also, Robert Underwood Johnson and Clarence Clough Buel, eds., *Battles and Leaders of the Civil War*, vol. 4 (New York: Thomas Yoseloff, 1956), p. 112. The text of both letters can be found in the appendix.

March 4, 1865, Saturday: A Sacred Effort

1. David Herbert Donald, *Lincoln* (New York: Simon & Schuster, 1995), p. 529.

2. Gideon Welles, *Diary of Gideon Welles: Secretary of the Navy under Lincoln and Johnson*, vol. 2 (Boston: Houghton Mifflin, 1911), p. 251.

3. Ibid., p. 252.

4. Ibid.

5. "Additional Details of the Inauguration Ceremonies," *New York Daily Herald*, March 5, 1865, p. 1.

6. *New York World*, March 6, 1865.

7. "From Washington: The Inauguration Ceremonies," *New York Times*, March 6, 1865, p. 1.

8. Ibid.

9. Quotes from the second inaugural address are from Abraham Lincoln, *The Collected Works of Abraham Lincoln*, ed. Roy P. Basler, vol. 8 (New Brunswick, NJ: Rutgers University Press, 1953), pp. 332–33. The text of the entire speech can be found in the appendix.

10. "The President's Address," *New York Daily Herald*, March 6, 1865, p. 5.

11. "From Washington: The Inauguration Ceremonies," *New York Times*, March 6, 1865, p. 1.

12. Carl Sandburg, *Abraham Lincoln: The Prairie Years and the War Years*, one vol. ed. (New York: Harcourt, Brace & World, 1954), p. 663.

13. *New York World*, March 6, 1865.

14. Lincoln, *Collected Works*, vol. 4, p. 271.

15. Frederick Douglass, *Life and Times of Frederick Douglass* (Boston: DeWolfe & Fiske, 1892), p. 402.

16. David Herbert Donald, *Lincoln* (New York: Simon & Schuster, 1995), p. 568.

March 5, 1865, Sunday: A Welcome Relief

1. "Service at the Capitol," *Evening Star* (Washington, DC), March 6, 1865, p. 3.

2. Dan Gilgoff, "Abraham Lincoln's Religious Uncertainty," *US News & World Report*, February 12, 2009, https://www.usnews.com/news/history/articles/2009/02/12/abraham-lincolns-religious-uncertainty.

3. Abraham Lincoln, *The Collected Works of Abraham Lincoln*, ed. Roy P. Basler, vol. 8 (New Brunswick, NJ: Rutgers University Press, 1953), p. 382.

4. Lincoln, *Collected Works*, vol. 7, p. 542.

5. "Life in the White House in the Time of Lincoln," in John Hay, *Addresses of John Hay* (New York: Century Co., 1907), p. 337. The Bible quote is from Luke 10:37.

March 6, 1865, Monday: Inauguration Ball

1. "The Inaugural," *New York Times*, March 6, 1865, p. 4.

2. *New York World*, March 6, 1865.

3. "The Inaugural," *Inquirer* (Philadelphia), March 6, 1865, p. 4.

4. "Topics of the Day: Mr. Lincoln," *Spectator* (London), March 25, 1865, p. 4.

5. Elizabeth Keckley, *Behind the Scenes: Thirty Years a Slave, and Four Years in the White House* (Buffalo, NY: Stansil and Lee, 1931), p. 155.

6. "News from Washington: The Grand Ball," *New York Times*, March 7, 1865, p. 4.

7. "Lincoln's Patent," Abraham Lincoln Online, 2018, http://www .abrahamlincolnonline.org/lincoln/education/patent.htm.

Part of the application reads, "Be it known that I, Abraham Lincoln, of Springfield, in the county of Sangamon, in the state of Illinois, have invented a new and improved manner of combining adjustable buoyant air chambers with a steam boat or other vessel for the purpose of enabling their draught of water to be readily lessened to enable them to pass over bars, or through shallow water, without discharging their cargoes."

8. William F. Richstein, *The Stranger's Guide-Book to Washington City, and Everybody's Pocket Handy-Book* (Washington, DC: W. F. Richstein, 1864), p. 25.

9. "News from Washington: The Grand Ball," *New York Times*, March 7, 1865.

10. "The Inauguration Ball," *Evening Star* (Washington, DC), March 7, 1865, p. 2.

11. Ibid.

12. Henry Adams, *The Education of Henry Adams* (Boston and New York: Houghton Mifflin, 1918), p. 107.

NOTES

March 7, 1865, Tuesday: Office Routine

1. Abraham Lincoln, *The Collected Works of Abraham Lincoln*, ed. Roy P. Basler, vol. 8 (New Brunswick, NJ: Rutgers University Press, 1953), p. 338–39.
2. Ibid., pp. 339–42.
3. Ibid., p. 339.
4. *Times* (London), May 25, 1864, p. 8.
5. Lincoln, *Collected Works*, p. 339.
6. Ulysses S. Grant, *Personal Memoirs of U. S. Grant: Two Volumes in One* (New York: Charles L. Webster, 1894), p. 592.
7. Ibid., pp. 592–93.
8. Ibid., p. 595–96.

March 8, 1865, Wednesday: Political Affairs

1. Abraham Lincoln, *The Collected Works of Abraham Lincoln*, ed. Roy P. Basler, vol. 8 (New Brunswick, NJ: Rutgers University Press, 1953), p. 345.
2. Ulysses S. Grant, *Personal Memoirs of U. S. Grant: Two Volumes in One* (New York: Charles L. Webster), p. 593.
3. Elisha Hunt Rhodes, *All for the Union: The Civil War Diary and Letters of Elisha Hunt Rhodes* (New York: Vintage Books, 1991), p. 210.

March 9, 1865, Thursday: Communications with General Grant

1. Abraham Lincoln, *The Collected Works of Abraham Lincoln*, ed. Roy P. Basler, vol. 8 (New Brunswick, NJ: Rutgers University Press, 1953), p. 346.
2. Ibid. p. 348.
3. Ibid.
4. Ibid., p. 347.
5. Ibid., p. 348.

6. Details of the Battle of Kilpatrick's Drawers are from a conversation with an acquaintance who lives in the area.

March 10, 1865, Friday: Day of Rest

1. George R. Agassiz, ed., *Meade's Headquarters, 1863–1865: Letters of Colonel Theodore Lyman* (Boston: Atlantic Monthly Press, 1922), pp. 324–25.
2. John Hay, "Life in the White House in the Time of Lincoln," in *Addresses of John Hay* (New York: Century Co., 1906), p. 339.
3. William Tecumseh Sherman, *Memoirs of General William T. Sherman*, two vols. in one ed. (New York: Da Capo, 1984), vol. 2, p. 297.

March 11 and 12, 1865, Saturday and Sunday: Life and Death Decisions

1. Abraham Lincoln, *The Collected Works of Abraham Lincoln*, ed. Roy P. Basler, vol. 8 (New Brunswick, NJ: Rutgers University Press, 1953), p. 350.
2. William Tecumseh Sherman, *Memoirs of General William T. Sherman*, two vols. in one ed. (New York: Da Capo, 1984), vol. 2, p. 297.

March 13, 1865, Monday: Not Sick, Just Tired

1. "Illness of the President," *New York Herald*, March 14, 1865, p. 4.
2. William Tecumseh Sherman, *Memoirs of General William T. Sherman*, two vols. in one ed. (New York: Da Capo, 1984), vol. 2, p. 297.
3. Douglas Southall Freeman, *R. E. Lee: A Biography* (New York: Charles Scribner's Sons, 1935), p. 544.
4. Clifford Dowdey, ed., *The Wartime Papers of R. E. Lee* (Boston: Little, Brown, 1961), p. 914.
5. "Black Confederate Soldiers," http://confederatelegion.com/Black_Confederate_Soldiers.html [site discontinued].

March 14, 1865, Tuesday: Cabinet Meeting

1. Gideon Welles, *Diary of Gideon Welles: Secretary of the Navy under Lincoln and Johnson*, vol. 2 (Boston: Houghton Mifflin, 1911), p. 297.
2. William Tecumseh Sherman, *Memoirs of General William T. Sherman*, two vols. in one ed. (New York: Da Capo, 1984), vol. 2, p. 299.
3. Elisha Hunt Rhodes, *All for the Union: The Civil War Diary and Letters of Elisha Hunt Rhodes* (New York: Vintage Books, 1991), p. 211.

March 15, 1865, Wednesday: Evening at Grover's Theatre

1. Abraham Lincoln, *The Collected Works of Abraham Lincoln*, ed. Roy P. Basler vol. 8 (New Brunswick, NJ: Rutgers University Press, 1953), p. 356. Thurlow Weed, who was also the editor of the *Albany Evening Journal*, predicted that Lincoln would never be reelected in 1864.
2. "The German Opera," *Evening Star* (Washington, DC), March 16, 1865, p. 2.
3. "Life in the White House in the Time of Lincoln," in John Hay, *Addresses of John Hay* (New York: Century Co., 1907), p. 332.
4. David Herbert Donald, *Lincoln* (New York: Simon & Schuster, 1995), p. 570.
5. The information concerning John Wilkes Booth's meeting at Gautier's Restaurant is based on three main sources: The Lincoln Assassination Suspect file, at the National Archives; Samuel B. Arnold, *Memoirs of a Lincoln Conspirator* (Bowie, MD: Heritage Books, 1996); and Michael W. Kauffman, *American Brutus: John Wilkes Booth and Lincoln Conspiracies* (New York: Random House, 2004), pp. 476–82.

March 16, 1865, Thursday: Tad

1. Margarita Spalding Gerry, comp. and ed., *Through Five Administrations: Reminiscences of Colonel William H. Crook, Body-Guard to President Lincoln* (New York: Harper and Brothers, 1910), p. 23.

2. William Tecumseh Sherman, *Memoirs of General William T. Sherman*, two vols. in one ed. (New York: Da Capo, 1984), vol. 2, pp. 300–301.

3. Ibid., pp. 302–303.

March 17, 1865, Friday: The President Thinks Ahead

1. Abraham Lincoln, *The Collected Works of Abraham Lincoln*, ed. Roy P. Basler, vol. 8 (New Brunswick, NJ: Rutgers University Press, 1953), p. 359.

2. Ibid., pp. 360–61.

3. Ibid., pp. 361–62.

4. Ibid., p. 362.

March 18 and 19, 1865, Saturday and Sunday: Executive Decisions

1. Abraham Lincoln, *The Collected Works of Abraham Lincoln*, ed. Roy P. Basler, vol. 8 (New Brunswick, NJ: Rutgers University Press, 1953), p. 364.

2. Gideon Welles, *Diary of Gideon Welles: Secretary of the Navy Under Lincoln and Johnson*, vol. 2 (Boston: Houghton Mifflin, 1911), p. 260.

3. Lincoln, *Collected Works*, p. 365.

4. William Tecumseh Sherman, *Memoirs of General William T. Sherman*, two vol. in one ed. (New York: Da Capo, 1984), vol. 2, p. 303.

5. Ibid., pp. 304–306.

6. Ibid., pp. 306–307.

7. Ibid., p. 314.

8. Ulysses S. Grant, *Personal Memoirs of U. S. Grant: Two Volumes in One* (New York: Charles L. Webster, 1894), p. 595.

9. Horace Porter, *Campaigning with Grant* (Secaucus, NJ: Blue and Grey, 1984), p. 402.

10. Welles, *Diary*, p. 261.

March 20, 1865, Monday: City Point

1. Horace Porter, *Campaigning with Grant* (Secaucus, NJ: Blue and Grey, 1984), p. 402.
2. Abraham Lincoln, *The Collected Works of Abraham Lincoln*, ed. Roy P. Basler, vol. 8 (New Brunswick, NJ: Rutgers University Press, 1953), p. 367.
3. Ulysses S. Grant, *Personal Memoirs of U. S. Grant: Two Volumes in One* (New York: Charles L. Webster, 1894), p. 596.

March 21, 1865, Tuesday: Lincoln Decides to Take a Trip

1. John S. Barnes, "With Lincoln from Washington to Richmond in 1865: I. The President Sees a Fight and a Review," *Appleton's Magazine* 9, no. 5 (May 1907): 518.
2. "At Old Fort Stevens: The Stars and Stripes Raised Over an Historic Spot," *Washington Times*, June 15, 1900, p. 3.
3. Ibid.
4. Abraham Lincoln, *The Collected Works of Abraham Lincoln*, ed. Roy P. Basler, vol. 8 (New Brunswick, NJ: Rutgers University Press, 1953), p. 369.
5. Ibid., p. 223.
6. Horace Porter, *Campaigning with Grant* (Secaucus, NJ: Blue and Grey, 1984), p. 402.
7. "German Opera," *Evening Star* (Washington, DC), March 22, 1865, p. 2.

March 22, 1865, Wednesday: A Flattering Letter

1. Abraham Lincoln, *The Collected Works of Abraham Lincoln*, ed. Roy P. Basler, vol. 8 (New Brunswick, NJ: Rutgers University Press, 1953), p. 371.
2. Ibid., pp. 371–72.

3. Garnet Wolseley, "A Month's Visit to the Confederate Head-quarters," in *The American Civil War: An English View: The Writings of Field Marshal Viscount Wolseley*, ed. James A. Rawley (Mechanicsburg, PA: Stackpole Books, 2002), p. 48.

4. Ward Hill Lamon, *Recollections of Abraham Lincoln, 1847–1865* (Lincoln, NE: University of Nebraska Press, 1994), p. 173.

5. William Tecumseh Sherman, *Memoirs of General William T. Sherman*, two vols. in one ed. (New York: Da Capo, 1984), vol. 2, p. 323.

6. Elisha Hunt Rhodes, *All for the Union: The Civil War Diary and Letters of Elisha Hunt Rhodes* (New York: Vintage Books, 1991), p. 213.

March 23, 1865, Thursday: Heading for City Point

1. Abraham Lincoln, *The Collected Works of Abraham Lincoln*, ed. Roy P. Basler, vol. 8 (New Brunswick, NJ: Rutgers University Press, 1953), p. 372.

2. John S. Barnes, "With Lincoln from Washington to Richmond in 1865: I. The President Sees a Fight and a Review," *Appleton's Magazine* 9, no. 5 (May 1907): 521.

3. "News from Washington," *New York Herald*, March 24, 1865, p. 1.

4. Lincoln, *Collected Works*, p. 373.

5. Margarita Spalding Gerry, comp. and ed., *Through Five Administrations: Reminiscences of Colonel William H. Crook, Body-Guard to President Lincoln* (New York: Harper and Brothers, 1910), p. 40.

March 24, 1865, Friday: Arrival

1. Abraham Lincoln, *The Collected Works of Abraham Lincoln*, ed. Roy P. Basler, vol. 8 (New Brunswick, NJ: Rutgers University Press, 1953), p. 373.

2. Ibid.

3. John S. Barnes, "With Lincoln from Washington to Richmond in 1865: I. The President Sees a Fight and a Review," *Appleton's Magazine* 9, no. 5 (May 1907): 521.

4. Julia Dent Grant, *The Personal Memoirs of Julia Dent Grant* (New York: G. P. Putnam's Sons, 1975), p. 142.

5. Ibid.

6. Ibid.

7. Adam Badeau, *Grant in Peace: From Appomattox to Mount McGregor: A Personal Memoir* (Hartford, CT: S. S. Scranton, 1887), p. 362. Also in Dent Grant, *Personal Memoirs*, p. 145.

March 25, 1865, Saturday: Visiting a Battlefield

1. Abraham Lincoln, *The Collected Works of Abraham Lincoln*, ed. Roy P. Basler, vol. 8 (New Brunswick, NJ: Rutgers University Press, 1953), p. 373.

2. Ibid., p. 374.

3. John S. Barnes, "With Lincoln from Washington to Richmond in 1865: I. The President Sees a Fight and a Review," *Appleton's Magazine* 9, no. 5 (May 1907): 521.

4. Lincoln, *Collected Works*, p. 373.

5. Jesse Grant Cramer, ed., *Letters of Ulysses S. Grant to His Father and His Youngest Sister, 1857–78* (New York: G. P. Putnam's Sons, 1912), p. 106.

6. Ulysses S. Grant, *Personal Memoirs of U. S. Grant: Two Volumes in One* (New York: Charles L. Webster, 1894), p. 597.

7. Ibid.

8. Horace Porter, *Campaigning with Grant* (Secaucus, NJ: Blue and Grey, 1984), p. 406.

9. Barnes, "With Lincoln from Washington," p. 521.

10. Ibid.

11. Margarita Spalding Gerry, comp. and ed., *Through Five Administrations: Reminiscences of Colonel William H. Crook, Body-Guard to President Lincoln* (New York: Harper and Brothers, 1910), p. 42.

12. Barnes, "With Lincoln from Washington," pp. 521–22.

13. Gerry, comp. and ed., *Through Five Administrations*, p. 43.

14. Porter, *Campaigning with Grant*, p. 406.

15. Ibid., p. 407.

16. Ibid., pp. 407–408.

17. Ibid., p. 408.

18. Ibid.

19. Ibid. p. 409.

20. Lincoln, *Collected Works*, p. 374.

March 26, 1865, Sunday: The Presidentress

1. Horace Porter, *Campaigning with Grant* (Secaucus, NJ: Blue and Grey, 1984), pp. 409–10. General John G. Parke sent this telegram: "The enemy attacked my front this morning at about 4.30 with three divisions under command of General [John B.] Gordon. By a sudden rush they seized the line . . . to the right of Fort Stedman, wheeled, and . . . took possession of the fort. . . . Our troops on either flank stood firm . . . the enemy were driven out of the fort, with the loss of a number of prisoners, estimated at about 1,600. . . ." Abraham Lincoln, *The Collected Works of Abraham Lincoln*, ed. Roy P. Basler, vol. 8 (New Brunswick, NJ: Rutgers University Press, 1953), p. 374.

2. Ibid.

3. Porter, *Campaigning with Grant*, p. 412.

4. Ibid.

5. Ulysses S. Grant, *Personal Memoirs of U. S. Grant: Two Volumes in One* (New York: Charles L. Webster, 1894), p. 599.

6. Ibid., p. 600.

7. Porter, *Campaigning with Grant*, p. 413.

8. John S. Barnes, "With Lincoln from Washington to Richmond in 1865: I. The President Sees a Fight and a Review," *Appleton's Magazine* 9, no. 5 (May 1907): 522.

9. Ibid., pp. 522–23.

10. Ibid., p. 523.

11. Ibid.

12. Ibid.

13. Ibid.

14. Ibid.

15. Ibid.

16. Porter, *Campaigning with Grant*, p. 413.

17. Ibid., p. 414.

18. Jean H. Baker, *Mary Todd Lincoln: A Biography* (New York: W. W. Norton, 1987), p. 239.

19. Porter, *Campaigning with Grant*, p. 414.

20. Barnes, "With Lincoln from Washington," p. 523 Photos of Mary Ord show her to be a fairly ordinary-looking middle-aged woman.

21. Baker, *Mary Todd Lincoln*, p. 239.

22. Adam Badeau, *Grant in Peace from Appomattox to Mount McGregor: A Personal Memoir* (Hartford, CT: S. S. Scranton, 1887), pp. 359.

23. Ibid., 360.

24. Julia Dent Grant, *The Personal Memoirs of Julia Dent Grant* (New York: G. P. Putnam's Sons, 1975), pp. 146–47.

25. Ibid., p. 147.

26. Porter, *Campaigning with Grant*, p. 414.

27. Barnes, "With Lincoln from Washington," p. 524.

28. Jackie Rosenhek, "The First Lady of Lunacy," *Doctor's Review*, November 2006, http://www.doctorsreview.com/history/nov06-history_medicine/.

29. Karen Springen, "Hellcat or Helpmate: A Look at Mary Todd Lincoln," *Newsweek*, September 18, 2007, http://www.newsweek.com/hellcat-or-helpmate-look-mary-todd-lincoln-100149.

30. Rosenhek, "First Lady of Lunacy."

31. "Mary Lincoln at Bellevue Palace," Abraham Lincoln Online, 2018, http://www.abrahamlincolnonline.org/lincoln/sites/bellevue.htm.

32. Barnes, "With Lincoln from Washington," p. 524.

33. Ibid.

34. Ibid.

35. Ibid.

36. Porter, *Campaigning with Grant*, p. 416.

37. Ibid.

38. Elisha Hunt Rhodes, *All for the Union: The Civil War Diary and Letters of Elisha Hunt Rhodes* (New York: Vintage Books, 1991), p. 213.

March 27, 1865, Monday: Aboard the *River Queen*

1. William Tecumseh Sherman, *Memoirs of General William T. Sherman*, two vols. in one ed. (New York: Da Capo, 1984), vol. 2, p. 324.

2. Horace Porter, *Campaigning with Grant* (Secaucus, NJ: Blue and Grey, 1984), pp. 417–18.

3. Ibid., p. 418.

4. Sherman, *Memoirs*, p. 234.

5. Ibid.

6. Porter, *Campaigning with Grant*, p. 419.

7. Sherman, *Memoirs*, p. 325.

8. Ibid.

9. Porter, *Campaigning with Grant*, p. 420.

10. John S. Barnes, "With Lincoln from Washington to Richmond in 1865: I. The President Sees a Fight and a Review," *Appleton's Magazine* 9, no. 5 (May 1907): 524.

11. Ibid.

12. Jean H. Baker, *Mary Todd Lincoln: A Biography* (New York: W. W. Norton, 1987), p. 240.

13. John S. Barnes, "With Lincoln from Washington to Richmond in 1865: II. The President Enters the Confederate Capital," *Appleton's Magazine* 9, no. 6 (June 1907): 743.

14. Ibid.

15. Ibid.

16. Abraham Lincoln, *The Collected Works of Abraham Lincoln*, ed. Roy P. Basler, vol. 8 (New Brunswick, NJ: Rutgers University Press, 1953), p. 375.

17. Ibid.

18. Ibid., p. 376.
19. Ibid.

March 28, 1865, Tuesday: "Let Them All Go"

1. Horace Porter, *Campaigning with Grant* (Secaucus, NJ: Blue and Grey, 1984), pp. 423.
2. William Tecumseh Sherman, *Memoirs of General William T. Sherman*, two vols. in one ed. (New York: Da Capo, 1984), vol. 2, p. 325.
3. Ibid.
4. Ibid., pp. 325–26.
5. Ibid., p. 329.
6. Ibid., p. 326.
7. Ibid.
8. Details of President Lincoln's conference aboard the *River Queen* are in Sherman, *Memoirs*, pp. 325–31.
9. David Herbert Donald, *Lincoln* (New York: Simon & Schuster, 1995), p. 574.
10. Sherman, *Memoirs*, p. 328.
11. Lloyd Lewis, *Sherman: Fighting Prophet* (New York: Harcourt, Brace, 1932), p. 542.
12. Sherman, *Memoirs*, p. 328.
13. Carl Sandburg, *Abraham Lincoln: The Prairie Years and the War Years*, one vol. ed. (New York: Harcourt, Brace & World, 1954), p. 679.
14. Sherman, *Memoirs*, p. 332.
15. Elisha Hunt Rhodes, *All for the Union: The Civil War Diary and Letters of Elisha Hunt Rhodes* (New York: Vintage Books, 1991), p. 215.

March 29, 1865, Wednesday: "Your Success Is My Success"

1. Horace Porter, *Campaigning with Grant* (Secaucus, NJ: Blue and Grey, 1984), p. 424.
2. Ibid., p. 425.

3. Julia Dent Grant, *The Personal Memoirs of Julia Dent Grant* (New York: G. P. Putnam's Sons, 1975), p. 149.

4. Porter, *Campaigning with Grant*, pp. 425.

5. Ibid., p. 426.

6. Ibid.

7. Abraham Lincoln, *The Collected Works of Abraham Lincoln*, ed. Roy P. Basler, vol. 8 (New Brunswick, NJ: Rutgers University Press, 1953), pp. 376–77.

8. Ibid., p. 376.

9. Ibid., p. 377.

10. Ibid.

11. Elisha Hunt Rhodes, *All for the Union: The Civil War Diaries and Letters of Elisha Hunt Rhodes* (New York: Vintage Books, 1991), p. 215.

12. Dent Grant, *Personal Memoirs*, p. 149.

13. William Crook's account of Smith/Surratt is from Margarita Spalding, comp. and ed., *Through Five Administrations: Reminiscences of Colonel William H. Crook, Body-Guard to President Lincoln* (New York: Harper and Brothers, 1910), pp. 45–47.

March 30, 1865, Thursday: War Nerves

1. Abraham Lincoln, *The Collected Works of Abraham Lincoln*, ed. Roy P. Basler, vol. 8 (New Brunswick, NJ: Rutgers University Press, 1953), p. 377.

2. Gideon Welles, *Diary of Gideon Welles: Secretary of the Navy under Lincoln and Johnson*, vol. 2 (Boston: Houghton Mifflin, 1911), p. 269.

3. John Y. Simon, ed., *The Papers of Ulysses S. Grant*, vol. 14 (Carbondale, IL: Southern Illinois University Press, 2005), p. 136.

4. Ibid.

5. Ulysses S. Grant, *Personal Memoirs of U. S. Grant: Two Volumes in One* (New York: Charles L. Webster, 1894), p. 601.

6. Ibid.

7. Horace Porter, *Campaigning with Grant* (Secaucus, NJ: Blue and Grey, 1984), pp. 427–28.

8. Ibid., p. 428.

9. Ibid., p. 429.

10. Lincoln, *Collected Works*, p. 377.

11. Ibid., p. 378.

March 31, 1865, Friday: Much Hard Fighting

1. Abraham Lincoln, *The Collected Works of Abraham Lincoln*, ed. Roy P. Basler, vol. 8 (New Brunswick, NJ: Rutgers University Press, 1953), p. 378.

2. Clifford Dowdey, ed., *The Wartime Papers of R. E. Lee* (Boston: Little, Brown, 1961), p. 922.

3. Lincoln, *Collected Works*, pp. 378–79.

4. Horace Porter, *Campaigning with Grant* (Secaucus, NJ: Blue and Grey, 1984), p. 431.

5. Ibid., 431–32.

6. Ibid., p. 433.

6. Lincoln, *Collected Works*, p. 378.

7. Gideon Welles, *Diary of Gideon Welles: Secretary of the Navy under Lincoln and Johnson*, vol. 2 (Boston: Houghton Mifflin, 1911), p. 269.

8. Ibid.

April 1, 1865, Saturday: Anxiety at City Point

1. David Herbert Donald, *Lincoln* (New York: Simon & Schuster, 1995), p. 573.

2. Abraham Lincoln, *The Collected Works of Abraham Lincoln*, ed. Roy P. Basler, vol. 8 (New Brunswick, NJ: Rutgers University Press, 1953), p. 381.

3. Doris Kearns Goodwin, *Team of Rivals: The Political Genius of Abraham Lincoln* (New York: Simon & Schuster, 2005), p. 715.

4. Ulysses S. Grant, *Personal Memoirs of U. S. Grant: Two Volumes in One* (New York: Charles L. Webster, 1894), p. 605.

5. Lincoln, *Collected Works*, p. 381.

6. Ibid., p. 380.

7. Horace Porter, *Campaigning with Grant* (Secaucus, NJ: Blue and Grey, 1984), p. 434.

8. Ibid., p. 439.

9. Ibid., pp. 442–43.

10. Ibid., p. 443.

11. Ibid., p. 444.

12. Ibid., pp. 444–45.

13. Lincoln, *Collected Works*, p. 382.

14. Margarita Spalding Gerry, comp. and ed., *Through Five Administrations: Reminiscences of Colonel William H. Crook, Body-Guard to President Lincoln* (New York: Harper and Brothers, 1910), p. 47.

15. Ibid.

April 2, 1865, Sunday: Messages for General Grant

1. Abraham Lincoln, *The Collected Works of Abraham Lincoln*, ed. Roy P. Basler, vol. 8 (New Brunswick, NJ: Rutgers University Press, 1953), p. 381.

2. Ibid., pp. 382–83.

3. Horace Porter, *Campaigning with Grant* (Secaucus, NJ: Blue and Grey, 1984), p. 445.

4. Julia Dent Grant, *The Personal Memoirs of Julia Dent Grant* (New York: G. P. Putnam's Sons, 1975), p. 147.

5. Lincoln, *Collected Works*, p. 383.

6. Ibid., pp. 383–84.

7. Ibid., p. 383.

8. Ibid.

9. Ibid., p. 384.

10. Clifford Dowdey, ed., *The Wartime Papers of R. E. Lee* (Boston: Little, Brown, 1961), p. 925.

11. Ibid., p. 924.

12. Porter, *Campaigning with Grant*, pp. 447–48.

13. Margarita Spalding Gerry, comp. and ed., *Through Five Administrations: Reminiscences of Colonel William H. Crook, Body-Guard to President Lincoln* (New York: Harper and Brothers, 1910), pp. 47–48.

14. Ibid., p. 48.

15. Porter, *Campaigning with Grant*, p. 448.

April 3, 1865, Monday: "Get Them to Plowing Once"

1. Abraham Lincoln, *The Collected Works of Abraham Lincoln*, ed. Roy P. Basler, vol. 8 (New Brunswick, NJ: Rutgers University Press, 1953), p. 384.

2. Ibid.

3. Ibid.

4. Ibid., pp. 384–85.

5. John S. Barnes, "With Lincoln from Washington to Richmond in 1865: II. The President Enters the Confederate Capital," *Appleton's Magazine* 9, no. 6 (June 1907): 744.

6. Ibid.

7. Horace Porter, *Campaigning with Grant* (Secaucus, NJ: Blue and Grey, 1984), p. 449.

8. Ibid., p. 450.

9. Ulysses S. Grant, *Personal Memoirs of U. S. Grant: Two Volumes in One* (New York: Charles L. Webster, 1894), p. 612.

10. Porter, *Campaigning with Grant*, p. 450.

11. Grant, *Personal Memoirs*, p. 613.

12. Porter, *Campaigning with Grant*, p. 451.

13. Grant, *Personal Memoirs*, p. 609.

14. Porter, *Campaigning with Grant*, p. 452.

15. Godfrey Weitzel, *Richmond Occupied: Entry of the United States Forces into Richmond, Va., April 3, 1865; Calling Together of the Virginia Legislature and Revocation of the Same*, ed. Louis H. Manarin (Richmond: Richmond Civil War Centennial Committee, 1965), p. 13.

16. Porter, *Campaigning with Grant*, p. 452.

17. Elisha Hunt Rhodes, *All for the Union: The Civil War Diary and Letters of Elisha Hunt Rhodes* (New York: Vintage Books, 1991), p. 219.

18. Gideon Welles, *Diary of Gideon Welles: Secretary of the Navy under Lincoln and Johnson*, vol. 2 (Boston: Houghton Mifflin, 1911), pp. 272–73.

19. "Grant, Richmond, and Victory! The Union Army in the Rebel Capital," *New York Times*, April 4, 1865, p. 1.

20. "Richmond Is Ours. The Old Flag Floats over the Rebel Capital," *Chicago Tribune*, April 4, 1865, p. 1.

21. Margarita Spalding Gerry, comp. and ed., *Through Five Administrations: Reminiscences of Colonel William H. Crook, Body-Guard to President Lincoln* (New York: Harper and Brothers, 1910), pp. 48–49.

22. Ibid., p. 49.

23. Ibid.

24. Ibid.

25. David Dixon Porter, *Incidents and Anecdotes of the Civil War* (New York: D. Appleton, 1885), p. 284.

26. Ibid., pp. 284–85.

27. Ibid., p. 285.

28. Barnes, "With Lincoln from Washington," p. 745.

29. Dixon Porter, *Incidents and Anecdotes*, p. 285.

30. Lincoln, *Collected Works*, p. 385.

31. Ibid.

April 4, 1865, Tuesday: The President Visits Richmond

1. Abraham Lincoln, *The Collected Works of Abraham Lincoln*, ed. Roy P. Basler, vol. 8 (New Brunswick, NJ: Rutgers University Press, 1953), p. 385. Also in US War Department, ed., *The War of the Rebellion: A Compilation of Official Records of the Union and Confederate Armies* (Washington, DC: Government Printing Office, 1891), series 1, vol. 46, part 3, p. 529.

2. Horace Porter, *Campaigning with Grant* (Secaucus, NJ: Blue and Grey, 1984), p. 452.

3. Ibid.

4. Elisha Hunt Rhodes, *All for the Union: The Civil War Diary and Letters of Elisha Hunt Rhodes* (New York: Vintage Books, 1991), p. 219.

5. Margarita Spalding Gerry, comp. and ed., *Through Five Administrations: Reminiscences of Colonel William H. Crook, Body-Guard to President Lincoln* (New York: Harper and Brothers, 1910), p. 50.

6. John S. Barnes, "With Lincoln from Washington to Richmond in 1865: II. The President Enters the Confederate Capital," *Appleton's Magazine* 9, no. 6 (June 1907): 747.

7. Gerry, comp. and ed., *Through Five Administrations*, p. 50.

8. Ibid., p. 52.

9. Barnes, "With Lincoln from Washington," p. 747.

10. Gerry, comp. and ed., *Through Five Administrations*, p. 53.

11. Ibid., p. 52.

12. Ibid., p. 53.

13. Ibid., p. 54.

14. Ibid.

15. Barnes, "With Lincoln from Washington," p. 748.

16. Gerry, ed., *Through Five Administrations*, p. 54.

17. Barnes, "With Lincoln from Washington," p. 748.

18. Ibid., p. 749.

19. Ibid.

20. Thomas Thatcher Graves, "The Occupation," in *Battles and Leaders of the Civil War*, ed. Robert Underwood Johnson and Clarence Clough Buel, vol. 4 (New York: Thomas Yoseloff, 1956), p. 728.

21. "Details of the Evacuation: The City on Fire," *New York Times*, April 8, 1865, p. 1.

22. Gerry, ed., *Through Five Administrations*, p. 56.

23. John A. Campbell, *Reminiscences and Documents Relating to the Civil War during the Year 1865* (Baltimore: John Murphy, 1887), p. 38.

24. David Herbert Donald, *Lincoln* (New York: Simon & Schuster, 1995), p. 577.

25. Campbell, *Reminiscences*, p. 39.

26. Ibid.

27. Gerry, ed., *Through Five Administrations*, p. 56.

28. Ibid.

29. Ibid., pp. 56–57.

30. David Dixon Porter, *Incidents and Anecdotes of the Civil War* (New York: D. Appleton, 1885), p. 307.

31. Gerry, ed., *Through Five Administrations*, p. 57.

32. Ibid.

33. Ibid.

34. Michael W. Kauffman, *American Brutus: John Wilkes Booth and the Lincoln Conspiracies* (New York: Random House, 2004), p. 194.

35. Porter, *Campaigning with Grant*, p. 453.

36. Rhodes, *All for the Union*, p. 219.

37. Ulysses S. Grant, *Personal Memoirs of U. S. Grant: Two Volumes in One* (New York: Charles L. Webster, 1894), p. 615.

April 5, 1865, Wednesday: Return to City Point

1. Abraham Lincoln, *The Collected Works of Abraham Lincoln*, ed. Roy P. Basler, vol. 8 (New Brunswick, NJ: Rutgers University Press, 1953), p. 386.

2. John A. Campbell, *Reminiscences and Documents Relating to the Civil War during the Year 1865* (Baltimore: John Murphy, 1887), p. 39.

3. Campbell, *Reminiscences and Documents*, pp. 39–40, and Lincoln, *Collected Works*, pp. 386–87. The terms that President Lincoln proposed are included in the appendix.

4. Lincoln, *Collected Works*, p. 387. Also in US War Department, ed., *The War of the Rebellion: A Compilation of Official Records of the Union and Confederate Armies* (Washington, DC: Government Printing Office, 1891), series 1, vol. 46, part 3, p. 575.

5. Ibid.

6. David Dixon Porter, *Incidents and Anecdotes of the Civil War* (New York: D. Appleton, 1885), p. 304.

7. Ibid., p. 305.

8. Ibid.

9. Margarita Spalding Gerry, comp. and ed., *Through Five Administrations: Reminiscences of Colonel William H. Crook, Body-Guard to President Lincoln* (New York: Harper and Brothers, 1910), pp. 57–58.

10. David Herbert Donald, *Lincoln* (New York: Simon & Schuster, 1995), p. 579.

11. Lincoln, *Collected Works*, p. 388.

12. Ibid.

13. Ibid., p. 387.

14. Ulysses S. Grant, *Personal Memoirs of U. S. Grant: Two Volumes in One* (New York: Charles L. Webster, 1894), p. 616.

15. William Tecumseh Sherman, *Memoirs of General William T. Sherman*, two vols. in one ed. (New York: Da Capo, 1984), vol. 2, p. 343.

16. The incident involving the scout Campbell is from Horace Porter, *Campaigning with Grant* (Secaucus, NJ: Blue and Grey, 1984), p. 455.

17. Grant, *Personal Memoirs*, p. 618.

18. Porter, *Campaigning with Grant*, p. 456.

19. Ibid.

20. Grant, *Personal Memoirs*, p. 618.

21. The Lincoln log for April 5, 1865, http://www.thelincolnlog.org/Results.aspx?type=CalendarDay&day=1865-04-05.

22. Jefferson Davis, *The Rise and Fall of the Confederate Government*, vol. 2 (Richmond, VA: Garret and Masie, 1938), p. 574.

The entire text of the proclamation can be found in the appendix.

April 6, 1865, Thursday: Bringing the Fighting to an End

1. Abraham Lincoln, *The Collected Works of Abraham Lincoln*, ed. Roy P. Basler, vol. 8 (New Brunswick, NJ: Rutgers University Press, 1953), p. 388.

2. Ibid., p. 389.

3. Ibid., p. 388.

4. Jean H. Baker, *Mary Todd Lincoln: A Biography* (New York: W. W. Norton, 1987), p. 241.

5. Marquis Adolphe de Chambrun, *Impressions of Lincoln and the Civil War: A Foreigner's Account* (New York: Random House, 1952), pp. 75–77.

6. Ulysses S. Grant, *Personal Memoirs of U. S. Grant: Two Volumes in One* (New York: Charles L. Webster), p. 620.

7. Elisha Hunt Rhodes, *All for the Union: The Civil War Diary and Letters of Elisha Hunt Rhodes* (New York: Vintage Books, 1991), pp. 219–20.

8. Ibid., p. 221.

9. Grant, *Personal Memoirs*, p. 620.

10. Ibid., p. 622.

11. Ibid.

April 7, 1865, Friday: "Let the *Thing* Be Pressed"

1. Abraham Lincoln, *The Collected Works of Abraham Lincoln*, ed. Roy P. Basler, vol. 8 (New Brunswick, NJ: Rutgers University Press, 1953), p. 389. Also in US War Department, ed., *The War of the Rebellion: A Compilation of Official Records of the Union and Confederate Armies* (Washington, DC: Government Printing Office, 1891), series 1, vol. 46, part 3, p. 640.

2. Lincoln, *Collected Works*, pp. 389–90.

3. Ibid., p. 390.

4. Ibid., pp. 390–91. Also *Official Records*, p. 596.

5. Lincoln, *Collected Works*, pp. 391–92.

6. Ibid., p. 392.

7. Ibid.; *Official Records*, p. 640.

8. Gideon Welles, *Diary of Gideon Welles: Secretary of the Navy under Lincoln and Johnson*, vol. 2 (Boston: Houghton Mifflin, 1911), p. 276.

9. Ibid.

10. Marquis Adolphe de Chambrun, *Impressions of Lincoln and the Civil War: A Foreigner's Account* (New York: Random House, 1952), p. 85.

11. Ibid.

12. Julia Dent Grant, *The Personal Memoirs of Julia Dent Grant* (New York: G. P. Putnam's Sons, 1975), pp. 149–50.

13. *Official Records*, p. 619.

14. Ibid.

15. Ulysses S. Grant, *Personal Memoirs of U. S. Grant* (New York: Charles L. Webster, 1894), p. 623.

16. Dent Grant, *Personal Memoirs*, p. 150.

17. Chambrun, *Impressions of Lincoln*, pp. 77–78.

18. Ibid., p. 78.

19. Elizabeth Keckley, *Behind the Scenes: Thirty Years a Slave and Four Years in the White House* (Buffalo, NY: Stansil & Lee, 1931), p. 169.

20. Dorus M. Fox, *History of Political Parties, National Reminiscences, and the Tippecanoe Movement* (Des Moines, IA: Iowa Printing, 1895), p. 218.

21. James Longstreet, *From Manassas to Appomattox: Memoirs of the Civil War in America* (New York: Konecky & Konecky, 1992), p. 619.

April 8, 1865, Saturday: A Hospital Visit and a Reception

1. Marquis Adolphe de Chambrun, *Impressions of Lincoln and the Civil War: A Foreigner's Account* (New York: Random House, 1952), p. 79.

2. Ibid., p. 80.

3. Elizabeth Keckley, *Behind the Scenes: Thirty Years a Slave and Four Years in the White House* (Buffalo, NY: Stansil & Lee, 1931), pp. 171.

4. John S. Barnes, "With Lincoln from Washington to Richmond in 1865: II. The President Enters the Confederate Capital," *Appleton's Magazine* 9, no. 6 (June 1907): 751.

5. Keckley, *Behind the Scenes*, pp. 171–72.

6. Chambrun, *Impressions of Lincoln*, p. 82.

7. Ibid.

8. Barnes, "With Lincoln from Washington," p. 750.

9. Chambrun, *Impressions of Lincoln*, p. 83.

10. Elisha Hunt Rhodes, *All for the Union: The Civil War Diary and Letters of Elisha Hunt Rhodes* (New York: Vintage Books, 1991), p. 221.

11. Ulysses S. Grant, *Personal Memoirs of U. S. Grant: Two Volumes in One* (New York: Charles L. Webster, 1894), p. 624.

12. Horace Porter, *Campaigning with Grant* (Secaucus, NJ: Blue and Grey, 1984), p. 461.

13. Grant, *Personal Memoirs*, p. 624.

14. US War Department, ed., *The War of the Rebellion: A Compilation of Official Records of the Union and Confederate Armies* (Washington, DC: Government Printing Office, 1891), Series 1, vol. 46, part 3, p. 641.

15. Porter, *Campaigning with Grant*, p. 462.

16. Ibid.

17. *Official Records*, vol. 46, part 3, p. 641.

18. Porter, *Campaigning with Grant*, p. 463.

19. Margarita Spalding Gerry, comp. and ed., *Through Five Administrations: Reminiscences of Colonel William H. Crook, Body-Guard to President Lincoln* (New York: Harper and Brothers, 1910), p. 59.

20. "The Sequel to the President's 'Peace Mission,'" *Sun* (New York), April 4, 1865, p. 2.

21. Gerry, comp. and ed., *Through Five Administrations*, p. 59.

22. John Russell Young, *Around the World with General Grant*, vol. 2 (New York: American News Company, 1879), p. 354.

April 9, 1865, Sunday: "Lee Has Surrendered"

1. John S. Barnes, "With Lincoln from Washington to Richmond in 1865: II. The President Enters the Confederate Capital," *Appleton's Magazine* 9, no. 6 (June 1907): 751.

2. Marquis Adolphe de Chambrun, *Impressions of Lincoln and the Civil War: A Foreigner's Account* (New York: Random House, 1952), p. 83.

3. William Shakespeare, *Macbeth*, in *The New Temple Shakespeare*, ed. M. R. Ridley (London: J. M. Dent & Sons, 1935), act 3, scene 2, p. 41.

4. Chambrun, *Impressions of Lincoln*, p. 83.

5. William Shakespeare, *Julius Caesar*, in *The New Temple Shakespeare*, ed. M. R. Ridley (London: J. M. Dent & Sons, 1935), act 3, scene 2, p. 35.

6. Barnes, "With Lincoln from Washington," p. 751.

7. Chambrun, *Impressions of Lincoln*, p. 84.

8. Ibid., pp. 85–86.

9. Ibid., p. 84.

10. Margarita Spalding Gerry, comp. and ed., *Through Five Administrations: Reminiscences of Colonel William H. Crook, Body-Guard to President Lincoln* (New York: Harper and Brothers, 1910), p. 58.

11. Ibid.

Abraham Lincoln's biographers have not written very much about his first hearing of General Lee's surrender. General Grant states that he telegraphed Secretary of War Stanton of the surrender at 4:30 p.m. Such an important message would have circulated throughout the city immediately. Julia Grant mentions that she was first given the news on "Sunday afternoon," but she does not specify the exact time. An account of Lincoln's visit to the recuperating Secretary of State Seward by his daughter Fanny, in her diary entry of April 9, 1865, puts the time later in the evening, when Secretary Stanton came to visit Secretary Seward. Doris Kearns Goodwin, in her book *Team of Rivals* (New York: Simon & Schuster, 2005, p. 725), states that Secretary of War Stanton showed Lincoln Grant's telegram when he reached the White House. It is more than possible that General Grant's "General Lee surrendered" telegram reached Washington by the time the president arrived from City Point, and that the word would have spread throughout the city immediately.

12. US War Department, ed., *The War of the Rebellion: A Compilation of Official Records of the Union and Confederate Armies* (Washington, DC: Government Printing Office, 1891), series 1, vol. 46, part 3, p. 644.

13. Ibid.

14. Horace Porter, *Campaigning with Grant* (Secaucus, NJ: Blue and Grey, 1984), p. 461.

15. *Official Records*, p. 665.

16. George A. Forsyth, *Thrilling Days in Army Life* (New York: Harper & Brothers, 1900), p. 187.

17. Joshua Lawrence Chamberlain, *The Passing of the Armies: An Account of the Final Campaign of the Army of the Potomac, Based Upon*

Personal Reminiscences of the Fifth Army Corps (New York: Bantam Books, 1993), p. 180.

18. Ibid., p. 181.

19. Ibid.

20. *Official Records*, p. 665.

21. Chamberlain, *Passing of the Armies*, p. 186.

22. Elisha Hunt Rhodes, *All for the Union: The Civil War Diary and Letters of Elisha Hunt Rhodes* (New York: Vintage Books, 1991), p. 222.

23. Julia Dent Grant, *The Personal Memoirs of Julia Dent Grant* (New York: G. P. Putnam's Sons, 1975), pp. 151–52.

24. Ibid., p. 152.

25. Ibid.

26. Ibid.

27. Fanny Seward's diary entry of April 9, 1865, in transcript by Patricia Carley Johnson, "Sensitivity and Civil War: The Selected Diaries and Papers, 1858–1866, of Frances Adeline (Fanny) Seward" (PhD thesis; Rochester, NY: University of Rochester, 1964).

28. Ibid.

29. Winston Churchill, *The Great Democracies*, vol. 4, *A History of the English Speaking Peoples* (New York: Dodd, Meade, 1958), p. 262.

30. "The End of the Rebellion," in *Evening Star* (Washington, DC), April 10, 1965, p. 2.

31. J. F. C. Fuller, *Grant and Lee: A Study in Personality and Generalship* (Bloomington, IN: University of Indiana Press, 1957), p. 245.

April 10, 1865, Monday: Return to the White House

1. Margarita Spalding Gerry, comp. and ed., *Through Five Administrations: Reminiscences of Colonel William H. Crook, Body-Guard to President Lincoln* (New York: Harper and Brothers, 1910), p. 60.

2. Ibid.

3. Ibid.

4. "Glory! Glory!! Glory!!! The Rebellion Ended!" *Detroit Free Press*, April 10, 1865, p. 1.

5. "Hang Out Your Banners, Union Victory!" *New York Times*, April 10, 1865, p. 1.

6. "General Lee and His Army Have Surrendered!" *Albany Evening Journal*, April 10, 1865, p. 4.

7. Gideon Welles, *Diary of Gideon Welles: Secretary of the Navy under Lincoln and Johnson*, vol. 2 (Boston: Houghton Mifflin, 1911), p. 278.

8. William Tecumseh Sherman, *Memoirs of General William T. Sherman*, two vols. in one ed. (New York: Da Capo, 1984), vol. 2, p. 343.

9. Marquis Adolphe de Chambrun, *Impressions of Lincoln and the Civil War: A Foreigner's Account* (New York: Random House, 1952), p. 93.

10. Ibid., p. 90.

11. Ibid., p. 91.

12. Gerry, comp. and ed., *Through Five Administrations*, p. 62.

13. Abraham Lincoln, *The Collected Works of Abraham Lincoln*, ed. Roy P. Basler, vol. 8 (New Brunswick, NJ: Rutgers University Press, 1953), p. 393. The complete version of the president's remarks can be found in the appendix.

14. Ibid., p. 394. The full text of the president's remarks can be found in the appendix.

15. Gerry, comp. and ed., *Through Five Administrations*, p. 62.

16. Ibid., p. 63.

17. Ibid.

18. Elisha Hunt Rhodes, *All for the Union: The Civil War Diary and Letters of Elisha Hunt Rhodes* (New York: Vintage Books, 1991), p. 222.

19. Joshua Lawrence Chamberlain, *The Passing of the Armies: An Account of the Final Campaign of the Army of the Potomac, Based Upon Personal Reminiscences of the Fifth Army Corps* (New York: Bantam Books, 1993), p. 188.

20. Horace Porter, *Campaigning with Grant* (Secaucus, NJ: Blue and Grey, 1984), p. 490.

21. Ibid.

22. Ibid., pp. 490–91.

23. Ulysses S. Grant, *Personal Memoirs of U. S. Grant: Two Volumes in One* (New York: Charles L. Webster, 1894), p. 634.

24. Porter, *Campaigning with Grant*, p. 491. In Charles Marshall's *An Aide-de-Camp of Lee: The Papers of Col. Charles Marshall* (Boston: Little, Brown, 1927, p. 275), Colonel Marshall states that General Grant asked General Lee to meet with Lincoln: "If you and Mr. Lincoln will agree upon terms, your influence in the South will make the Southern people accept what you accept, and Mr. Lincoln's influence in the North will make reasonable people of the North accept what he accepts, and all my influence will be added to Mr. Lincoln's." The colonel went on to say, "I think myself, and have always thought, that if General Lee and Mr. Lincoln would have met as General Grant proposed, we could have had immediate restoration of peace and brotherhood among the people of these States." But according to Horace Porter, General Grant never said any such thing.

25. Porter, *Campaigning with Grant*, p. 491.

April 11, 1865, Tuesday: A Fair Speech

1. Benjamin F. Butler, *Autobiography and Personal Reminiscences of Major-General Benjamin F. Butler* (Boston: A. M. Thayer, 1892), p. 904. *Daily National Republican*, April 12, 1865.

2. Abraham Lincoln, *The Collected Works of Abraham Lincoln*, ed. Roy P. Basler, vol. 8 (New Brunswick, NJ: Rutgers University Press, 1953), pp. 396–98.

3. Gideon Welles, *Diary of Gideon Welles: Secretary of the Navy under Lincoln and Johnson*, vol. 2 (Boston: Houghton Mifflin, 1911), p. 279.

4. Marquis Adolphe de Chambrun, *Impressions of Lincoln and the Civil War: A Foreigner's Account* (New York: Random House, 1952), pp. 92–93.

5. Margarita Spalding Gerry, comp. and ed. *Through Five Administrations: Reminiscences of Colonel William H. Crook, Body-Guard to President Lincoln* (New York: Harper and Brothers, 1910), p. 63.

6. "The Celebration Last Night," *Evening Star* (Washington, DC), April 12, 1865, p. 1.

7. The quotes from Lincoln's speech are from Lincoln, *Collected Works*, pp. 399–405.

8. Elizabeth Keckley, *Behind the Scenes: Thirty Years a Slave and Four Years in the White House* (Buffalo, NY: Stansil & Lee, 1931), pp. 174–75.

9. Michael W. Kauffman, *American Brutus: John Wilkes Booth and Lincoln Conspiracies* (New York: Random House, 2004), p. 210.

10. Lincoln, *Collected Works*, p. 405. The full text of the president's address can be found in the appendix.

11. Chambrun, *Impressions of Lincoln*, p. 93.

12. Gerry, comp. and ed., *Through Five Administrations*, p. 64.

13. *New-York Tribune*, April 12, 1865.

14. "A Grand Illumination—Speech by the President," *Evening Star* (Washington, DC), April 12, 1865, p. 1.

15. Chambrun, *Impressions of Lincoln*, p. 93.

16. Ibid.

17. Ibid., pp. 93–94.

April 12, 1865, Wednesday: Only a Dream

1. Abraham Lincoln, *The Collected Works of Abraham Lincoln*, ed. Roy P. Basler, vol. 8 (New Brunswick, NJ: Rutgers University Press, 1953), p. 405.

2. Ibid.

3. Ibid., p. 406.

4. Ibid.

5. Gideon Welles, *Diary of Gideon Welles: Secretary of the Navy under Lincoln and Johnson*, vol. 2 (Boston: Houghton Mifflin, 1911), pp. 279–80.

6. Lincoln, *Collected Works*, p. 407.

7. Ibid., pp. 406–407.

8. Joshua Lawrence Chamberlain, *The Passing of the Armies: An Account of the Final Campaign of the Army of the Potomac, Based upon Personal Reminiscences of the Fifth Army Corps* (New York: Bantam Books, 1993), p. 195.

9. Ibid., pp. 195–96.

10. Ibid., p. 196.

11. Ibid., pp. 200–201.

12. Ibid., p. 201.

13. Ibid., p. 202.

14. William Tecumseh Sherman, *Memoirs of General William T. Sherman*, two vols. in one ed. (New York: Da Capo, 1984), vol. 2, p. 344.

15. Ibid.

16. Ibid.

17. Ibid.

18. The description of Lincoln's dream is from Ward Hill Lamon, *Recollections of Abraham Lincoln, 1847–1865*, ed. Dorothy Lamon Teillard (Washington, DC: published by the editor, 1911), pp. 115–17.

April 13, 1865, Thursday: "Melancholy Seemed to Be Dripping from Him"

1. Maunsell B. Field, *Memories of Many Men and of Some Women* (New York: Harper & Brothers, 1874), p. 321.

2. Abraham Lincoln, *The Collected Works of Abraham Lincoln*, ed. Roy P. Basler, vol. 8 (New Brunswick, NJ: Rutgers University Press, 1953), p. 408.

3. Ibid., p. 409.

4. Margarita Spalding Gerry, comp. and ed., *Through Five Administrations: Reminiscences of Colonel William H. Crook, Body-Guard to President Lincoln* (New York: Harper and Brothers, 1910), p. 68.

5. Julia Dent Grant, *The Personal Memoirs of Julia Dent Grant* (New York: G. P. Putnam's Sons, 1975), p. 154.

6. Justin G. Turner and Linda Levitt Turner, eds., *Mary Todd Lincoln: Her Life and Letters* (New York: Alfred A. Knopf, 1972), p. 257.

7. "The Grand Display Last Night," *Evening Star* (Washington, DC), April 14, 1865, p. 1.

8. Dent Grant, *Personal Memoirs*, p. 154.

9. Gerry, comp. and ed., *Through Five Administrations*, p. 65.

April 14, 1865, Friday: Ford's Theatre

1. Abraham Lincoln, *The Collected Works of Abraham Lincoln*, ed. Roy P. Basler, vol. 8 (New Brunswick, NJ: Rutgers University Press, 1953), pp. 410–12.

2. Gideon Welles, *Diary of Gideon Welles: Secretary of the Navy under Lincoln and Johnson*, vol. 2 (Boston: Houghton Mifflin, 1911), p. 282.

3. Ibid., pp. 282–83.

4. Ibid., p. 291.

5. Ibid.

6. Gideon Welles, "Lincoln and Johnson: Their Plan of Reconstruction and the Resumption of National Authority," *Galaxy* 13, no. 4 (April 1872): 526.

7. Ibid.

8. Charles Dana, *Recollections of the Civil War: With the Leaders at Washington and in the Field in the Sixties* (New York: D. Appleton, 1902), pp. 273–74.

9. Ibid., p. 274.

10. Horace Porter, *Campaigning with Grant* (Secaucus, NJ: Blue and Grey, 1984), p. 497.

11. The story of the messenger inviting Mrs. Grant to Ford's Theatre is from Julia Dent Grant, *The Personal Memoirs of Julia Dent Grant* (New York: G. P. Putnam's Sons, 1975), p. 155.

12. Porter, *Campaigning with Grant*, p. 497.

13. *Evening Star* (Washington, DC), April 14, 1865, p. 2.

14. Porter, *Campaigning with Grant*, pp. 497–98.

15. Dent Grant, *Personal Memoirs*, pp. 155–56. A footnote explains that "Confederate Colonel John S. Mosby's partisan rangers" had come close to capturing General Grant in Virginia in 1864.

16. Porter, *Campaigning with Grant*, p. 498.

17. Dent Grant, *Personal Memoirs*, p. 156.

18. Porter, *Campaigning with Grant*, pp. 498–99.

19. John Russell Young, *Around the World with General Grant*, vol. 2 (New York: American News Company, 1879), p. 356.

20. William Tecumseh Sherman, *Memoirs of General William T. Sherman*, two vols. in one ed. (New York: Da Capo, 1984), vol. 2, pp. 345–46.

21. Ibid., pp. 346–47.

22. Ibid., p. 347.

23. "Fort Sumter: Restoration of the Stars and Stripes," *New York Times*, April 18, 1865, p. 8.

24. Blain Roberts and Ethan J. Kytle, "When Old Glory Returned to Fort Sumter," *New York Times*, April 16, 2015, https://opinionator.blogs.nytimes.com/2015/04/16/when-old-glory-returned-to-fort-sumter/#more-156636.

25. "Fort Sumter: Restoration of the Stars and Stripes," *New York Times*, April 18, 1865, p. 8.

26. Roberts and Kytle, "When Old Glory Returned."

27. Marquis Adolphe de Chambrun, *Impressions of Lincoln and the Civil War: A Foreigner's Account* (New York: Random House, 1952), p. 36.

28. Lincoln, *Collected Works*, vol. 7, p. 376.

29. Charles W. Johnson, ed., *The Official Proceedings of the First Three Republican National Conventions: 1856, 1860, and 1864* (Minneapolis, MN: Charles W. Johnson, 1893), p. 242.

30. "The Nomination of Mr. Lincoln—How the News Is Received," *New York Times*, June 9, 1864, p. 4.

31. Hans L. Trefousse, *Andrew Johnson: A Biography* (New York: W. W. Norton, 1989), p. 192.

32. Lincoln, *Collected Works*, vol. 8, p. 410.

33. Mary Bushrod's story is from Esther May Carter, *She Knew Lincoln* (Cuyahoga Falls, OH: published by the author, 1930), pp. 5–11.

34. Justin G. Turner and Linda Levitt Turner, eds., *Mary Todd Lincoln: Her Life and Letters* (New York: Alfred A. Knopf, 1972), p. 284.

35. Ibid., p. 285.

36. Margarita Spalding Gerry, comp. and ed., *Through Five Administrations: Reminiscences of Colonel William H. Crook, Body-Guard to President Lincoln* (New York: Harper and Brothers, 1910), p. 65.

37. William Crook's description of his walk to the War Department

and back with President Lincoln are from Gerry, comp. and ed., *Through Five Administrations*, pp. 65–68.

38. Lincoln, *Collected Works*, vol. 8, p. 413. Congressman Ashmun framed the card and placed it next to a card of his own, upon which he wrote, "The above is the last autograph of President Lincoln. It was written & given to me at half past 8 P.M. April 14, 1865, just as he and Mrs. Lincoln were starting off for the Theatre where he was assassinated."

39. Noah Brooks, *Mr. Lincoln's Washington: The Civil War Dispatches of Noah Brooks* (South Brunswick, NJ: Thomas Yoseloff, 1966), p. 443.

40. Timothy Noah, "Our American Cousin Revisited," *Slate*, February 11, 2009, http://www.slate.com/articles/news_and_politics/chatterbox/2009/02/our_american_cousin_revisited.html.

41. Richard Byrne, "Our American Cousin: A Sort of Defense (Revised)," *Balkans via Bohemia* (blog), February 13, 2009, http://richbyrne.blogspot.com/2015/04/our-american-cousin-sort-of-defense.html.

42. George S. Bryan, *The Great American Myth* (New York: Carrick & Evans, 1940), p. 176.

43. Ruth Painter Randall, *Mary Lincoln: Portrait of a Marriage* (Boston: Little, Brown, 1953), p. 382.

44. Annie F. F. Wright, "The Assassination of Abraham Lincoln," *Magazine of History*, February 1909. In the confusion immediately following the assassination, people gave conflicting accounts of what they had seen and heard. Most biographies agree that John Wilkes Booth shouted "Sic semper tyrannis," which is also the state motto of Virginia. Booth claimed that he said the phrase just after shooting the president, not after he jumped onto the stage.

45. Ibid.

46. "The Autopsy of President Lincoln," in Visible Proofs: Forensic Views of the Body, US National Library of Medicine, last updated June 5, 2014, https://www.nlm.nih.gov/visibleproofs/galleries/cases/lincoln.html.

47. Dr. Blaine Houmes, who has studied Lincoln's assassination from a medical standpoint, states, "Today if you treat someone with an injury like Lincoln had, despite all of our advances, despite all of our equipment,

despite all the drugs we're able to give, and the procedures available, if you look in the medical literature, the fatality rate is still 100 percent." Blaine Houmes, "A Doctor's View of the Lincoln Assassination," interview with Abraham Lincoln Online, 2018, http://www.abrahamlincolnonline.org/lincoln/education/medical.htm.

48. Ibid.

49. Marquis Adolphe de Chambrun, *Impressions of Lincoln and the Civil War: A Foreigner's Account* (New York: Random House, 1952), pp. 95–96.

50. Ibid., p. 96.

51. US War Department, ed., *The War of the Rebellion: A Compilation of Official Records of the Union and Confederate Armies* (Washington, DC: Government Printing Office, 1891), series 1, vol. 46, part 3, pp. 744–45.

52. The description of General and Mrs. Grant receiving the news of Lincoln's assassination is from Dent Grant, *Personal Memoirs*, p. 156.

53. Ibid.

54. *Official Records*, p. 756.

55. Porter, *Campaigning with Grant*, p. 499.

56. Dent Grant, *Personal Memoirs*, p. 157.

57. "The Assassination: The Murderous Assault upon Mr. Seward," *Evening Star* (Washington, DC), April 18, 1865, p. 1.

58. The description of Gideon Welles visiting Secretary Seward and President Lincoln after the attacks upon them is from Welles, *Diary*, vol. 2, pp. 284–87. Frederick Seward recovered fully and later became a member of the New York State Assembly.

April 15, 1865, Saturday: A New World

1. Blaine Houmes, "A Doctor's View of the Lincoln Assassination," interview with Abraham Lincoln Online, 2018, http://www.abrahamlincolnonline.org/lincoln/education/medical.htm.

2. David Herbert Donald, *Lincoln* (New York: Simon & Schuster, 1995), p. 598.

3. Gideon Welles, *Diary of Gideon Welles: Secretary of the Navy under Lincoln and Johnson*, vol. 2 (Boston: Houghton Mifflin, 1911), p. 288.

3. Gideon Welles, *Diary of Gideon Welles: Secretary of the Navy under Lincoln and Johnson*, vol. 2 (Boston: Houghton Mifflin, 1911), p. 288.

4. Ibid.

5. John G. Nicolay and John Hay, *Abraham Lincoln: A History*, vol. 10 (New York: Century, 1890), p. 302.

6. "Special Cabinet Meeting," *Evening Star* (Washington, DC), April 15, 1865, p. 2.

7. Welles, *Diary*, p. 288.

8. "The New President," *New York Times*, April 17, 1865, p. 1.

9. Welles, *Diary*, p. 290.

10. Ibid.

11. "New President," *New York Times*, April 17, 1865. The complete text of Andrew Johnson's speech was printed in the *New York Times*, and can be found in the appendix.

12. Marquis Adolphe de Chambrun, *Impressions of Lincoln and the Civil War: A Foreigner's Account* (New York: Random House, 1952), p. 103.

13. Horace Porter, *Campaigning with Grant* (Secaucus, NJ: Blue and Grey, 1984), p. 501.

14. Ulysses S. Grant, *Personal Memoirs of U. S. Grant: Two Volumes in One* (New York: Charles L. Webster, 1894), p. 641.

15. "Awful Event: President Lincoln Shot by an Assassin," *New York Times*, April 15, 1865, p. 1.

16. *Atlas & Argus* (Albany, NY), April 17, 1865.

17. Deuteronomy 34:4.

18. "Our Great Affliction," *Chicago Tribune*, April 17, 1865, p. 1.

19. Margarita Spalding Gerry, comp. and ed., *Through Five Administrations: Reminiscences of Colonel William H. Crook, Body-Guard to President Lincoln* (New York: Harper and Brothers, 1910), p. 68.

20. Ibid., pp. 73–74.

21. John S. Barnes, "With Lincoln from Washington to Richmond in 1865: II. The President Enters the Confederate Capital," *Appleton's Magazine* 9, no. 6 (June 1907): 751.

22. Ibid.

23. Elisha Hunt Rhodes, *All for the Union: The Civil War Diary and Letters of Elisha Hunt Rhodes* (New York: Vintage Books, 1991), p. 223.

24. The description of General Chamberlain hearing the news of President Lincoln's death is from Joshua Lawrence Chamberlain, *The Passing of the Armies: An Account of the Final Campaign of the Army of the Potomac, Based upon Personal Reminiscences of the Fifth Army Corps* (New York: Bantam Books, 1993), pp. 210–13.

25. *New York Tribune*, April 17, 1865.

26. Walter Stahr, *Seward: Lincoln's Indispensable Man* (New York: Simon & Schuster, 2012), p. 438.

27. The description of Jefferson Davis receiving the news of Lincoln's death is from Jefferson Davis, *The Rise and Fall of the Confederate Government*, vol. 2 (Richmond, VA: Garrett and Massie, 1938), p. 550.

28. Beth G. Crabtree and James W. Patton, eds., *"Journal of a Secesh Lady": The Diary of Catherine Ann Devereux Edmondston, 1860–1866* (Raleigh, NC: Division of Archives and History, Dept. of Cultural Resources, 1979), p. 702.

29. "Mournful Intelligence: Assassination of President Lincoln," *Daily Standard* (Raleigh, NC), April 18, 1865, p. 2.

30. "The Situation," *Texas Republican* (Marshall, TX), April 28, 1865, p. 2.

31. "The Assassination of President Lincoln," *Tri-Weekly News* (Winnsboro, SC), May 20, 1865, p. 1.

32. "Glorious News: Lincoln and Seward Assassinated," *Demopolis Herald* (Alabama), April 19, 1865.

33. John Rhodehamel and Louise Taper, eds., *"Right or Wrong, God Judge Me": The Writings of John Wilkes Booth* (Urbana: University of Illinois Press, 1997), pp. 130–31.

34. Ibid., p. 154.

35. Ibid.

Epilogue: "The Loss This Country Has Suffered"

1. William Manchester, *The Glory and the Dream: A Narrative History of America, 1932–1972*, vol. 2 (Boston: Little, Brown, 1973), p. 1384.

2. Marquis Adolphe de Chambrun, *Impressions of Lincoln and the Civil War: A Foreigner's Account* (New York: Random House, 1952), p. 105.

3. Ibid., p. 112.

4. Ibid., p. 106.

5. Ulysses S. Grant, *Personal Memoirs of U. S. Grant: Two Volumes in One* (New York: Charles L. Webster, 1894), p. 641.

6. Chambrun, *Impressions of Lincoln*, pp. 109, 111.

7. Albert Castel, *The Presidency of Andrew Johnson* (Lawrence, KS: University Press of Kansas, 1979), p. 20.

8. "Restoration: President Johnson's Amnesty Proclamation," *New York Times*, May 30, 1865, p. 1.

The entire text of the proclamation was published in the *New York Times* and is included in the appendix.

9. Andrew Johnson, "Proclamation 135—Reorganizing a Constitutional Government in North Carolina," Washington, DC, May 29, 1865, http://www.presidency.ucsb.edu/ws/index.php?pid=72403.

10. William Tecumseh Sherman, *Memoirs of General William T. Sherman*, two vols. in one ed. (New York: Da Capo, 1984), vol. 2, p. 347.

11. Ibid., p. 349.

12. Grant, *Personal Memoirs*, p. 641.

13. US War Department, ed., *The War of the Rebellion: A Compilation of Official Records of the Union and Confederate Armies* (Washington, DC: Government Printing Office, 1891), series 1, vol. 47, part 3, pp. 243–44.

14. Ibid.

15. Horace Porter, *Campaigning with Grant* (Secaucus, NJ: Blue and Grey, 1984), p. 504.

16. Ibid.

17. "Sherman's Army—Gen. Sherman Negotiating with Gen. Johnston—His Actions Repudiated by the President and the Cabinet," *New York Times*, April 24, 1865, p. 5.

18. Grant, *Personal Memoirs*, p. 644.

19. The description of General Chamberlain's memorial service for Lincoln is from Joshua Lawrence Chamberlain, *The Passing of the Armies: An Account of the Final Campaign of the Army of the Potomac, Based upon Personal Reminiscences of the Fifth Army Corps* (New York: Bantam Books, 1993), pp. 214–17.

20. Julia Dent Grant, *The Personal Memoirs of Julia Dent Grant* (New York: G. P. Putnam's Sons, 1975), p. 170.

21. Robert E. Lee Jr., comp., *Recollections and Letters of Robert E. Lee* (New York: Barnes and Noble, 2004), p. 147.

22. J. William Jones, *Life and Letters of Robert Edward Lee: Soldier and Man* (Washington, DC: Neale Publishing, 1906), p. 390.

23. Castel, *Presidency of Andrew Johnson*, p. 111.

24. Ibid.

25. Ibid.

26. Ibid., p. 229.

27. Margarita Spalding Gerry, comp. and ed., *Through Five Administrations: Reminiscences of Colonel William H. Crook, Body-Guard to President Lincoln* (New York: Harper and Brothers, 1910), p. 80.

28. Ibid., pp. 83–84.

29. Arthur M. Schlesinger Jr., *A Thousand Days: John F. Kennedy in the White House* (Boston: Houghton Mifflin, 1965), p. 675.

INDEX